Procedural Natural Law

Procedural Natural Law

Rodney Jay Blackman

Carolina Academic Press
Durham, North Carolina

Library of Congress Cataloging-in-Publication Data

Blackman, Rodney Jay, 1936–
Procedural natural law / Rodney Jay Blackman.
p. cm.
Includes bibliographical references.
ISBN 0-89089-688-7
1. Natural law. 2. Law—Philosophy. I. Title.
K474.B54 A3 1999
340'.112—dc21 99-048920

Carolina Academic Press
700 Kent Street
Durham, North Carolina 27701
Telephone (919) 489-7486
Fax (919) 493-5668
E-mail: cap@cap-press.com
www.cap-press.com

Printed in the United States of America

Contents

Acknowledgments

I would like to thank my students, Kirstin Muller, John Depke, Daniel Meyer, Thomas McInerney, Michelle Touhy, Daniel DeLeo, Todd Hunnewell, Jonathan Cole, Brandon Kroft, John Hayes and Cassel McClure for their research in helping me prepare this book. Also, my colleagues, Susan Bandes, Margit Livingston and Mark Weber, deserve thanks for their helpful suggestions (though not for any criticism). And so does Joel Feinberg for reading and agreeing with a portion of an earlier version of this manuscript.

In addition, I would like to thank the *Arizona Law Review*, where a substantial portion of this material originally appeared in article form (Vol. 37, No. 1, 1995), for agreeing to waive any copyright claim it might have and allowing me to publish this expanded version in the book that follows.

About the Author

Rodney Jay Blackman has been a professor of law at DePaul College of Law in Chicago for many years. He teaches Jurisprudence, Constitutional Process and a First Amendment seminar. He received his J.D. from Harvard Law School and his Ph.D. in philosophy from the University of Wisconsin in Madison.

Procedural Natural Law

1

Introduction

I start this book with the assumption that you, dear reader, like many intelligent people, are skeptical of the notion that there is such a thing as natural law.[1] In the pages that follow I will provide a brief definitional description of natural law. Then I will summarize some natural law theories. I will try to persuade you that a limited version of the concept makes sense. Indeed, I suspect that you already understand this version of natural law when others use it. Further, so far as you talk about the subject, you too probably use this version even if you are not aware of engaging in natural law talk. Indeed, I hope to persuade you that it is so obvious that this limited version of natural law is part of your understanding of language that it is no longer a live issue for you, that is, it is a settled matter, a closed book.

What I am referring to when I mention a limited version of natural law is legal procedure or what I call 'procedural natural law.' I also use other terms interchangeably with procedural natural law, such as, 'legality,' 'the rule of law,' 'law as an ideal,' 'the idea of law' and 'law.' In discussing this procedural natural law, I will have the burden of showing that it is indeed a version of natural law, albeit a limited one. I will attempt to meet this burden by suggesting that 'law' necessarily involves rules and procedures.

The originator of this limited version of natural law was Lon Fuller[2] and I shall make some effort to spell out what his view of the concept (as well as mine and others') entails. But unlike Fuller who, for the most part did not explain the basis for his assertion that there was such a thing as procdedural natural law, I shall attempt to show that it exists as part of our language. Thus, if a government's legal system lacks this element, it does not come within a commonly understood use of the concept 'law.'

---

1. As one legal philosopher put it, "One label...is particularly dreaded; no one wants to be called a natural lawyer." Dworkin, Ronald, "*'Natural' Law Revisited*," 34 *U. Fla. L. Rev*. 165 (1982).

2. However, it has antecedents in English law. *See* Nance, Dale A., *Law and Justice, Second Edition*, 1999, at 271.

Let us assume that I persuade you that this limited version of natural law exists as part of our use of language (yours as well as mine and the community's), my next step is to persuade you that an awareness and acceptance of procedural natural law has value. Its value lies in its use in characterizing and assessing regimes, both by propagandists who seek to deflect charges that the regimes that they serve violate this version of natural law and by the critics of these regimes. For a regime to be justifiably charged with violating this concept is generally regarded as containing a serious flaw.

I will then show that to some extent even some of the staunchest critics of natural law theory in large measure accept this limited version of the concept. So that despite their assertions to the contrary, even for these critics there is no real basis for a dispute.

In addition, I will attempt to ward off some common charges that might be leveled against procedural natural law. One of these charges is that the book's argument derives an ought from an is. This charge assumes my assertion that the concept 'law' involves the existence of procedure as a factual element as to how the concept is used, but rejects what the critic thinks follows from this factual element, namely, that the concept 'law' ought to contain procedure.

Another charge provisionally accepts the notion of procedural natural law as a Western convention, but rejects its having universal meaning or value. If the concept of procedural natural law is an artifact of a particular group of language users in Western Europe and North America, then what is the point of using this concept to characterize regimes elsewhere as violating a concept that is not used in their cultures?

Finally, some critics might regard procedural natural law as either a tool of the ruling elites designed to keep the masses in their place or else as not providing people significant or sufficient protection against the abuses of these elites.

I will attempt to respond to these various charges.

2

What Is Natural Law?

Traditionally, natural law was thought of as a law of nature. Just as other natural phenomena consistently follow a set pattern, such as, the acorn becoming an oak or the sun "rising" in the morning, so there is a "law" which people in power (in some sense) have to or ought to follow. One critic of this traditional view put it as "a metaphysical theory of law [that] pretends to discover a natural law imminent in nature."[3]

This definitional understanding of natural law is sufficiently easy to attack that any defense of natural law based on it labors under a substantial handicap. One difficulty is that humans, unlike other natural phenomena, do not appear to be governed by stringent laws of nature, such as, the law of gravity.

Another more contemporary definitional analysis of natural law is more defensible. This definition asserts that there is a necessary (noncontingent) connection between law and morality.[4] This definition avoids the problems associated with the earlier posited definition in terms of a law of nature. The application of this newer definition asserts nothing about the laws of human nature or about deriving an ought from an is. But it seemingly does not escape the difficulty that if law has a necessary connection with morality, how does one explain the fact that those in power, such as, Hitler, Stalin, Mao and a parade of other evil leaders, often flout whatever consensus might exist about moral standards? Does one assert that, contrary to this possible consensus, that these leaders exhibit the necessary morality? If the answer that these leaders exhibit the necessary morality is unac-

---

3. Kelsen, Hans, *Pure Theory of Law*, translated by Max Knight, 1989, at 77.

4. Hart, H. L. A., *The Concept of Law*, 1961, at 151, 181; Wueste, Daniel E., "Book Review: Fuller's Processual Philosophy of Law," 71 *Cornell L. Rev.* 1205 (1986). *See also* MacCormick, Neil, "Natural Law and the Separation of Law and Morals," George, Robert T. ed., *Natural Law Theory*, 1992, at 120. Joseph Raz calls for the rejection of natural law theory because "there [is] no necessary connection between law and moral values." Raz, Joseph, "The Purity of the Pure Theory," Freeman, M. D. A., *Lloyd's Introduction to Jurisprudence*, Sixth Edition, 1994, at 328.

ceptable (as we probably would all agree), then the only avenue left for one asserting that there is a necessary connection between law and morality is that these leaders are violating legality. But can this proposition be made credible?

At the very least if natural law theory is viewed as asserting a necessary connection between law and morality, then it is obvious that there are two terms which need further explication, 'law' and 'morality.' The idea mentioned above that evil political leaders might violate a notion of legality suggests that the term 'legality' could have several definitions, one associated purely with power and control of territory and the other containing a normative (moral) element. As noted below in the text, this is the tack that I propose to take to explain how some evil political leaders can both understandably assert that whatever they do bears the stamp of legality and at the same time be viewed by outsiders as violating the outsiders' notion of legality.

In opposition to any version of natural law theory, including my version based on how the term 'law' is used, there stand the positivists. Positivists like John Austin, Hans Kelsen, H.L.A. Hart and Joseph Raz reject the idea that there is a necessary connection between law and morality. There are several expressions of this view that go back to Austin. One of these is, "[t]he existence of law is one thing, its merit or demerit is another."[5] Another more pungent example is his statement that "to say that human law which conflicts with the Divine law are not *binding*, that is to say, are not laws, is to talk stark nonsense."[6] Or as Kelsen put it, "The concept of a legal obligation refers exclusively to a positive legal order and has no moral implication whatever."[7] Contrary to my thesis, the positivists believe that law can be described without ascribing to it any moral dimension.

Thus, the issue is joined. To make sense of it, we must not only focus on the term 'law' but also on the term 'morality.' As to 'moral-

---

5. Hart, H. L. A., "Positivism and the Separation of Law and Morals," quoting J. L. Austin, Feinberg, Joel and Gross, Hyman eds., *Philosophy of Law*, 1991, at 64.

6. Austin, John, *The Province of Jurisprudence Determined*, 1994, at 158.

7. Kelsen, *Pure Theory of Law, supra*, at 117. Raz summed up Kelsen's view as well as his own, stating that "Kelsen does not regard the law as necessarily good or justified in any sense." Raz, Joseph, *The Concept of a Legal System*, 1980, at 132.

ity' or 'ethics', two terms that I use interchangeably,[8] one philosopher has defined it as "concerned with providing the general outlines of a normative theory to help us answer problems about what is right or ought to be done."[9] Another philosopher has put it simply as "how one should treat other persons."[10] A third relates it to "how best to behave in situations where it is in our power to counteract the extreme vulnerability of others by being thoughtful and considerate."[11] One explicit or implicit common element in these and other definitions is the normative ought element.

Another element either implicit or explicit in these various definitions is that morality is confined to persons. Ordinarily we do not think of government as coming within the category of morality, that is, acting either morally or immorally. The post office's prompt delivery of your mail is thought of as efficient rather than as moral. And the IRS's delay in returning your tax refund is thought of as inefficient or incompetent rather than as immoral.

But if natural law theory based on a necessary connection between law and morality is to make any sense, then some exception must be found to the ordinary way of viewing institutional action such as that of the government. One reason for finding this exception is that sometimes moral judgments can be applied to institutions as well as to persons. To explicate this point I cite Colbe and Kohlberg who have posited a hierarchical series of stages of moral development. At the third stage of this hierarchy people will live up to other people's expectation of them in their roles. But living up to expectations (as a moral concept) can be applied to government as well. Under what we think of as the rule of law, a term referring to the procedural natural law concept I have already introduced and will be developing below, government can be expected to fulfill its general rules.[12] This would

8. *The Compact Edition of the Oxford English Dictionary, Vol. 1*, 1982, at 654. This usage seems more consistent with ordinary language than Habermas' stipulated distinction between morality, which is freed of reference to self interest or one's group, and ethics, which is not. Habermas, Jurgen, *Between Facts and Norms*, translated by William Rehg, 1996, at 97.

9. Frankena, William, *Ethics*, 1963, at 5.

10. Machan, Tibor, *Individuals and their Rights*, 1989, at 33.

11. Habermas, Jurgen, *Moral Consciousness and Communicative Action*, translated by Christian Lenhardt and Shierry Weber Nicholsen, 1991, at 137.

12. "Law consists of the exploitation of conflict perspectives for the formation and reproduction of congruently (temporally/objectively/socially) generalized behavioral

be done when, say, those in charge of the criminal law apparatus only seek to prosecute those whom they have reason to believe are guilty of some crime.

At stage five in their hierarchy Colbe and Kohlberg posit that the rules relative to the group "should usually be upheld... in the interest of impartiality." Here too the rule of law involves a similar moral dimension, namely, impartially treating similars similarly. At stage six "universal principles of justice [and] equality of human rights" are discussed. Again, natural law theory generally and procedural natural law specifically purport to apply principles universally, that is, cross culturally. Thus, if a regime uses its "laws" to treat its least favored members substantially differently than it does its own elite and a disinterested outsider can find no rational explanation for this difference in treatment, then there is a violation of both the procedural rule of law and the Colbe/Kohlberg paradigm.[13]

Another reason for finding an exception to the usual view of government and other institutions as not coming within the category of morality (or immorality) is found in our ordinary language use.[14] For example, the statement that "in firing her without notice, the company acted immorally" makes perfectly good sense to us. Likewise, we understand "even though there is no legal way to recover the money, by misappropriating the pension funds the union violated the workers' rights." Similarly, it is appropriate to assert that "the government acted unfairly when it informed the alien that if he left the country he could return, and then when he did leave refused to allow him back in." In each instance one can argue whether it is the institution that has acted immorally or only some persons within it. But re-

expectations." Luhmann, Niklas, "The Unity of the Legal System," translated by Bielefeld, Teubner, Gunther, ed., *Autopoietic Law: A New Approach to Law & Society*, 1988, at 27.

13. Colbe, Anne & Kohlberg, Lawrence, *The Measurement of Moral Judgment*, 1987, at 18-19.

14. "[W]hat we are after is accounts of how certain words work...." Ryle, Gilbert, "Ordinary Language," Caton, Charles E., ed., *Philosophy and Ordinary Language*, 1963, at 126. "To know what an expression means involves knowing what can (logically) be said with it and what cannot (logically) be said with it." Ryle, Gilbert, *The Theory of Meaning*, at 143. Ryle also referred to Wittgenstein's famous expression in the Philosophical Investigations, "Don't ask for the meaning ask for the use...." *Id.* at 143.

gardless of how one resolves this argument, we understand the use of language that ascribes moral terminology to institutions.[15]

If one accepts that it sometimes makes sense to make moral judgments about governmental and other institutions, what criteria would one use to make such judgments? One appropriate common sense criterion is to make moral judgments about government on the same basis as such are made in purely interpersonal relationships. That basis would entail understanding how people believe institutions such as government ought to treat them.

In the context of this text, the moral argument runs as follows. If a government sets forth and follows a legal procedure,[16] then people can attempt to act in accordance with it. They can plan their interactions and futures in accordance with what the government has indi-

---

15. Here is one philosopher's use of procedural natural law language similar to what I propose to use to make moral judgments about a government's actions:

> A telling example of the value people do practically attach to the observance of legality has been provided by recent developments in the Warsaw Pact countries [countries held within the Soviet bloc between 1945 and the late 1980s-early 1990s by the force of Russian and other troops]. At all stages of the revolutions against one-party Communist governments, there has been expressed *inter alia* a claimant and persistent demand for a restoration of the Rule of Law, and this has been plainly a moral demand. Those who have protested against and denounced the arbitrary rule and arbitrary self-preferences of presidents like Ceausescu and party officials like Honecker have not been asking for technically efficient law. They have been demanding the instatement in public life of basic elements of fairness.... [People] can agree that whatever property and contract regime is fixed by law, the situation will be better—better in moral terms—if the regime is applied fairly and openly and in accordance with the Rule of Law.

MacCormick, Neil, "Natural Law and the Separation of Law and Morals," George, Robert P. ed., *Natural Law Theory*, 1992, at 123-4.

Implicit in the following remark is the view that what I call procedural natural law (or what is called here the internal morality of procedure) provides moral protection to individuals:

> Despite [their] disagreements, [Oakshott, Hayek, Dworkin and Finnis] were nevertheless united in their conviction that the particular rights which defined the basic entitlement of the individual citizen to due process in the administration and enforcement of law ranked as fundamental requirements of justice. It was for this reason that the theorists were drawn to the conclusion that the justice of law depended, in part at least, on conformity to an internal morality of procedure which was given in the very concept of law itself.

Covell, Charles, *The Defence of Natural Law, supra*, at 27.

16. I here postpone any discussion of the nature of the precedure provided.

cated it demands through the rule of law. This lends stability to their lives. This stability has a moral dimension because it satisfies, however minimally, the criterion of having the characteristic of what people believe government ought to have, namely, providing a path that makes it easier for people to get through the government's bureaucratic maze. One analogy is to a promise breaker. Unless such a person has a good excuse, he is likely to be thought of as acting immorally. Another analogy is to a scientist leading a rat through a maze. Just as a thinking rat would regard the scientist as immoral who consistently but randomly shut doors in the maze that were once open, so people would feel the same way if government were to consistently but arbitrarily change and shut off the avenues through its bureaucracy so that no security was possible.

So, to summarize the remarks of this section, I have defined natural law as a necessary connection between law and morality. If morality is defined in terms of how persons reasonably expect to be treated by other persons or by institutions, then it makes sense to ascribe moral values to the way in which government treats persons. Further, the government's having in place legal procedures can be regarded as providing such a moral value because it fulfills personal expectations. Thus, government action can be judged in moral terms. Of course, the nature of these legal procedures must be fleshed out in order to know what personal expectations are to be regarded as morally desirable. This will come below.

3

Substantive Natural Law Theories

Applying either the traditional definition of natural law (a law of nature) or the one I accept (a necessary connection between law and morality), this concept has its obverse, namely, what is called positivism. Positivists reject both versions of natural law theory in favor of the view that law has no necessary connection either to nature or morality. According to positivists the only law that exists is that which states (and primitive societies) employ. The elements of 'law' can be and are described by these positivists.

By contrast, natural law theorists believe that what states do in the name of law can sometimes be attacked as violating the principle of natural law. Natural law theory can be divided into two categories, substantive natural law and procedural natural law. The terms 'substance' and 'procedure' cannot be distinguished with precision in the context of natural law theory. Still, substantive natural law theorists assert that law must have as its end conformity with human needs or human nature, must contain certain self evident, indemonstrable truths about human beings[17] or some arrangement that elucidates human interaction. Procedural natural law theorists assert that law must contain certain formal elements (like rules of a game) regardless of the ends it serves.

Procedural natural law theory, which I will defend in the main portion of the book, has a 20th Century pedigree, going back to the writings of Lon Fuller in the middle of this century. By contrast, substantive natural law theories go back to the writings of Homer and Sophocles in ancient Greek fiction,[18] China[19] and the Hebrews.[20] Some reference to natural law can also be found in Aristotle, Cicero and Justinian.

---

17. This version of natural law is thought to give rise to natural rights.

18. Weinreb, Lloyd, *Natural Law and Justice*, 1987, at 15-24.

19. Needham, J., *Science and Civilisation, Vol.* 2, Chap. 18, 1956, at 518 and following.

20. Silving, H., "The Jurisprudence of the Old Testament," 28 *N. Y. U. L. Rev.* 1129 (1953).

But the most developed exposition of traditional substantive (content based) natural law theory was provided by Thomas Aquinas. Aquinas believed that natural law consisted in the rational human participation in the divine law. When this natural law was put into effect, it would be positive law in the desired sense of the word 'law.' This natural law would involve the commands of the prince based on reason and having as their end the well-being of the whole community. The precepts of natural law would correspond to natural human inclinations. These included self preservation, sexual relationship, rearing of offsprings, to do good, to live in society and to know the truth about God.[21]

A contemporary British philosopher, John Finnis, has provided a spirited defense of an Aquinian version of natural law. Finnis posits certain self-evident basic values or aspects of human (and societal) good, namely, life, knowledge (for its own sake as well as instrumentally), play, aesthetic experience, friendship and sociability, practical reasonableness (choosing one's goals and determining how to get to them from here) and religion (concern about cosmological and transcendent issues even if one is not a believer).[22] The focal (but not the only) meaning of the term 'law' is for the appropriate governmental authority to enact reasonable rules that are then used by the appropriate governmental authority to reasonably adjudicate disputes applying appropriate sanctions. The rules are enacted and adjudicated for the common good in accordance with the basic values listed above.[23]

Another substantive approach to natural law and natural rights comes out of the social contract traditon. Under the traditional versions, human beings live in a state of nature, that is, by themselves and without a governmental structure. But then for one reason or another, they agree to enter into a community with a governmental structure. The three muskateers of this tradition were Hobbes, Rousseau and Locke. Of the three only Locke has had a strong impact on the development of natural law and natural rights tradition in the U.S. going back to Jefferson's Declaration of Independence and certain constitutional provisions, such as the Ninth Amendment, but

21. Aquinas, Saint Thomas, "Law," *Summa Theologiae*, translated and edited by Timothy McDermott, 1989, at 280-9.

22. Finnis, John, *Natural Law and Natural Rights*, 1980, at 81-94.

23. *Id.* at 276-7, 351-2.

the social contract tradition generally has inspired later political and legal theories.

For Hobbes the state of nature was the human equivalent of a snake pit where every person was at war with every other, and the life of each was solitary, poor, nasty, brutish and short. Because the need for government was so great, the agreement among people left government virtually unrestrained, a Leviathan.[24] The only right the person had to resist an overbearing government was to defend herself against that government; that is, she did not have to testify against herself, did not have to voluntarily submit to imprisonment, torture or being killed by the government.[25]

Another soical contract version was provided by Rousseau. Rousseau posited a state of nature rather than asserted its existence. But in that state man was an animal with his instincts governing his reason. Once he joined with others to form a civil society, then his reason governed his desires. Still, he did not join with others to provide a civil society without assuring that there would have to be unanimity (a general will) before governmental action could be taken. However, if a person refused to obey the general will of society as expressed by the government, he could be forced by that society to be free, that is, to obey. It would be the civil society that protected his property.[26]

Because Hobbes' natural law version led to a very strong government with limited protection to the person against governmental excess and Rousseau's version could be read as providing no protection at all to the person against governmental excess,[27] most Anglo-Amer-

---

24. Freeman, *Lloyd's Introduction to Jurisprudence, supra*, at 137-8.

25. Hobbes, Thomas, *Leviathan*, 1950, at 109.

26. Rousseau, Jean Jacques, *The Social Contract and Discourses, Book I*, Chs. V-IX, translated by C. D. H. Cole, 1950, at 12-22.

27. Rousseau has had much more influence among tyrants than democrats or natural law theorists. For example, the poet, Heinrich Heine, noted: "Mark this, ye proud men of action...; ye are nothing but unconscious instruments of the men of thought, who... have appointed you to your inevitable task. Maxmillian Robespierre was merely the hand of Jean Jacques Rousseau..." Popper, Karl R, *The Open Society and its Enemies, Vol.* 2, 1962, at 109. As this quote indicates, Rousseau influenced the French Revolution. That revolution, in turn, influenced the Soviet Revolution which, in turn, influenced the Chinese Communist Revolution.

But democratic continental philosophers have sometimes appreciated Rousseau more than Anglo-American ones have. For example, Habermas uses Rousseau's emphasis on ican defenders of natural law theory have looked to the third thinker for inspiration, John Locke. For Locke the reason for a person in a state of nature to join with others and enter into civil society was to safeguard her life and possessions against possible assault by others. However, since a person in a state of nature is obliged by reason not to destroy herself or anybody else as all other persons are equal to her, she cannot agree to give to a state the arbitrary power to take away her life, liberty or property. The state's power is limited to the pursuit of the public good of society, and cannot be used to destroy, enslave or impoverish the people.[28]

As will be noted below, the social contract theory has had significant influence on later political theory. Before doing so, however, I turn to another philosopher who has had a substantial influence on moral (and to a lesser extent on political) theory, namely, Immanuel Kant. Kant believed that man's accepting an obligation without being externally or internally caused (motivated) reflects his noumenal (in and of itself) free will or freedom. All people have this same possibility to act autonomously, freely, without being caused.[29]

Morality consists in a person's acting autonomously to undertake an obligation. A moral obligation is expressed by the categorical (non-contingent) imperative: "Act according to a maxim [a subjective principle] which can be adopted at the same time as a universal law,"[30] that is, act as if everybody were to act in the same way. A further maxim, in effect, is to regard man always as an end in himself rather than simply as a means to your own end: "man . . . and . . . every

---

the general will as a basis of support for his discourse theory. Under that theory in an ideal democratic society where there is a dispute one makes an argument with "the intention of winning the assent of a universal audience . . ." even though in reality one will not convince everybody. One does so in a non-coercive way based on the best information and reasons. Habermas, *Between Facts and Norms, supra*, at 228, 300-1.

Even in the United States there is an echo of Habermas' approach as well as Rousseau's general will in T. M. Scanlon's recent work when he states: ". . . the subject matter of judgements of right and wrong . . . are judgments about what would be permitted by principles that could not reasonably be rejected . . ." McGinn, Colin, *Reasons and Unreasons*, a book review of T. M. Scanlon's *What We Owe to Each Other, The New Republic*, May 24, 1999, at 34.

28. Locke, John, *Treatise of Civil Government*, edited by Charles L. Sharman, 1937, at 5-12, 63-85.

29. Weinreb, *Natural Law and Justice, supra*, at 90-96.

30. Kant, Immanuel, *The Philosophy of Law*, translated by W. Hastie, 1887, at 35.

rational being exists as an end in himself and not merely as a means to be arbitrarily used by this or that will....The practical imperative, therefore, is...: Act so that you treat humanity...always as an end and never as a means only."[31] It is only in this way that people can live in harmony.

Kant wrote of both natural right and natural law. Natural right is determined by philosophic knowledge. It is from natural right that the immutable principles of positive (existing) legislation are derived by lawyers and legislatures.[32] Natural right is innate and belongs to each of us by nature, that is, independent of positive laws. Right is the condition present when "the voluntary actions of any one person can be harmonized in reality with the voluntary actions of every other person, according to a universal law of freedom."[33] Each person's equal freedom consonant with everybody else's is the one natural right belonging to each of us by virtue of our humanity. My freedom is independent of the compulsory will of all others by virtue of a universal law which provides to these others their freedom to the same extent as mine.[34] This natural right is a reality when one has entered into a state where "every one can have what is his own secured against the action of every other."[35] A republican form of government would be the most desirable way to bring about natural right, and the existence of such governments generally is the best hope for perpetual peace among states.[36]

Kant's natural law theory as distinguished from his morality is given a certain spin by Jurgen Habermas. While morality is uncoerced, law by necessity is coercive except among saints. For Habermas morally uncoerced adherence to law exists only if, assuming contrary to fact one had the freedom to choose, that is, the law deserved to be followed: "[a]lthough legal claims are coupled with authorized coercion, they must always be such that subjects can comply on account of their normative validity as well..."[37]

---

31. Kant, Immanuel, *Grundlegung Zur Metaphysik Der Sitten*, Gottlieb, Stephen E., *Jurisprudence*, 1993, at 448; *See also* Bloch, Ernst, *Natural Law and Human Dignity*, translated by Dennis J. Schmidt, 1987, at 242.

32. Kant, *The Philosophy of Law, supra*, at 43-4.

33. *Id.* at 45.

34. *Id.* at 56.

35. *Id.* at 55.

36. *Id.* at 230-1.

37. Habermas, *Between Facts and Norms, supra*, at 29.

In fact, however, Kant's view diverged from Habermas'. While Kant posited the existence of natural laws that are recognized by reason as obligatory in advance of the experience of their having been imposed as positive laws (a priori), the first of these is the presupposition of the authority of a lawgiver who by right could subject others to obligations through his own will.[38] Contrary to Habermas' requirement that law must deserve to be followed, Kant concluded that any opposition to a legal system is opposition to the possibility of living in a community governed by the moral law: "[i]t is duty of the People to bear any abuse of the Supreme Power, even ... it should be considered unbearable."[39]

Several American political philosophers have developed theories that reflect Locke's social contract (though not his belief in an original state of nature) as well as Kant's emphasis on natural rights (though not his ultimate conclusion that man must submit to oppressive regimes). One of these, Robert Nozick's *Anarchy, State and Utopia*,[40] to some extent echoes Locke and Kant. Each individual is inviolable. No one can be involuntarily sacrificed as a means to another's ends.[41] This leads him to begin his analysis with the premise that the existence of a state must be justified over anarchy. A minimal state is justified in order to protect the person, her liberty and property against violence, theft and fraud. If wealth is accumulated through violence, theft or fraud, then a transfer of this wealth is justified in order to rectify the injustice. But except apparently to provide a welfare baseline,[42] the state is not justified in engaging in redistributions of wealth where the wealth was not originally obtained or transferred unjustly.

Another political philosopher, John Rawls, has a much more expansive understanding of the value of the state than Nozick. In his *A Theory of Justice*[43] Rawls posits a thought experiment. If we were ignorant of all of our specific attributes, talents, our economic and social positions, what societal structure would we agree upon as free

---

38. Kant, *The Philosophy of Law, supra*, at 33.

39. *Id.* at 177.

40. Nozick, Robert, *Anarchy, State, and Utopia*, 1974.

41. *Id.* at 30-31. But Nozick quickly denies that a person cannot be constrained against her will. *Id.* at 31.

42. *Id.* at 177; Freeman, *Lloyd's Introduction to Jurisprudence, supra*, at 371.

43. Rawls, John, *A Theory of Justice*, 1971.

and equal moral persons.[44] The basic structure of society distributes primary goods, that is, things that every rational person would want. These are the social bases of self respect, basic liberties (freedom of thought, conscience), freedom of movement and free choice of occupation, powers and perogatives of offices and positions of responsibility and income/wealth.[45] He believes that in such a situation our first principle of justice would be an equal right to the most extensive liberty possible compatible with a similar system of liberty for all.[46] The basic liberties of citizens include the right to vote, the right to be eligible for public office, freedom of speech and assembly, liberty of conscience, freedom of thought, freedom (and integrity[47]) of the person, the right to hold (personal) property and freedom from arbitrary arrest and seizure. The second principle (less important than the first) would require both fair equality of opportunity and that any unequal distribution of social and economic inequalities be justified on the ground that it benefits everybody, particularly the least advantaged.[48] He calls that portion of the second principle referring to unequal distribution of inequalities the difference principle.

In his later work, *Political Liberalism*, his model is still a contractual one.[49] But instead of examining political justice from the perspective of a hypothetical veil of ignorance, he attempts to work from an initial agreement to produce both the basic constitutional value of justice in a liberal democracy and what would constitute an accept-

44. Rawls rejects the idea that he is creating an updated version of natural rights theory. "Rather, [the] foundation [of his principles of justice] is in the conception of the person and of social cooperation most likely to be congenial to the public culture of a modern democratic society." Rawls, John, *Political Liberalism*, 1993, at 339. Despite this assertion, his political philosophy, though hypothetical rather than historical, is explicitly based on the social contract tradition of John Locke and the moral philosophy of Immanuel Kant. Thus, it comes out of the natural law and natural rights tradition and, perhaps more importantly, seems like natural law and natural rights theory.

45. *Id.* at 308-9.

46. His exact wording is: "Each person is to have an equal right to the most extensive total system of equal basic liberties compatible with a similar system of liberty for all." Rawls, *A Theory of Justice, supra*, at 302. He later modifies his first principle to read: "Each person has an equal right to a fully adequate scheme of equal basic liberties which is compatible with a similar scheme of liberties for all." Rawls, *Political Liberalism, supra*, at 291.

47. *Id.* at 291.

48. Rawls, John, *A Theory of Justice, supra*, at 17-19, 60-65, 136-138, 302-3.

49. Rawls, *Political Liberalism, supra*, at 257-9.

able public reason for pursuing our political values in contradistinction to our comprehensive religious, philosophical and moral doctrines. While he does not posit the veil of ignorance of his earlier work, that is, he does not posit that we lack knowledge of our own situation, he does reiterate and expand on the first principle of the earlier book. He asks, given a background structure which establishes an agreement of "free and equal moral persons,"[50] what would they actually agree to? In analyzing this question, he assumes that these "persons...[are] capable of being normal and fully cooperating members of society over a complete life."[51]

Rawls posits an agreement for the purpose of maximizing equal liberty. This would include liberty of general thought and speech, as well as freedom of association and movement. While the ageement would not include the difference principle of the earlier book (that is, economic and social inequalities have to be justified as advantageous to the least well off class), it does include a requirement that basic needs of citizens be met so that they can take part in political and social life.[52]

As the last sentence's reference to citizens would suggest, in *Political Liberalism* Rawls does not deal with how government is to treat non-citizens. But he does touch upon this subject in a contemporaneous piece.[53] There he posits that a just political society would recognize human rights for people who are in good standing. Indeed, without these rights, the regime lacks legitimacy. One does not have to be a citizen to have such rights, only that the person be a responsible and cooperating member of society. These rights include the right to life and security, personal property, liberty of conscience and freedom of association, the right to emigrate and the rule of law.[54]

---

50. *Id.* at 286.

51. *Id.* at 301.

52. *Id.*, at 38-40, 145-168.

53. Rawls, John, "The Law of Peoples," Shute, Stephen and Hurley, Susan, *On Human Rights*, 1993.

54. *Id.* at 60-71.

4

Contra Substantive Natural Law

Each of these substantive natural law theories, specifically including Aquinas, Finnis, Locke, Kant, Nozick and Rawls, has aspects which resonate with me. But I have two fundamental problems with each of them. One problem is that their basic premises must be accepted as either self evidently true or on faith. Another problem is that I do not perceive any negative consequence flowing from a government's failure to abide by their understanding of natural law (or natural rights). Thus, in response to someone's pointing out that a government violated a principle of natural law as set forth by Aquinas et al., the government leader could say "so what?" What meaningful response to this could Aquinas provide?

Turning to the first problem, namely, the difficulty of justifying each philosopher's basic premise(s), suppose I play devil's advocate and make an effort to deny the universality (and therefore the self evident nature) of each theorist's basic premise(s). Playing devil's advocate does not necessarily mean that I agree with the argument I am making or that I want the substantive natural law theory to fail, only that I think the argument I am making is plausible. Let me start with the emphasis on reason found not only in Aquinas and Finnis, but also in Kant[55] and Rawls.[56]

But how can we be sure that we humans are rational creatures. A plausible argument can be made that we are primarily irrational (emotional, sexually oriented) creatures. As such our actions are not based on reason, though we might attempt to mask our irrationality through rationalizations.[57]

---

55. Kant points out that when he refers to a person's will, he means the faculty of practical reason. He states that "[l]aws arise from the Will, viewed generally as Practical Reason..." Kant, *The Philosophy of Law, supra*, at 35.

56. "[Primary] goods are defined as things that, from the standpoint of the original position, it is rational for the parties to want whatever their final ends (which are unknown to them). They serve as generalized means... for realizing all, or most all, rational systems of aims." Rawls, *Political Liberalism, supra*, n. 13, at 278.

57. Freud's biographer, Ernest Jones, comes close to asserting that Freud made such a claim:

Examining Aquinas' specific points, he posits that under natural law theory the commands of the sovereign would have as their end the well-being of the whole community. If one accepts the apparent utilitarian premise underlying this thesis (that is, the greatest good for the greatest number),[58] then one might argue that Aquinas' view of natural law encompasses the killing of part of the community for the benefit of the majority as the majority perceived it. If so, many governments that we deem evil (such as, Hitler's, Stalin's, Mao's, Idi Amin's, Saddem Hussein's) might satisfy Aquinas' natural law theory.

In Aquinas' defense, these dictators do not seem to have had as their end the well being of the whole community. Hitler was quite willing to see Germany destroyed in the last months of World War II.[59] And Mao believed that while the occurrence of nuclear war would be a bad thing, if it did occur and half of mankind were destroyed, China would triumph.[60]

Nontheless, even if one of the brutal dictatorships mentioned above would not come within Aquinas' natural law theory, other, less brutal dictatorships might. As long as a regime could be regarded as concerned with the well-being of the majority, the fact that it disregarded the interests of the minority would be irrelevant. Such a regime would pass muster as reflecting this aspect of Aquinas' natural law thesis.

> Three ideas, of equal importance in Freud's way of thinking now come together in his mind. The primary processes that had to be bound before the pleasure principle could operate emanated from internal stimulation and so belonged to the instincts. The tendency to repetition was also pretty evidently of an instinctual nature. *It also was more fundamental than the pleasure principle and contrasted with it in its "demonic" character*; the [pleasure principle] was often refined into a "reality principle." The tendency toward stability, also called the "constancy principle," was a fundamental attribute of the mind.

Jones, Ernest, *The Life and Work of Sigmund Freud, Vol. 3*, 1957, at 270 (emphasis added). I believe that Freud's reality (pleasure) principle, which Freud asserted was less fundamental than instincts, is the basis for the self-interested rational choices of substantive natural law theorists. So, Freud's bottom line is that instincts are more fundamental than the basis for rational activity.

58. Finnis rejects utilitarianism: "[a]s a general strategy of moral reasoning, utilitarianism . . . is irrational." Finnis, *Natural Law and Natural Rights*, *supra*, at 112. If one reads Finnis' rejection back into Aquinas (as I am not doing in the text), then Aquinas too is rejecting utilitarianism and my critique of him in the text would be inapplicable.

59. Fest, Joachim C., *Hitler*, 1975, at 725.

60. Spence, Jonathan D., *The Search for Modern China*, 1990, at 576.

Aquinas also posited various aspects of human nature with which a regime would be expected to comply. One central problem with his list is that human nature is arguably too varied to fit within it.[61] For example, he posits that we have a natural inclination to self preservation.[62] Again, playing devil's advocate, I wonder whether this is so clearly correct as Aquinas (and Finnis) suggest. Freud posited a death instinct, thantos, that conflicted with life and love (eros).[63] The apparent human willingness to continuously wage war some place around the earth at every moment of recorded history suggests that people do not always regard self preservation as their principle value. To reinforce this skepticism, I here point out some of man's dangerous sports and activities, ones that are exciting at least in part because they involve playing with the possibility of death: rock climbing, mountain climbing, automobile racing, boxing, sky diving, hang gliding, bungee jumping and smoking.

Next on Aquinas' list of natural inclinations is sexual relations. Again, while I do not personally advocate abstinence, it is worth noting that sexual relations have not always been universally praised. Saint Paul, for example, damned sex with the faint praise that it is preferable for a husband to have sex with his wife than to burn.[64] And indeed, some Christians and Buddhists have advocated sexual abstinence as desirable.

Aquinas regarded the rearing of offsprings as a natural inclination. Living in a large city and listening to the local news every night, I conclude by the number of people who are reported as killing, abandoning or neglecting their children that child rearing is not as universal an inclination as was once thought. Strengthening this perception is an awareness that more and more people have chosen not to have

---

61. "[Alan Gewirth's] criticism of [natural law] tradition [includes that] human nature is too varied to provide a determinate set of principles...." Hittinger, Russell, "Natural Law and Virtue: Theories at Cross Purposes," George, Robert ed., *Natural Law Theory*, 1992, at 50.

62. This goes back to Aristotle who said that "we all see that men cling to life even at the cost of enduring great misfortune, seeming to find in life a natural sweetness and happiness." Aristotle, *The Politics, Book III*, c.6, 1943, Benjamin Jowett ed., p. 137.

63. "...Freud [posited] two opposing forces in the mind: he termed them Life Instincts and Death Instincts..., the former being entitled *Eros*. They were...in constant struggle with each other, although the latter inevitably won in the end." Jones, *The Life and Work of Sigmund Freud, Vol. 3, supra*, at 273.

64. *See* I Corinthians 7:9, *The Interpreter's Bible, Vol. 10*, 1981, at 78.

children. Women in particular are no longer quite so much compelled by societal mores to have children they might not want.

Aquinas also claimed that people have a natural inclination to do good. How does one define doing good? Helping others? I would doubt that most of us spend any considerable time helping others. But assuming contrary to this assertion that we do collectively spend a fair amount of time helping others, how would we characterize this activity? Perhaps one would say that the helpful person is an altruist. But our language also suggests other, more pejorative, terms, such as, "do gooder," "goody two shoes," "busybody," and, more pretentiously, "officious intermeddler."

What sort of government would most clearly correspond to the value of doing good? I would think that the answer would be a strongly socialist one. But is this the most desirable form of government? Regardless, it would seem that in a capitalistic and individualistic society like the U.S., doing good for others is generally subordinated to looking out for oneself.[65]

Next on Aquinas' list of natural inclinations is living in society.[66] While most people undoubtedly share this inclination, it is not uni-

---

65. One commentator has suggested that the current American ethos both accepts that looking out for onself is desirable but also that government should look out for oneself as well:

> [Based on polling data t]he consensus represents a national embrace of a kind of one-way libertarianism. Its main assumption is that the government has a very serious obligation to the middle class: it must provide a degree of protection. On the other hand, the middle class is in no way obligated to commit time or money to larger national projects — anything from military service to solving problems that are off somewhere out of immediate view.

Lemann, Nicholas, "The New American Consensus," Sec. 6, *The New York Times Magazine*, Nov. 1, 1998, at 68.

This turns the language of John F. Kennedy's inaugural address ("Ask not what your country can do for you; Ask what you can do for your country.") on its head. *See* Kennedy, John, *To Turn the Tide*, 1962, at 10.

66. This view goes back to Aristotle who pointed out that man is a social animal:

> The proof that the state is a creation of nature and prior to the individual is that the individual, when isolated, is not self-sufficing...; [H]e who is unable to live in society, or who has no need because he is sufficient for himself, must be either a beast or a god: he is no part of a state. A social instinct is implanted in all men by nature...

Aristotle, *The Politics, supra, Book I*, C.2, at 55.

versally perceived to be desirable. In the United States and Canada, for example, some people live and presumably enjoy living where there are open spaces with few people, for example, in Montana, Idaho, Wyoming, the Dakotas, Alaska and Northern Canada.

Finally, Aquinas regards as a natural inclination the value of knowing the truth about God. Aquinas' version of this value seems limited to the transcendent God of the Western religions, that is, Judaism, Christianity and Islam or perhaps to Christianity alone. Obviously, this is not a universal value if one includes within one's purview Buddhists, Hindus, Confucianists, Shintoists, agnostics and atheists. So, instead of dealing with Aquinas' version, I would turn to John Finnis, who defends Aquinas' natural law generally, and provides a much broader and easier to defend version of a similar value:

> But is it reasonable to deny that it is...peculiarly important to have thought reasonably and (where possible) correctly about these questions of the origins of cosmic order and of human freedom and reason—whatever the answer to those questions turns out to be, and even if the answers have to be agnostic or negative?[67]

I can understand why thinking about cosmic order is so important if one concludes that there is a transcendent God who would admit you into heaven only if you believed in Him. But a lot of religious people do not believe this, including members of the religious traditions that do adhere to this position. And it can also be argued that thinking a lot about the cosmic order takes time away from other, more constructive pursuits, such as, making a more comfortable living and supporting oneself. So, is it so obvious that one ought to pursue thinking about the origin and nature of the cosmic order?

In summary, each one of Aquinas' natural inclinations can be disputed, some more successfully disputed than others, as not universally applicable. If the disputation seems plausible , then the bases for his natural law theory are severely undercut.

But what about his modern defender, John Finnis? What about his seven self evident basic aspects of human good (life, knowledge, play, aesthetics, friendship and sociability, practical reasonableness and religion)? Are there fundamental differences between Finnis and Aquinas with respect to how universal these values have to be and

67. Finnis, *Natural Law and Natural Rights, supra*, at 89.

whether they are regarded as self evidently good? I don't think so. When Finnis refers to these as basic values, just like Aquinas he is making a claim about human beings universally. For example he states: "[a]ll human societies show a concern for the value of human life; in all, self-preservation is generally accepted as a proper motive for action, and in none is the killing of other human beings permitted without some fairly definite justification."[68]

There is one substantive difference with Aquinas, however, namely, Finnis emphasizes that these are aspects of human good rather than simply natural human (and in some categories, animal,) inclinations. He makes it clear that he is referring to what in a rational, practical (prudential) sense is good for one's well being, not what she regards as morally good.[69] He also makes it clear that animals do not share in these aspects of human good.[70] Still, I fail to see how this puts Finnis' list of aspects of human good in any more impregnable position than Aquinas' list of natural inclinations.

This leads me to conclude that, just as with Aquinas, if I can show that we humans do not (nearly universally) act as though these are self evident values, then this substantially weakens Finnis' thesis. But I have already demonstrated this with respect to several of Finnis' values, namely, life, practical reasonableness, friendship and sociability and religion. I now turn to his other basic values, speculative knowledge, play and aesthetic experience.

The first of these, the desire to learn, to know, probably characterizes everyone who is reading this book. But it does not characterize everybody. It does not necessarily characterize many of those television couch potatoes who stay home to watch the daily daytime dose of soap operas, talk shows and game shows or those fixated on evening and weekend viewing of sporting events. The idea that the average person is genuinely interested in speculative knowledge beyond what is contained in gossip columns, sports pages, comics and the magazines available at the checkout counters at grocery stores ("what inquiring minds want to know") is easy to attack.

Finnis' other basic values, play and aesthetic experience, however, are more difficult to attack. Still, the ability and willingness to play,

68. *Id.* at 83.
69. *Id.* at 86-7.
70. *Id.* at 194-5.

even though desirable in the abstract, seem to have eroded among a fair number of workaholic white collar and executive adults in the economically advanced countries of North America, Western Europe and Japan. It is not uncommon to hear of people working 60 to 80 hours a week and commuting to and from the job three hours a day or more. Then one can throw in time spent taking care of children, doing household chores and buying the food and clothing necessities of life. For such people the amount of time, energy and inclination available for play would seem minimal to non-existent.

While I would expect that virtually everybody, if asked, would rank aesthetic experiences (beauty) as important, I think that it is quite possible that in reality many people demonstrate that they do not especially value such experiences. Some people who could do otherwise do not live in physically attractive surroundings, do not regard their physical appearance as all that important, do not throw all of their garbage in the appropriate containers, do not fight to keep their communities free of unnecessary pollution, do not visit the national parks or areas of beauty available to them and do not go to art museums. If the previous statement has the ring of truth, then the near universality of the basic value of aesthetic experience can reasonably be questioned.

In summary, Finnis' basic values, like Aquinas' natural inclinations, can be attacked. Once these divinely inspired or self evident values become somewhat more problematic, then the natural law theories based on them become more problematic as well. Even though both Aquinas and Finnis make room for a number of basic self evident values, indeed provide lists of them, human nature cannot be so easily pigeonholed: "human nature itself [is] contradictory."[71]

Well then, what about the premises underlying the natural law theories of Locke, Kant, Nozick and Rawls? How air tight are these premises? Of the four, Locke's social contract theory is easiest to attack. Influenced by the experience of the colonists in the new world, he apparently believed literally in a social contract, that is, people came together to agree to form a government.

In fact, however, from what we know of our human history as well as our nearest relatives, the chimps, the orangutans and the great

---

71. Ignatieff, Michael, *Isaiah Berlin*, 1998, at 202.

apes, people probably always lived in groups. This is because, despite my efforts at being a devil's advocate above, Aristotle,[72] Aquinas and Finnis are right, namely, the vast majority of people (but not all or nearly all) are social and cannot easily survive without others. From this one can develop an argument that goes contrary to Locke and Nozick, namely, that the polity is logically prior to the person. Since persons virtually always live in groups, it makes no sense to assert that their individual rights and liberties are prior to the social unit in which they live. After a certain level of organization is reached, peoples' social unit becomes the polity. In short, a theory based on group interests is right and natural rights theories are wrong. Carried further, this argument concludes that positivism is right, for it is the state and only the state (as a successor to the family, the tribe, the group) that decides upon our rights, if any, through the positive law and not some natural law thesis that can rationally explain how individual rights are independent of what the state grants and takes away.

Kant's basic premise is that it makes sense to refer to our basic noumenal (uncaused, unmotivated) freedom to obligate ourselves. But it can be argued that this subjective sense of freedom is an illusion. If freedom is an illusion, then this destroys his natural law argument because it is premised on the assertion that the lawgiver ought to enact laws that would comply with every person's freedom.

As to the argument based on illusion, the assertion goes as follows: when we undertake a moral obligation, we are always motivated by something or other. Freud would say that we are motivated by having internalized the values of our parents and the community (what he calls the superego and we would call conscience) to do what they believe we should be doing.[73] So, under this argument there is not really the freedom, in fact, that Kant emphasized.

---

72. "A social instinct is implanted in all men by nature..." Aristotle, *The Politics, Book I, c. 2. supra*, at 55.

73. Here is one commentator's take on this aspect of Freud's understanding of the super ego:

> Children first choose their parents as objects of their love and then, forced to relinquish these choices as unacceptable, identify with them by taking their attitudes-their norms, injunctions, and prohibitions—into themselves. In short having begun by wanting to *have* their parents, they end by wanting to *be* like them. But not precisely like them—they construct their identifications as Freud put it, "not on the model of their parents but on that of the parental superego."
>
> In this way the superego becomes "the vehicle of tradition, of all the time-

Not only can it be argued that freedom is an illusion, it also can be argued that we are sometimes, though not usually, aware that it is an illusion. Our awareness that free will is an illusion depends on our awareness in general. As we are educated, particularly in psychology, we develop the ability to analyze and question why we undertake obligations. The awareness gained sometimes enables us to be cognizant of what motivates us to undertake obligations.

Also, for Kant if there is to be a community acting in conformity with the moral law, it will occur only through people acting in accordance with the lawful authority. Thus, the bottom line for Kant is that we must give obeisance to the lawful authority because otherwise the community cannot comply with the moral law.[74] But this gives the dictator free rein to enact whatever laws he wishes and demand obedience from the subjects as their obligation under Kantian theory.

Further, Kant seems to be asserting that the leader ought to enact laws that would accord with each person's moral freedom. But why should he? From the dictator's perspective, there is no particularly good reason as to why he should.

Next I turn to Rawls. One possible difficulty arises because Rawls assumes a background structure in which free and equal moral persons agree on the maximization of equal liberty. One can attack his assumption from two conflicting perspectives, one that denies the assumption altogether and the other that regards it as too restrictive. The first objection rejects the notion of moral equality which underlies Rawls' background structure on which his hypothetical agreement in *Political Liberalism* is based. This objection, though not easily accepted by contemporary democrats, might have met with the approval of Aristotle. Although Aristotle believed that a political entity "ought to be composed, as far as possible, of equals[75]," he also believed in natural slavery.[76]

---

resistant valuations that have thus propagated themselves across generations." Hence the superego, at once preserving cultural values and attacking the individual it inhabits, becomes the agent of life and death alike.

Gay, Peter, *Freud*, 1989, at 415.

74. Freeman, *Lloyd's Introduction to Jurisprudence*, Sixth Edition, at 109.

75. Aristotle, *The Politics, Book IV*, c. 11, *supra*, at 191.

76. *Id.* c. 6, at 137.

To make the argument that we are not morally equal, I suggest a thought experiment. Suppose you were a fireperson attempting to rescue people from a burning building. Because you were familiar with the building and its occupants, you would know who the occupants were and where they were. Would you treat them all as morally equal? Or would you be likely to rescue the kids and younger women first, leaving the old folks to die? Would you be more likely to rescue the distinguished but disabled scientist, say Stephen Hawking, rather than the parolee who had served time for raping his daughter?[77] If the answer is yes, are you not denying that moral equality which Rawls asserts as a condition for the agreement that is the basis of his natural law theory?

The second objection to Rawls' notion of moral equals agreeing to the principles he enunciates is based on its underinclusiveness. Rawls attributes to them as moral persons two capacities, one for a sense of justice (to understand, apply and act from the principles of justice) and the other for a conception of the good life. This focus creates a problem, for one can argue that the obligations of a just society arise independently of people's capacity to reasonably agree on certain reciprocal principles of justice. Under Rawls' thesis,[78] infants, the seri-

77. As I write this, I have fresh in my mind the obituary of Andre Weil. According to the obituary, Weil, a brilliant mathematician considered the intellectual equal of the great scientists and mathematicians of our age, was a French citizen who avoided the draft at the beginning of World Ward II. He stated that "[a]s a soldier, I would be entirely useless, but as a mathematician, I could be of some use." Burkhart, Ford, "Andre Weil, Who Reshaped Mathematics, Is Dead at 92," *The New York Times*, Aug. 10, 1998. A17.

Although one can dismiss Weil's statement as a self interested desire to avoid the possibility of dying masquerading as a rational argument, I suggest that we examine it as though it were a rational assertion. One can argue that Weil was not asserting that his moral superiority justified escaping the draft but rather that his intellectual superiority did so. But the effect of the argument is that he has a right to live while others might die and this is equivalent in effect even if not in intention to the position that he has a moral right to live while others might die. Is it so clear that, given his extraordinary intelligence and productivity, he was wrong?

78. The next step is to take the two moral powers as the necessary and sufficient condition for being counted a full and equal member of society in questions of political justice. Those who can take part in social cooperation over a complete life, and who are willing to honor the appropriate fair terms of cooperation, *are regarded as equal citizens*.

Rawls, *Political Liberalism, supra*, at 302 (emphasis added).

ously "mentally challenged" and the senile would be in no position to agree on the obligations of justice and seemingly not be entitled to its benefits. In short, the contract principle of justice, even one like Rawls' that is not intended as reflecting historical reality, limits those included within its ambit of mutual obligations to people with certain intellectual capacities, those able to sustain the two moral powers of a sense of justice and a capacity for justice. It is not our humanness (or, more broadly, our sentience) which creates mutual obligations, but rather our having certain capacities. To restate, this leaves out of the equation obligations to the comatose, the psychotic, the senile, the severely retarded, and those too young to have developed the necessary capacities.[79]

Another possible difficulty with Rawls' thesis is that it requires a fairly interventionist state. In his earlier work, *A Theory of Justice*,

---

79. To a lesser extent a similar argument can be made against Alan Gewirth's defense of human rights.

Gewirth's argument goes as follows. that every actual or prospective performer of an action requires freedom (or voluntariness) and well-being (purposiveness or intentionality) as necessary conditions for the successful completion of the action. Since the person who seeks to engage in a successful action must deny that other persons have the right to interfere in her action, she therefore claims a right to freedom and well being. Logically, once she makes the claim of a right to freedom and well being, the claim must be universalized. Thus, she must accord the same right to freedom and well being to every other prospective purposive agent. Gewirth, Alan, "The Epistemology of Human Rights," *Social Philosophy and Policy, Vol. 1*, 1984, 1-24.

The argument applicable to Rawls is less applicable to Gewirth, for Gewirth includes within his ambit of those with rights prospective purposive agents. This would include infants. But it would not include the comatose. And it might not include the severely retarded, the psychotic and the senile. The following statement by Gewirth implicitly acknowledges this point:

> Since for any prospective agent the point of having and respecting the generic rights derives from their necessary contribution to action in pursuit of purpose-fulfillment, persons who are not capable of such action have the right to freedom only to the extent to which their free conduct would not directly interfere with the conditions of their own freedom and well-being or with the generic rights of other persons. *But to the extent to which mentally deficient persons have human potentialities*, the [Principle of Generic Consistency] requires both that these be protected and that efforts be made to effect whatever improvements may be possible in the direction of normal agency.

Gewirth, Alan, *Reason and Morality*, 1978, at 142 (emphasis added).

When Gewirth writes that to the extent a mentally deficient person has the human potentiality to act as a purposive agent she should be protected, he is implying that to the extent she lacks the potentiality to act as a purposive agent she need not be protected.

his second basic principle includes the difference principle, namely, that social and economic inequalities must be justified on the ground that they benefit the least advantaged. In *Political Liberalism* Rawls assures us that the difference principle does not involve government micro managing the economy by redistributing assets at the level of individual transactions that are fairly entered into: "[t]he objection that the difference principle enjoins continuous corrections of particular distributions and capricious interference with private transactions is based on a misunderstanding."[80] Instead, taxes would be used in a forseeable way to redistribute wealth to the less favored. As a means to producing a just social order, inequalities would be allowed only so long as they improve everyone's situation. The least favored "have, so to speak, a veto"[81] over allowing inequalities that result.

However, presumably everything comes to a halt while the least well off (or their representatives) are pondering whether to allow the widget to be manufactured or the entertainer to perform. The possibilities for bureaucratic delays and mistakes are enormous. To give the least favored (or the government acting on their behalf) a veto over inequalities is an invitation to stultification and stagnation of the economic process.

Further, how can the least educated and least well off (or anybody else for that matter) calibrate which inequalites improve everyone's situation and therefore can be approved and which do not and therefore must be vetoed? Did the wealth accumulated by Elvis Presley or Michael Jordan benefit everyone's situation? The idea that this should be and can be measured seems difficult to defend. Rawls' work steers clear of an economic analysis.[82] But isn't the economic feasibility of his moral conception of the difference principle relevant to its practical value and usability?

Another possible weakness in Rawls' defense of massive wealth redistribution to the least favored is that it promotes a welfare state. The weakness is twofold. First, it harms the recipient of the government help. This harm occurs because the redistribution at best is likely to undermine the development of a strong work habit and at worst is likely to promote laziness. Nor is it clear that getting some-

80. Rawls, *Political Liberalism, supra*, at 283.
81. *Id.* at 282.
82. *See Id.* n. 21 at 306.

thing from the government because one cannot earn it on one's own promotes self respect.

And secondly, having the government redistribute the wages of the haves to the have nots (except where inequalities can be shown to be to the advantage of the have nots) is likely to promote a sense in the haves that the system is disadvantageous to them, economically inefficient and perhaps even unfair. Thus, despite Rawls' positing of a sense of justice on the part of the haves that would make them willing to endure the redistribution of a sizeable portion of their wealth and income to the less well off, it is quite likely that he is mistaken. Rather than suffer in the name of justice, the haves would be likely to vote against the wealth redistribution either before it was instituted or later once it was observed in operation.

Perhaps, as Rawls indicates in another context, his response to the argument of the last paragraph would go along the following path: the sense of justice is exercised not for its own sake but rather "as the best way to stabilize just social cooperation and thereby advance the determinate concepts of the good...."[83] To put this another, less positive way: one should accept the difference principle (with the least favored obtaining a veto over economic inequalities) because it is the best way to insure social cooperation. In short, if the least favored are bribed by the most favored with economic goodies, then social cooperation will follow. But if this is what a cynical reading of Rawls' theory indicates that he is asserting, then his theory, while a means to produce social peace, does not carry that much weight as a moral principle or as a natural law principle.

So far, acting as devil's advocate, I have raised possible theoretical objections to the premises of the various substantive natural law theories presented. I have attacked the factual premises of Aquinas' and Finnis' version. I have attacked Locke's and Nozick's defense of natural rights on the ground that humans are social animals, and therefore the social was probably always prior to the individual. I have attacked Kant's notion that we subjectively necessarily feel we are freely entering into obligations. And I have attacked Rawls, both on his underlying background assumption that we are morally equal when in at least some contexts we might not be and on his use of the

83. *Id.* at 318.

difference principle that gives the have nots a veto over economic development that will add to economic and social inequalities.

Another ground for attacking substantive natural law theory is based on Hume's notion that it is a logical fallacy to go from an is to an ought.[84] What is involved is a shift from a factual premise concerning human nature to a prescriptive conclusion about how rulers ought to behave.[85] Although not dealing with rulers, the following remark by Locke illustrates this approach. Locke asserted that in their earlier history humans lived in a state of nature, only to contract later with one another to enter into civil society. Still, in the earlier state of nature phase there was a law of nature that governed human interaction. That law was reason. "[R]eason, which *is* [that law of nature], teaches all mankind who will but consult it, that being all equal and independent, no one *ought* to harm another in his life, health, liberty or possessions...."[86] (emphasis added).

As I mentioned, according to Hume one cannot derive an ought from an is. Thus, if one asserts as Locke did that humans have a certain nature, say, ability to reason, vulnerability to being injured when physically assaulted, it does not logically follow that law ought to be reasonable or protect people from attack. The evil dictator who wishes to stay in power above everything else might decide that the best way to do so is by making the laws sufficiently irrational with the likely consequence that many citizens would be randomly injured or killed. As a result, the citizens would remain in fear for their lives and too passive to organize a revolt. And the dictator would more likely survive in power.

Another difficulty with natural law arises if the definition of natural law couples 'law' with what those in power must do. One exam-

---

84. Hume, David, *A Treatise of Human Nature, Book III*, Pt. I, sec. 1, edited by L. A. Selby-Bigge, 1888.

85. At one point I would also have included as an example of this alleged fallacy Thomas Aquinas' going from how humans are, such as, each person attempts to preserve his own life, to an ought, namely, how government ought to deal with its citizenry. But according to Finnis, Acquinas was not, contra Hume, deriving oughts from what is. Rather, the oughts of government are self evident or indemonstrable truths. Finnis, *Natural Law and Natural Rights, supra*, at 33-4, 47. (Whether or not Finnis is right about Aquinas is a question I need not decide.)

86. Locke, *Two Treatises of Government*, Freeman, *Lloyd's Introduction to Jurisprudence, supra*, at 139.

ple is Thomas Aquinas' assertion that "...the *ruler's will is law* [only] on the proviso that the ruler's will is ruled by reason; otherwise a ruler's will is more like lawlessness."[87] Another example is that of the legal philosopher, H. L. A. Hart.[88] Hart asserted that where human survival is the goal, then a legal system must take into consideration certain facts about the human condition, specifically, our vulnerability, our approximate equality, our limited altruism, our limited understanding and strength of will and the existence of limited resources.[89] But as Hart would have agreed[90], there are many examples in which those in power have not followed any such principles of law as laid down by Aquinas or even by Hart.

Thus, it is reasonable to ask, how would natural law theorists respond to a dictator who did not choose to follow their theories? This mental exercise is reminiscent of Oliver Wendell Holmes' admonition to look at the positive (existing) law, say of Massachusetts, from the perspective of the "Bad Man" whose only interest in obeying it is his fear that otherwise he would be punished.[91] Why should a cynical dictator follow the various versions of substantive natural law proposed by these thinkers? Indeed, my parade of horribles, namely, Hitler, Stalin, Mao Tse Tung, Pol Pot, Nicolae Ceausescue and Saddem Hussein, come to mind immediately as people who refused to follow any of the above versions of natural law theory.

---

87. Aquinas, Thomas, *Summa Theologica, supra,* Qu. 90.1 at 280.

But according to Finnis, Aquinas' way of dealing with the problem was not to deny that an evil ruler could act lawfully. Rather, Aquinas was asserting that in one sense of the term, which Finnis calls the focal sense, an evil ruler is not acting lawfully. Finnis, John, *Natural Law and Natural Rights, supra,* at 363-366.

88. Despite appearances here, Hart basically rejected natural law theory as will be noted below.

89. Hart, H. L. A., *The Concept of Law,* 1961, at 188-193,

90. ...Hart does not seek to suggest that, even if this analysis of human society is accepted, this must inveitably lead to a system of even minimal justice within a given community. On the contrary, he accepts the fact, as indeed is hardly to be denied, that human societies at all periods of history have displayed a melancholy record of oppression and discrimination in the name of security and legal order, as, for instance, in the case of systems based on slavery, or systems based on positive religious or racial discrimination, all too familiar in the modern world.

Freeman, *Lloyd's Introduction to Jurisprudence, supra,* at 120.

91. Holmes, Oliver Wendell, "The Path of the Law," *Collected Papers,* 172-3.

What could these theorists say in response to the evil dictator? Aquinas could say that the dictator did not participate in divine truth. Finnis could say that the dictator did not recognize self evident truth. Locke could say that the dictator violated an historic social contract. Nozick could say that the dictator, in infringing on personal and property rights, extended the state's power beyond justified limits. Rawls could say that he violated the basic principle of equal liberty. A number of natural law theorists could say that he acted illogically and unreasonably.

What could the dictator say in response? He could say "I do not accept your premises including your notion of rationality as true, or if true, as binding on me. And, therefore, I do not choose to act in accord with your theories." Is there any persuasive response to this assertion of the dictator? If there is, I am not sure what it would be.

5

Procedural Natural Law

Procedural natural law theory does not provide the same degree of protection to the person against a government's excesses or the same level of psychic satisfaction to someone studying it as its substantive natural law sibling provides. Indeed, the critic who asserts that there is not the same level of psychic satisfaction in reciting the elements of procedural natural law as to be obtained by the writings of some substantive natural law theorists (say, John Locke or Thomas Jefferson's *Declaration of Independence*) makes a good point. I too get more pleasure out of rereading the Declaration of Independence's reference to the self evident truths that all men are created equal and that from this equal creation they derive the inalienable rights of life, liberty and the pursuit of happiness than I get out of reciting elements of procedural natural law. But despite its being less emotionally satisfying and less protective of the person, procedural natural law theory can be defended more easily against some of the attacks that prove so troubling when employed against the substantive version.

As far as I know, Lon Fuller was the first legal philosopher to focus his attention on procedural natural law.[92] He was the principal exponent of the view that the concept 'law' contains a necessary proce-

---

92. James Boyle has pointed out that Henry Hart and Albert Sachs, two professors at Harvard Law School at the same time as Lon Fuller was there, took the same procedural approach as Fuller did. See James Boyle, "Legal Realism and the Social Contract: Fuller's Public Jurisprudence of Form, Private Jurisprudence of Substance," 78 *Cornell L. Rev.* 371, 377 (1993). If so, this would muddy the waters as to whether Fuller originated the concept. But my memory of the Hart and Sachs material leads me to conclude that they were dealing with the value of analyzing 'law' in the context of Anglo-American law rather than making claims about what the concept 'law' contains that transcended what existed in any particular culture.

As I indicated in an earlier footnote, in editing an article by R. A. Duff for his book, *Law and Justice*, Second Edition, 1999, at 271, Dale A. Nance refers to Duff's use of the term 'Natural Justice.' Nance's gloss on this term, which is consistent with Duff's use of it, is that "'Natural Justice' is a term used in English jurisprudence to refer to normative principles of procedural justice." This reference (which appears to be a less conceptualized and abstract version of procedural natural law) would suggest that the concept has a pedigree in British jurisprudence that Fuller might have adopted.

dural moral element or what he called procedural natural law. One version of Fuller's idea of procedural law (or what he sometimes refered to as the inner morality of the law) comes in the form of eight principles: (1) made laws must be sufficiently general (that is, there must be rules); (2) they must be publicly promulgated; (3) they must be sufficiently prospective; (4) they must be clear and intelligible; (5) they must be free of contradiction; (6) they must be sufficiently constant through time so people can order their relations accordingly; (7) they must not require the impossible; and (8) they must be administered in a way sufficiently congruent with their wording so people can abide by them.[93] Another facet of Fuller's procedural morality is the requirement of "'justice itself'...that like cases be decided alike."[94] Elsewhere, Fuller fleshed out his idea of procedural law by explicating what would constitute a violation:

> When a system calling itself law is predicated upon a general disregard by judges of the terms of the laws they purport to enforce, when this system habitually cures its legal irregularities, even the grossest, by retroactive statutes, when it has only to resort to forays of terror in the street, which no one dares to challenge, in order to escape even those scant restraints imposed by the pretence of legality—when all these things have become true of a dictatorship, it is not hard for me, at least, to deny to it the name of law.[95]

What was Fuller doing when he set forth these criteria for the concept 'law'? I believe that he was attempting to define the concept.[96]

---

93. Summers, Robert L., *Lon L. Fuller*, 1984, at 28. *See also*, Fuller, Lon, *The Morality of Law*, 1964, at 39, 46-91.

94. Summers, *Lon L. Fuller, supra*, at 28.

95. Fuller, Lon L., "Positivism and Fidelity to Law—A Reply to Professor Hart," 71 *Harv. L. Rev.* 630. 660 (1958).

96. One scholar regards Fuller's analysis as a deduction from the meaning of law: "[W]hen Fuller describes the 'morality that makes law possible,' he has in mind a set of formal criteria that define, or perhaps it would be better to say are deduced from, the very meaning of law." Boyle, "Legal Realism and the Social Contract," *supra*, at 372.

I have my doubts whether Professor Boyle is right about this. But whether he is or not, the version of procedural natural law developed in this book is not deduced from the meaning of law. Rather, the criteria developed here are elements that we are aware belong to the concept 'the rule of law' because we recognize that as we use language these elements are generally included within the concept.

This view is reinforced by Fuller's statement that he is denying that certain government actions come within the name of law. It should be noticed that Fuller is not asserting that any violation of the principles he enunciates means that the government is not acting in accordance with the concept 'law.' Rather, he refers to a "general" disregard by judges of the laws and the system's "habitually curing" its legal irregularities.

This indicates Fuller's awareness that the issue of what constitutes legality is not an all or nothing affair. If, as he indicated, a government could violate his principles on occasion and still continue to be operating a legal system, to me this would indicate that he was examining the concept 'legality' in terms of its use rather than arbitrarily stipulating a concept that he wished to apply even though it lacked any substantial connection to our actual use of language. This was the approach suggested by Ludwig Wittgenstein who asked, "isn't the meaning of the word also determined by...[its] use?"[97] After I first point out that other legal and non-legal philosopers have followed Fuller's emphasis on the procedural aspects of law, I will attempt to show that this assertion is rooted in our language.

Another point worth mentioning before getting into Fuller's approach is Professor Boyle's assertion that Fuller's approach is based on a social contract: "...Fuller is clearly adopting the structure and rhetoric of the social contract in his analysis of the bonds between government and citizen." *Id.* at 377. *But see* Covell, Charles, *The Defence of Natural Law*, 1992, at 50.

Whether or not there is an implicit or explicit social contract element in Fuller's analysis, I make no use of a social contract approach in defending the procedural natural law position taken here. Rather, as stated below, the defense is based on linguistic usage.

97. Ludwig Wittgenstein, *Philosophical Investigations*, 3rd ed., sec.139, translated by G.E.M. Anscombe, 1953, at 54.

Others have made a similar point:

"[W]ords are not, or not merely, labels but often signals; that language is learned from instances of use, and consequently meaning is compounded out of instances of use and that meaning is context-dependent...." Pitkin, Hannah F., *Wittgenstein and Justice*, n. 16 at 85.

"[E]veryday language is also the medium by which the intersubjectivity of a shared world is maintained." Habermas, Jurgen, *Moral Consciousness and Communicative Action*, translated by Christian Lenhardt and Shierry Weber Nicholsen, 1991, at 199.

6

Philosophers Use the Language of Procedural Natural Law

But before showing that the concept 'legality' is rooted in our language, I will suggest that other philosophers and legal thinkers support the notion of procedural natural law to a greater or lesser extent. So far as I succeed in this endeavor, I also strengthen my assertion that our language accommodates this way of speaking and writing and that it is not just my own (and Fuller's) idiosyncratic vision. Surprisingly enough, one of these legal philosophers was H. L. A. Hart. The reason why my enlisting Hart's support for procedural natural law is surprising is that Hart was a positivist who rejected the idea that law contained a necessary moral element and therefore refused to accept any general (substantive) natural law theory. Nontheless he explicitly followed Fuller's lead in accepting the idea that law contains a procedural element:

> If we attach to a legal system the minimum meaning that it must consist of general rules—general both in the sense that they refer to courses of action, not single actions, and to multiplicities of men, not single individuals—this meaning connotes the principle of treating like cases alike, though the criteria of when cases are alike will be, so far, only the general elements specified in the rules. It is, however, true that *one* essential element of the concept of justice is the principle of treating like cases alike. This is justice in the administration of the law, not justice of the law. So, there is, in the very notion of law consisting of general rules, something which prevents us from treating it as if morally it is utterly neutral, without any necessary contact with moral principles. Natural procedural justice consists therefore of those principles of objectivity and impartiality in the administration of the law which implement just this aspect of law and which are designed to ensure that rules are applied only to what are genuinely cases of the rule or at least to minimize the risks of inequality in this sense.[98]

---

98. Hart, H.L.A., "Positivism and the Separation of Law and Morals," in *Philosophy*

This statement clearly indicates that Hart accepted a very minimal version of what he called natural procedural justice. Hart did include in his criteria of legal procedure that the rules be general, and that the judge decide impartially and objectively. In asserting that law consists of general rules, he was directing his assertion at governmental officials and what they must do to make these general rules, thereby delineating procedural rules as well.

The general rules would be required to be administered by treating similars similarly. But as this phrase would indicate, Hart's version of procedural natural law was rather limited. Similar cases were to be treated similarly. This meant the administrators of the existing positive law would be required to treat similars similarly rather than that the legal rules themselves would be required rationally to treat similars similarly. He explicitly rejected the idea that it makes any sense to judge whether the regime is treating similars similarly based on transcendent criteria, that is, from outside the regime's own purported criteria for similarity. If a revolutionary regime, say the Khymer Rouge in Cambodia, were to adopt a rule calling for the killing of all those who wore glasses or whose eyes looked like they had worn glasses (on the ground that they were probably dangerous intellectuals), then under Hart's analysis and his terminology one could examine whether natural procedural justice had been done, that is, had virtually all eye glass wearers been killed? However, he would not examine whether it was somehow a violation of law as an ideal to kill eye glass wearers (under substantive natural law theory) or a violation of the idea of law to distinguish between eye glass wearers and non-eye glass wearers (under procedural natural law theory). That is, under Hart's criteria for what actions of the regime are consistent with law, he would have allowed for an analysis of the regime's stated criteria to determine that they were being applied but not an analysis of the regime's actions based on universal criteria that transcended what the regime purported to apply.

Although the genocide perpetuated by the Khymer Rouge clearly violates any acceptable moral code (acceptable to me or to Hart or, I presume, to you), as I have previously indicated I am not persuaded that there is a convincing justification for applying a version of substantive natural law theory to attack that regime's actions. By con-

---

of Law, 4th ed., edited by Joel Feinberg and Hyman Gross, 1991, at 76.

trast and in disagreement with Hart, I do believe that the procedural version of natural law, explicated by Fuller and to some extent by Hart himself, could be used to attack the Khymer Rouge as well as other horrendous regimes. Although I will not tie it specifically to the Khymer Rouge regime, later in the text I will attempt to justify this attack.

Returning to Hart's analysis of legal procedure, he distinguished between primary rules of a mature legal system, which require persons to do or abstain from certain actions, and secondary rules, which do not impose similar duties on persons. It is the primary rules which correspond to the traditional legal category of the substantive element of law and the secondary rules[99] which roughly correspond to the procedural element. From Hart one learns that the secondary rules, the legal procedures, are not directed at the general public in the way that the primary rules are.

The primary (substantive) rules are exemplified by the prohibitory norms of criminal law and the laws empowering persons to enter into contracts. By contrast legal procedures are directed to those who interact with the government, particularly officials of the system, including judges and lawyers, to inform them how to decide what primary rules to apply, how to change the primary and secondary rules and how to decide legal disputes. As Hart put it, "the primary rules may be conclusively ascertained, introduced, eliminated, varied and the fact of their violation conclusively determined."[100] When Hart referred to the primary rules being violated, he indicated that in order for a sanction to be applied the person must have done something, that is, the primary rules deal with action rather than status.

Various philosophers in addition to Fuller and Hart have provided elements of the concept of an ideal legal procedure while presenting more general philosophical ideas. These philosophers include Rawls, Finnis and Habermas. In *A Theory of Justice* John Rawls, recognizing a debt to Lon Fuller, also develops a procedural understanding of the idea of law as well as his more general, substantive political/legal ideal outlined above. Although not adopting Fuller's terminology of procedural natural law, Rawls does refer to the rule of law (formal

---

99. Specifically, Hart called these secondary rules rules of recognition, change and adjudication. *Id.* at 89-95.

100. *Id.* at 92. *See also* 78-79.

justice) as including: the regular, consistent and impartial administration of public rules which are known, promulgated, general and non-retroactive; the good faith belief by those who enact and enforce rules that can be obeyed; and the absence of bribery, corruption and the abuse of the legal process to punish political enemies. Further, judges must be impartial and independent and trials must contain rules of evidence that promote rational procedures of inquiry.[101] He defines a legal system as:

> a coercive order of public rules addressed to rational persons for the purpose of regulating their conduct and providing the framework for social cooperation. When their rules are just they establish a basis for legitimate expectations. They constitute grounds upon which persons can rely on one another and rightly object when their expectations are not fulfilled.[102]
>
> . . .
>
> If deviations from justice as regularity are too pervasive, a serious question may arise whether a system of law exists as opposed to a collection of particular orders designed to advance the interests of a dictator or the ideal of a benevolent despot.[103]
>
> . . .
>
> [O]ught implies can.... [A system of rules] must not impose a duty to do what cannot be done.... Legislators and judges, and other officials of the system, must believe that the laws can be obeyed....[104]
>
> . . .
>
> The rule of law also implies the precept that similar cases be treated similarly.[105]
>
> . . .
>
> [L]aws [must] be known and expressly promulgated...[106]

101. Rawls, *A Theory of Justice, supra*, 1971, at 235-241.
102. *Id.* at 235.
103. *Id.* at 236.
104. *Id.* at 236-7.
105. *Id.* at 237.
106. *Id.* at 238.

...

> A tyrant might change laws without notice, and punish (if that is the right word) his subjects accordingly, because he takes pleasure in seeing how long it takes them to figure out what the new rules are from observing the penalities he inflicts. But these rules would not be a legal system, since they would not serve to organize social behavior by providing a basis for legitimate expectations.[107]

In the last of these several quotes Rawls provides the basis for regarding the rule of law as having a moral dimension and therefore constituting an element of natural law theory, namely, people can organize their behavior in reliance on the promulgated governmental rules.

Other aspects of Rawls' rule of law include avoidance of bills of attainder and retroactive penal "laws." In addition, Rawls introduces what he refers to as the precepts of natural justice. These precepts are guidelines intended to preserve the integrity of the judicial process.[108] They include open trials, rules of evidence guaranteeing rational procedures of inquiry, judicial independence and impartiality. Like Fuller before him, in this section Rawls outlines much of the idea of what law entails. Like Hart, however, he believes that treating similars similarly does not go beyond using the criteria laid out by the regime's own rules: "we must suppose that the criteria of similarity are given by the legal rules themselves and the principles used to interpret them."[109]

Although I have referred to John Finnis as a reformulater of Thomas Aquinas' substantive natural theory, with the benefit of Fuller's writings Finnis pays much more explicit attention to the procedural aspect of natural law than Aquinas did. For example, he refers to "features of specificity, minimization of arbitrariness, and maintenance of a quality of reciprocity [stability and predictability] between the subjects of the law both amongst themselves and in their relations with the lawful authorities."[110]

---

107. *Id.* at 238.

108. *Id.* at 238.

109. *Id.* at 237.

110. Finnis, John, *Natural Law and Natural Rights, supra*, at 276-7, [287].

Some of the same points are made by J.R. Lucas:

> A legal system must satisfy certain conditions if it is to count as a legal system at all: the laws must be generally known, and for the most part be of general appli-

In the process of setting forth a more general theory as to how to justify democratic politics through a theory of discourse, the philosopher, Jurgen Habermas, also sets forth what he regards as the rule of law and criteria for its justification. Ostensibly, he rejects natural law theory[111] in favor of a theory of democratic legitimacy wherein there is a discursively achieved agreement whereby the "citizens should always be able to understand themselves also as authors of the law to which they are subject as addressees."[112] Instead of rights being secured through a higher natural law, they are secured by the community of citizens themselves through rational discourse. The question they must answer is, "what rights must citizens mutually grant one another if they decide to constitute themselves as a voluntary association of legal consociates and legitimately to regulate their living together by means of positive law?"[113] The rights must include that liberty which assures private autonomy or else there cannot be positive law.[114] It is only through positive law that our common life is orga-

> cation; there must be general agreement about what are to be accepted as laws, and a generally recognized way of adjudicating doubtful cases, with due regard to the arguments on either side.

Lucas, J.R., *On Justice*, 1980, at 32.

Lucas includes some elements of what he regards as natural justice by indicating what would constitute its absence. He does this by listing judicial situations where a procedural or formal element is missing and therefore where natural justice is lacking: where a judicial decison lacks reasonableness, where it is arbitrary, where it is based on irrelevant factors, where it lacks available reasons, where it reflects a bias, where the person rendering it is incompetent, where the judge does not give one of the parties a chance to be heard and cross examine witnesses, where he decides against the accused in a criminal case without there being evidence of guilt, where he does not treat similar cases similarly and where he punishes a person for doing something which that person could not reasonably have known was wrong. *Id.*, at 72-123.

111. Habermas, Jurgen, *Between Facts and Norms, supra*, at 199. "[R]ights are a social construction...." *Id.* at 226. "The proceduralist view is...incompatible with the Platonistic idea that positive law can draw its legitimacy from a higher law..." *Id.* at 450. If law were viewed as subordinated to morality, then there would be the adoption of a natural law theory. But (according to Habermas) it is not. *Id.* at 452-3. To assert that law is subordinate to morality burdens law with misleading natural law connotations. Whereas morality deals with simple face-to-face interactions, by contrast "the principle of democracy [through its laws] regulates relations among legal persons who understand themselves as bearers of rights." *Id.* at 233. *See also* 457.

112. *Id.* at 449.

113. *Id.* at 453. *See also* 459.

114. *Id.* at 455.

nized.[115] Each free and equal citizen (person) in association with the others agrees on a procedure embedded in a consitution employing the rule of law.[116]

In addition, law imposes limits on the realization of communitarian or utilitarian goals[117] and allows individuals to bring claims in order to protect their rights[118] against violations[119] and to secure their autonomy.[120] Procedural law regulates the basis for communication between legislators, legal advocates and the courts.[121]

Norms (or statutes) must normally be formulated in writing, must be public, must not be retroactive, must be general and consistent, and must treat comparable cases in the same way.[122] As to this last requirement of treating comparable cases in the same way, legal norms are different from moral norms. Moral norms are abstract and universalizable, that is, they say what is equally good for all human beings: "...private autonomy, in the sense of this universal right to equal liberties, implies a universal right of equality, that is, the right to equal treatment according to norms that guarantee substantive legal equality."[123] Legal norms, however, are concrete and addressed to a particular legal community: "[b]y contrast, a spatiotemporally localized *legal community* protects the integrity of its members only insofar as they acquire [from the state] the status of bearers of individual rights [that is, citizenship]."[124] Still, legal norms are general in that those addressed are treated similarly. "Ideally, legal rules [also] regulate a matter in the equal interest of all those affected...."[125] and

115. *Id.* at 460.

116. *Id.* at 496. Here Habermas writes of persons rather than citizens. Despite this language, the context of this section itself suggests and the rest of the book indicates that he accords legal protection to citizens rather than persons. I think that he believes that ideally (morally) each person coming within the jurisdiction of the state is a citizen. But his theory in general protects citizens rather than persons.

117. *Id.* at 159, 180.

118. Rights are derived from legitimately produced norms. *Id.* at 419.

119. *Id.* at 172.

120. *Id.* at 410.

121. *Id.* at 235.

122. *Id.* at 143-4.

123. *Id.* at 401.

124. *Id.* at 452.

125. *Id.* at 151-4.

so far as they are just they harmonize with moral norms.[126] Thus, a just society is one where each person is given the promise of human dignity and is emancipated and autonomous: "[i]n a legal community, *no one* is free as long as the freedom of one person must be purchased with another's oppression."[127] Further "[t]he law of a concrete legal community..., if it is to be legitimate [must] at least be compatible with moral standards that claim universal validity beyond the legal community.[128]

From these remarks I read Habermas as asserting that legal rights extend to citizens and not necessarily to persons generally living within the legal community. Like Hart and Rawls Habermas denies that a regime applying procedural natural law need provide similar treatment to those whom it deems non-citizens. But, so far as the community's legal institutions also reflect universal moral values, then basic legal rights will also be extended to persons generally.

Habermas goes on to assert that laws not only confer jurisdiction on governmental institutions, but they also regulate its power.[129] Thus, administrative power comes from and is limited by statutory authorization[130] as applied by courts.[131] While Habermas recognizes a connection between law and politics, he insists on the requirement that law maintains its legal form and not "be *absorbed* into politics."[132] "[L]aw has a structure all its own and is not arbitrarily malleable...."[133] If an undemocratic political reality violates the proce-

---

126. *Id.* at 156.

127. *Id.* at 418.

> [The] status [of legal rights belonging to those within a legal community] does not contradict the universalistic meaning of the classical liberties that include all persons as such and not only all members of a legal community. Even as basic legal rights, they extend to all persons insofar as the latter simply reside within the jurisdiction of the legal order: to this extent, everyone enjoys the protection of the constitution.

Id. at 456.

128. *Id.* at 282.

129. *Id.* at 144. Habermas is here referring to what H. L. A. Hart calls secondary rules. This will be discussed further below.

130. *Id.* at 150. Habermass recognizes, as I do, that administrative power is not always very well controlled. *Id.* at 190.

131. *Id.* at 169. *See also* 386.

132. *Id.* at 152. *See also* 352-4, 378.

133. *Id.* at 428.

> The idea of the rule of law sets in motion a spiraling self-application of law,

dural safeguards for democratic legislation and judicial decisions set forth in the constitution, then the juridical form of the rule of law may appear to be maintained but its reality has been lost.[134] The rule of law provides a barrier against citizens being overpowered by the use of illegitimate power and stabilizes behaviorial expectations. Thus, like Rawls Habermas indicates the basis for my assertion that a government complying with law stabilizes peoples' behavioral expectations by reducing governmental arbitrariness and irrationality.[135] This provides law with a moral dimension.

Independent courts with their own procedures[136] must exist to decide impartially, rationally[137] and appropriately. Each person must be given equal treatment before the law (due process), including equal claim to a legal hearing and equality in the application of the law.[138] Indeed, rationality is determined by the fact that citizens are treated equally before the law.[139] How does one determine that the citizens are being treated equally? They are treated equally if the reasons for their treatment (as similars and/or dissimilars) are "rationally acceptable [to] the...citizens as authors of the legal order."[140]

> which is supposed to bring the internally unavoidable supposition of political autonomy to bear against the facticity of legally uncontrolled social power that penetrates law *from the outside*. The development of the constitutional state can be understood as an open sequence of experience-guided precautionary measures against the overpowering of the legal system by illegitimate power relations that contradict its normative self-understanding.

Id. at 39.

134. *Id.* at 429.

135. *Id.* at 143. Later in the text Habermas can be read as making a procedural natural law claim using some of the same concepts that I will be referring to later in my text: "By rendering authoritative decisions about what is legal and illegal in individual cases, the judiciary treats existing law as law, namely, from the normative standpoint of stabilizing behavioral expectations." If (as I think) by the term 'normative' he means morally normative, then he is asserting that the concept 'law' has a necessary moral element because it stabilizes people's expectations as to how they can interact with each other and the government without incurring any sanctions.

136. *Id.* at 178.

137. "The judiciary cannot make whatever use it likes of the reasons packaged in, and linked to, statutes..." *Id.* at 192.

138. *Id.* at 109, 114, 125.

139. *Id.* at 414.

140. *Id.* at 415.

Procedural guarantees include the prohibition against double jeopardy and ad hoc courts.[141] Influenced by Kant, Habermas asserts that what confers legal legitimacy on lawmaking is that the citizenry could agree (though not necessarily would agree) on the legislation under the assumption that they could participate fully in the process of communication among themselves and with the legislators.[142] In a constitutional state the legislative enactments can be reviewed by a court to determine their conformity with the constitution.[143] As part of the procedure of ideally rendering a judicial decision, Habermas posits that the lawyers representing the various positions can present their arguments equally without anyone, regardless of his power, having an unfair advantage.

What Habermas regards as his proceduralist understanding of law depends on there being undistorted forms of public communication, that is,

---

141. *Id.* at 126.

142. He posits what he calls the democratic principle. The democratic principle states that only those statutes may claim legitimacy which can meet with the assent of all citizens through what he calls the discourse principle. The discourse principle regards statutes as valid when all possibly affected persons could agree on them as participants in rational discourse. Rational discourse occurs when communication allows for the free processing of topics, contributing information and reasons in the public sphere. *Id.* at 107-8, 110, 121. "[T]he only law that counts as legitimate is one that could be rationally accepted by all citizens in a discursive process of opinion-and will-formation." *Id.* at 135. When law making occurs through a public process through which reasons, information, topics and contributions are filtered, it has the presumption of rational acceptability. *Id.* at 151. Legal legitimacy requires that laws and judicial decisions be "rationally grounded...so that all participants can accept them as rational decisions." *Id.* at 198. His discourse theory also allows for bargaining, that is, there are to be procedures put in place for negotiating compromises where all the interested parties have an equal opportunity to pressure one another so that a fair agreement could be reached. *Id.* at 166-7, 283. He agrees with Ronald Dworkin that positive law unavoidably absorbs a moral content because moral reasons enter into law through the democratic procedure of legislation and fair bargaining. *Id.* at 204.

He goes on to assert that it is the rule of law or legal legitimization that creates basic rights, including the right to the greatest possible measure of equal liberties, the basic right to equal opportunities to participate in the creation of public opinion and the right to have safe living conditions. *Id.* at 122-3. Although not viewed by Habermas as reflecting a natural law position, his rights are substantive rather than procedural. It is apparently his discourse theory which enables Habermas to view what he has set forth as dispensing with natural law theory. *Id.* at 149.

143. *Id.* at 168.

no one having unfair advantage or influence.[144] The judge will then decide the issue in a way coherent with precedents and statutes by applying good reasons that represent the enlarged intersubjective perspective of the community generally.[145] A similar process with different actors operates at the legislative level. In neither case is what constitutes good reasons some Platonic idea transcending the contextual community: rather, under discourse theory reason resides in the intrinsically rational character of a democratic process. This process exists where the relevant information that facilitate deliberative politics flows. When this occurs, there is a presumption that what is produced is fair and rational.[146]

What Habermas and other philosophers from various traditions, specifically, Fuller, Hart, Finnis and Rawls, reveal is an overlapping idea of what legal procedure either does or ought to include. So far as their ideas of the ideal against which to measure the reality of what governments do mirror our use of the language of law, they are setting forth what I would consider, though Habermas in particular would not, a version of procedural natural law. Unlike the examples I will give below in the section dealing with how we think and use language, however, except for Fuller these philosophers are not basing their analyses on our ordinary language understanding of this ideal concept 'law.' Rather they are stipulating what they believe this ideal ought to contain. Still, what they are doing is not altogether alien to us. We understand what they are setting up as the ideal is connected with our ordinary understanding of law.

Collectively, these philosophers (specifically, Fuller, Hart, Rawls and Habermas) have made some of the following points: law ideally consists of general rules (Fuller, Hart, Rawls, Habermas); the rules are to be publically promulgated (Fuller) and prospective (Fuller,[147] Rawls, Habermas); the law concerns activity rather than status (Fuller,[148] Hart, Rawls); decisions are based on the terms of the law to

144. *Id.* at 408.

145. *Id.* at 225-228. Habermas distinguishes his position from that of Ronald Dworkin whose ideal judge, Hercules, decides the issue applying her own principles rather than that of the community.

146. *Id.* at 285, 296, 486.

147. Summers, *Lon L. Fuller, supra*, at 28.

148. This is suggessted by Fuller's requirements that laws be such that: (1) people can order their relations accordingly; (2) people can abide by them and (3) they not require the impossible.

be enforced (Fuller, Hart); similars are to be treated similarly (Fuller,[149] Hart, Rawls); decisions are to be rational (Habermas) and based on rational procedures of inquiry (Rawls); decisions are to cohere with precedent and avoid double jeopardy (Habermas); the judge is to decide impartially and objectively (Fuller,[150] Hart, Rawls, Habermas); courts have the power to review the constitutionality of legislation (Habermas).[151]

---

149. In describing Fuller's view James Boyle asserts that it is "ethically thin." He also suggests that Fuller regards "autonomy [as] more legitimately the concern of the state than equality."

Boyle, *Legal Realism and the Social Contract, supra*, at 394.

Assuming that the concept 'thin ethic' means that it fails to provide as many substantive answers to specific questions as a thick ethic, I would agree that an ethic that emphasizes process is thinner than an ethic that emphasizes substance. Still, by ignoring Fuller's requirement of formal equality (that similars must be treated similarly), Boyle treats Fuller's ethic as thinner than it is.

Also, as I assert below as an element of procedural natural law (though not in Fuller's version), equal treatment requires the regime's spokesperson to explain to a disinterested outsider why it treats less favored persons within its control worse than it treats its own elite. Once this element is added to a procedural ethic, the regime cannot escape criticism as violating the notion of legality simply by asserting that the less favored are all treated fairly according to the regime's own criterion. Once the legal ethic allows the critic to hold a regime accountable for violating a transcendent criterion of treating similars similarly (assuming that the regime treats its elite better than others and cannot justify this distinction to the disinterested outsider), then the legal process ethic can no longer be criticized so easily as being insufficiently "thick."

150. Fuller, Lon, *The Morality of Law*, 1964, at 33-8.

151. Another legal philosopher who makes some of these same points is J.R. Lucas:

> A legal system must satisfy certain conditions if it is to count as a legal system at all: the laws must be generally known, and for the most part be of general application; there must be general agreement about what are to be accepted as laws, and a generally recognized way of adjudicating doubtful cases, with due regard for the arguments of either side.

Lucas, J.R., *On Justice, supra*, at 32.

"Legality is also a concomitant of the principle of treating like cases alike..." *Id.* at 77.

Still yet another legal scholar summarizing aspects of the rule of law is Andrew Altman:

> This liberal conception of the rule of law...incorporates...institutional arrangements...[which] include an independent judiciary to interpret and apply the authoritative norms; access to the courts by the population; and the guarantee of

The criteria of law as an ideal set forth by Fuller, Hart, Finnis, Rawls and Habermas among others reflect our use of language to delineate the boundary where a regime's compliance with legality ends and its extra-legal use of power begins. Thus, if, as suggested, one accepts what these thinkers have articulated as reflecting the idea of legal procedure as it exists in our linguistic discourse if not always in reality, then one can articulate, as was done above, various aspects of the idea of procedural law.

> a hearing, fairly conducted, in which the relevant parties to any case can present their sides of the story. Such arrangements are designed to secure the rule of law by insuring *due process* of law.

Altman, Andrew, *Critical Legal Studies*, 1990, at 26.

7

Further Explication of the Ideal of Legal Procedure

Procedure as Distinguished from Substance

So far, while I have delineated a thesis of procedural natural law and set forth what several philosophers have said about it, I have not systematically examined what constitutes this procedure. A further discussion will be undertaken here.

One might say that as the term is used in law, procedure is contrasted with substance. There is good reason for hesitating to pursue this approach, however. As any law student who has struggled with the terms 'procedure' and 'substance' knows, it is difficult if not impossible to provide satisfactory, non-circular defining characteristics of these terms.

Still, the following mind game might help to bring the substance/procedure dichotomy into greater focus. Assume that you are at the information desk at the entrance to a great university in a country whose culture is relevantly similar to our own. You want to know where to go to learn how the culture treats various issues. So you ask a series of questions: (1) in what academic discipline would I learn about human nature?; (2) in what academic discipline would I learn about how government goes about satisfying human aspirations and goals?; (3) in what academic discipline would I learn about how government ought to further the common good?; (4) in what academic discipline would I learn about basic human rights?; and (5) in what academic discipline would I learn about what constitutes the rule of law?

Some of the answers would be overlapping. The answer to question one might include biology and psychology. The answer to question two might include political science and sociology. The answer to questions three and four might include political science (theory) and philosophy. And the answer to question five might include philosophy and, you guessed it, law school. It is because there is a specialized discipline called the law that is concerned with what is distinctively legal, including what constitutes the idea of law, that we can refer to the search for the distinguishing methodology of the law as a procedural one.

My focus on how language is used suggests another guide to distinguishing between substantive and procedural natural law. The difference lies in what the former theorists are focusing on as compared to the latter: substantive natural law theorists, such as Aquinas[152] and Finnis,[153] are concerned about the nature of human beings, their rights and their basic needs,[154] to which law ought to conform,[155] whereas procedural natural law theorists, such as Fuller, are concerned about the meaning of the concept 'law' itself.[156]

---

152. [T]he law in us by nature...command[s] us to do whatever reason, when planning action, naturally grasps to be good for man, whatever man naturally seeks as a goal. That includes...whatever accords with the natural tendency every substance has to try and preserve its natural being...[,] mating between the sexes and bringing up one's young.

Aquinas, *Summa Theologiae, supra*, sec. 94, at 287.

153. "The basic forms of good grasped by practical understanding are what is good for human beings with the nature they have." Finnis, *Natural Law and Natural Rights, supra,* at 34. "[E]ach reader must ask himself: What *are* the basic aspects of my well-being?"..."What, then, are the basic forms of good for us?" *Id.* at 85-86. For Finnis, the answers are: life, knowledge, play, aesthetic experience, friendship, practical reasonableness and religion.

154. Here is the language of a similar approach taken by a contemporary substantive natural law philosopher: "I am proposing that we cannot effectively go beyond positivism without first examining certain basic philosophical and theological assumptions concerning human nature." Alexander, Frank S. "Beyond Positivism: A Theological Perspective," 20 *Ga. L. Rev.*Rev. 1089, 1090 (1986).

155. The antecedents of substantive natural law go back to Plato and Aristotle, "[who] recognized no fundamental conflict between the condition of political society and the condition of human nature. On the contrary, they conceived the state...as an ethical form of human association, which made possible the full realization of the ends essential to the rational nature of the human agent." Covell, Charles, *The Defence of Natural Law*, 1992, at 5.

156. I have interpreted Fuller as implicitly making a judgment about how we talk. My support for this assertion can be found in his statement quoted earlier in this book to the effect that if a government were to sufficiently violate the ideal of legality (what he called the inner morality of law), he would refuse to give it the name of law.

Rationality Explicated

Some of the criteria of the ideal of procedural law are relatively self explanatory. One criteria of this ideal that is not self explanatory is that of 'rationality.' Each person's judgment of whether a regime is acting rationally begins with her filtering that regime's actions through her understanding of what constitutes being rational.[157] Each person's judgment of the regime's rationalaity is then filtered through the collective wisdom of the community when it is accessible to subjective interpersonal agreement.[158]

But for my purpose here, this is not enough. A person's notion of rationality and that of her family and tribal community reflect what that person or her tribal community thinks is in her or its best interest. What the person thinks is in her best interest is perfectly compatible with indifference or hostility toward the other, the outsider, even the outsider living within the same state. As David Hume put it: "[t]is not contrary to reason to prefer the destruction of the whole world to the scratching of my finger."[159]

---

157. "If we cannot find a way to interpret the utterances and other behavior of a creature as revealing a set of beliefs largely consistent and true by our own standards, we have no reason to count that creature as rational, as having beliefs, or as saying anything at all." Ramberg, Bjorn, *Donald Davidson's Philosophy of Language*, 1989, n. 8 at 82 (quoting Donald Davidson).

But what is rationality exactly? Here is one philosopher's definition.

> First, that rationality is a matter of reasons. A belief's rationality depends upon the reasons for holding that belief. These will be reasons for thinking the belief is true (or perhaps for thinking that it has some other desirable cognitive virtue, such as explanatory power).
>
> Second, that rationality is a matter of reliability. Does the process or procedure that produces (and maintains) the belief lead to a high percentage of true beliefs? A rational belief is one that arises through some process that reliably produces beliefs that are true (or that have some other desirable cognitive virtue).

Nozick, Robert, *The Nature of Rationality*, 1993, at 64.

"Rationality involves taking into account of reasons for *and* against." *Id.* at 72.

"[R]ationality involves some degree of self-consciousness. Not only reasons are evaluated, but also the process by which information arrives, is stored, and is recalled. A rational person will try to be alert to biases in these processes and take steps to correct those biases he knows of." *Id.* at 74.

158. I am applying a coherence theory of truth.

159. Hume, David, *A Treatise of Human Nature, Book II, Part III*, 1888, at 416.

(cont. on next page)

Thus, it is not an oxymoron to refer to a person having rational paranoia. In the American Wild West as well as in the literal and figurative battle fields of life it sometimes pays to destroy a possible enemy first and ask questions later. If two people (or peoples) are disputing ownership or control over a piece of land, then one of them might kill the other as a rational preventative measure to secure the land. This might be viewed as rational as long as the killer lacks a conscience. She would sleep better at night if she could get away with killing all of her perceived enemies.

But the notion of rationality as part of 'law as an ideal' cannot be limited to what would be considered rational by a person or a tribal community reflecting this egocentric or ethnocentric bias. What is required of 'rationality' as part of the legal ideal, however, is a perspective that is divorced from that of the particular person, her family or her tribal community. What is required is that the state apparatus acts according to the abstract general principles reflective of the rule of law.[160] The abstract perspective must be divorced from named particular persons. Even if the person, her family or her tribal community controlled the mechanisms of the state's power, he or they would have to apply this abstract notion of rationality to come within the legal ideal.

'Rationality' as part of the legal ideal is circumscribed more than 'rationality' would be circumscribed as applied to the person or her tribal community. While the paranoid person may rationally seek to destroy his perceived enemies before they destroy him, the paranoid operators of a state complying with the rule of law cannot act in this way. The state is certainly entitled to defend itself against perceived

---

Obviously, Hume cannot literally mean this statement. For one thing, almost all of us depend on others for food, clothing and shelter, in short for our very survival. For another thing, I am part of the world, so if the world is going to be destroyed, I will be destroyed along with it.

160. Is this a circular definition of rationality? I am asserting that rationality as part of procedural natural law is given a limited meaning, namely, as punishing actions of persons rather than "punishing" them based on their status. And that such punishment must be justifiable to neutral outside observers. Thus, rationality as part of the legal ideal is limited to what I claim describes the legal ideal. 'Rationality' does not explicate the legal ideal but rather is defined by it.

But I believe that the limited meaning of rationality that I put forth is consistent with our common sense understanding of how the ideal of the rule of law is contained within limits much more extensive than what would be regarded as rational as applied to persons or their extensions, the family or tribe. And as such, the limited meaning of 'rationality' does explicate the concept 'the rule of law' and, therefore, has value even if it is ultimately circular.

external and internal enemies. But to the extent that it operates within the rule of law, the state must provide the sorts of procedural protections I have been discussing even if it means that the state is defended less well. Those operating the state cannot decide that some residents within their control are enemies based simply on their race, ethnicity, religious background, sexual orientation or any other special status characteristic without also determining that each particular person in question has done something deserving of special (negative) treatment. And the burden is on the state to be able to demonstrate to neutral, outside observers that each person's punishment is justified based on his or her actions rather than his or her status.[161] The requirement that the regime's spokespeople must be able to justify its actions to neutral outside observers is to insure that those controlling the regime are not simply reflecting their personal and tribal biases or paranoia in treating the disfavored according to status rather than actions justifying sanctions. 'Rationality' as applied to the state's actions against perceived enemies within are subject to a secular, earth bound equivalent of Spinoza's sub species aeternitatis. As part of this effort at judging the regime's legal rationality, the neutral outside observers must also attempt to eliminate her personal biases.[162]

An analogy might be helpful in fleshing out the secular, earth bound position sub species aeternitatis of the disinterested and neutral outside observer. Let us liken this person to a baseball fan watching a game on television between two teams as to which he has no special allegiance. The umpire calls a batter out at first base when the fan believes that the television screen and replays clearly show that the batsman was safe. It makes perfect sense for the television watcher to assert, despite the finality of the umpire's call, that the umpire got it wrong or, in an extreme situation, that the umpire must have been blind or bribed. While the umpire's judgment is final, it need not be correct. And if the umpire is involved in an unusual call of a disputed play, he may feel forced by the public outcry and the media to explain his decision. Again, the decision is final even if it,

161. "Justice is reasonable. Some say it simply is embodied reason. Certainly, the word 'justify' in English means simply to give reasons." Ramberg, *Donald Davidson's Philosophy of Language, supra*, at 35.

162. "A rational person will try to be alert to biases...and will take steps to correct those biases he knows of." Nozick, *The Nature of Rationality, supra*, at 74.

See also, Rawls, John, *A Theory of Justice, supra*, at 18-22 (discussion of the original position).

along with an explanation (including the appeal to the rules), is unpersuasive to the baseball fan who does not care about who wins this particular game. Finally, there can be a general consensus among disinterested fans of the game that the umpire got it wrong.

Returning to various features of 'rationality,' another feature is that of non-arbitrariness. This involves deliberating, evaluating[163] and determining how well what is at issue fits into a pattern of what is already considered rational.[164] Rationality also involves consistency and coherence.[165] In addition, whoever is making a judgment will be expected to interpret texts, taking into consideration how they are currently understood. There is no license to interpret the texts in a way that is wholly arbitrary.[166] Rationality involves using the accepted[167] tools of deductive and inductive logic.[168]

---

163. "To term something rational is to make an *evaluation*; its reasons are *good* ones (of a certain sort), and it meets the standards (of a certain sort) that it *should* meet." Nozick, *The Nature of Rationality, supra*, at 98.

164. "The rationality of a belief is connected to a dense network of reasoning, inference and evaluation of evidence in chains of overlapping statements." *Id.* at 71.

"The idea of rationality is that of the ability, given certain present and particular data, to unite or relate them with other data in certain appropriate ways." Bennett, Jonathan, *Rationality*, 1964, at 85.

165. *See* MacCormick, Neil, *Legal Right and Social Democracy*, 1982, at 129.

166. [W]e can be sure that some contexts will be irrelevant:

> ...The Rule of Law cannot operate unless legal materials (which in theory, are what bind persons) are iterable. The Rule of Law presupposes that the same corpus of legal materials will be applied to case A as to case B. If a different rule were applied in each case we would not have the Rule of Law. However, the author's legal intent when she creates legal materials is not iterable; it is forever lost at the moment of creation. All that remains is the sign, the existence of which makes intersubjective communication possible. The iterability of the sign of the author's intent, and not the intent itself, is essential to the operation of the Rule of Law....The statute's claim to legal authority is derived not from the intent of its framers, but from its present signification....The purpose of the deconstruction is not to establish that any interpretation of the text is acceptable, but that the yearning for originary meaning...is incomplete...The intent theory and a theory of free play must coexist in an uneasy alliance in which neither can be master nor servant.

Balkin, *Deconstructive Practice and Legal Theory, supra*, at 780-84.

167. "[W]e define a rational belief as one which is arrived at by the methods which we now consider reliable." Rorty, Richard, *Philosophy and the Mirror of Nature*, 1979, at 337 (quoting A. J. Ayer).

168. Gewirth, Alan, *Reason and Morality*, 1978, at 46.

Rationality also involves an appropriate dispassionate effort to determine facts and to fit these facts into a general rule which these facts are supposed to come within. Assuming that the facts are novel and do not comfortably fit into any particular rule, one might use either Rolf Sartorius' concern to produce a logical fit[169] or Ronald Dworkin's Herculean effort to combine fit with justification.[170]

Another basis for rejecting a regime's claim of rationality is its unwillingness to accept empirical counter-examples to its thesis and unwillingness to adjust and reject its thesis when these examples become too numerous to ignore. If Hitler believed that Caucasions were superior fighters to Asians, then he would be hard pressed to explain away the Japanese defeat of the British at Singapore in the early stages of World War II. If Hitler believed that Jews lacked physical courage, then he would be hard pressed to explain the Warsaw ghetto uprising. At some point a rational person would be forced to change his view of such matters based on the empirical evidence whereas Hitler refused to do so.

Treating Similars Similarly

Because we may be judging a regime's adherence to the concept 'the rule of law' while standing outside the regime, we need to be able to use this concept across geographic and cultural boundaries. Because we may be making judgments about another country's legality, the principle applied must transcend the issue of how to decide a particularly hard or novel case within a particular state's jurisdiction. This principle begins with the assumption that human beings are similar.[171] Rationality involves treating similars similarly.[172]

---

169. Altman, *Critical Legal Studies, supra*, at 40.

170. Dworkin, Ronald, *Law's Empire*, 1986, at 255.

171. [A]ll social rules treat individuals as abstractions.

> It is not only possible for individuals to be treated in that way; it is essential to human social life. Where there are social rules, people must regard themselves and others as "just anybody" or "no one special" to borrow Sartre's suggestive term.... When the Jew, the black, or the homosexual is regarded as "just anybody" by the existing system of legal rules, he or she is protected from the inclinations of intolerance and prejudice that could well play a role in more context-sensitive modes for regulating public and private power.

Altman, *Critical Legal Studies, supra*, at 190, 192-3.

172. One might wonder how this possible reliance on human rationality distinguishes this version of natural law from the various versions of substantive natural law, such

The notion that similars must be treated similarly is a moral concept as well as a legal one. As a moral concept it was expressed by Kant as the Categorical Imperative: "[a]ct according to a Maxim which can be adopted at the same time as a Universal Law."[173] But in Western civilization, it goes back to the *Old Testament* injunction, "love thy neighbor as thyself."[174] This concept appears to have universal appeal, for variants of the Golden Rule exist cross-culturally. In Judaism, there is Hillel's response to the non-Jew asking for the *Torah* to be explained while standing on one foot: "[w]hat is hateful to you, do not do to your neighbor."[175] In Christianity, it is expressed in *Matthew* 7:12 as: "[t]herefore all things whatsoever ye would that men should do to you, do ye even so to them."[176] In Islam, "[s]eek for mankind that of which you are desirous for yourself."[177] In the Hindu *Mahabharata*: "[d]o not to others what ye do not wish Done to yourself."[178] In the *Pali* canon of Buddhism it states: "[m]ake *thine own self the measure of the others*, And so abstain from causing hurt

as, Aquinas' and Finnis', that I have discussed above. In both instances there is a reliance on human nature.

In response, I note several differences.

One is that, contrary to the substantive natural law theorists who make an assertion about human nature, namely, that rational humans would choose certain substantive legal concepts, I assert that legal procedure is by definition (based on our ordinary language) necessarily rational.

Also, to the extent that I am making an assertion about human nature, it is quite minimal. I assert that regardless of culture ordinary people unconnected to their governments would understand that when their government acts in accordance with procedures of law, it is acting more desirably than when it acts arbitrarily and by whim. Thus a government that acts in accordance with law treats persons better rather than worse. The preference for being treated better rather than worse constitutes part of what it means for a person to be rational. (As I indicate in the text, personal rationality is not the same as legal rationality.)

By contrast to my minimal assertion that a rational person would prefer to be treated better rather than worse, the substantive natural law philosopher (Finnis) posits a more substantial and problematic assertion, namely, that people wish to know whether God exists. Even the substantive natural law assertion that people prefer to live is more sweeping and therefore more problematic than my assertion that while alive, they would prefer to be treated better rather than worse.

173. Kant, Immanuel, *The Philosophy of Law*, 1887, at 34.

174. Leviticus 19:18.

175. Rost, H. T. D., *The Golden Rule*, 1986, at 69.

176. *Id.* at 76.

177. *Id.* at 103.

178. *Id.* at 28.

to them."[179] In Confucianism: "[w]hat you do not want done to yourself, do not do to others."[180] What all of these versions ethical maxims have in common is that they do not limit who the other can be; and they do not say that the utterer need treat the other like the self only if he feels like it.

Why should the legal ideal necessarily limit who is included in the term 'the other' more than the ethical ideal does? I find no good reason to think it should be. As in the various ethical versions set forth above, in treating similars according to the legal ideal I posit no explicit limit as to who is included. Of course, a government can provide reasons that justify differential treatment. But unless the government does so, that is justify distinguishing say, between resident and citizen or between tribal outsider and tribal insider, all who come within the state's control will be expected to be treated similarly.

As to a state's treatment of the alien differently than its treatment of its citizen, sometimes this difference in treatment can be justified as consistent with the rule of law as when a regime decides to deport a resident alien who has committed a felony but does not deport a citizen who has committed a similar crime. But in terms of the ideal of law rather than how it has been or is sometimes actually practiced, the burden of persuasion falls on the regime's spokespersons to explain and justify to a disinterested outside observer (namely, ourselves, or those of us who have no special bias) why it is deviating from the general principle of similar treatment of persons within its control. The outside observer making the judgment (namely, potentially each of us) is expected to study the issue to the best of her ability with the requisite seriousness and knowledge of the scientific or other facts and not simply accept the regime's spokespersons' assurances to the effect that, say, the Jew is relevantly different from the German or that Cambodians who were killed because they wore glasses were relevantly different from Cambodians who weren't killed because they didn't wear the glasses. So, in so far as the regime treats different people differently, the regime's spokesperson must explicate both the regime's general rules and its decision making process in individual cases in language that would make some sense to a disinterested outside observer.

179. *Id.* at 39.
180. *Id.* at 49.

The assumption I make is that this evaluation will produce a general consensus, at least in extreme cases, even cross-culturally. That is, in an extreme case disinterested outside observers from various cultures would generally agree on their assessment of a regime's assertion that it is treating similars similarly and rationally distinguishing between those whom it asserts are not similar. In order to insure this consensus, additional assumptions might be required, namely, that these disinterested outside observers might need to have a certain level of intelligence, education and knowledge of science, such as, what constitutes a human being.

Let us assume that a regime propounds two separate laws. First, any person who seeks a job in a police department must meet the height requirement of being at least five foot eight inches tall. And second, any person residing within the territory controlled by the regime who is a member of a disfavored racial group will be killed regardless of the person's age or prior indication of hostility to the regime. I believe that, regardless of the culture of the outside disinterested observers, the second of these two laws will appear both clearly irrational and also more irrational than the first of these laws.[181] That there might or might not be a consensus as to the existence of a rational justification for the first law (because it presumably is a borderline case) would not detract from the likely consensus as to the second law.

John Rawls makes a similar point about rationality in his explication of what he calls the veil of ignorance:

> [N]one [of the parties in a veil of ignorance] would urge that special privileges be given to those exactly six feet tall or born on a sunny day. Nor would anyone put forward the principle that basic rights should depend on the color of one's skin or the texture of one's hair.... The rationality of

181. Suppose you think abortion is murder and that it makes no difference whether the pregnancy is the result of rape. Would you not think that a statute prohibiting abortion except in the case of rape distinctly better than a statute prohibiting abortion except to women born in one specified decade each century? At least if you had no reason to think either would in fact allow more abortions? You see the first of these statutes as a solution that gives effect to two recognizable principles of justice, ordered in a certain way even though you reject one of the principles. You cannot treat the second that way; it simply affirms for some people a principle it denies to others.

Dworkin, Ronald, *Law's Empire*, 1986, at 183.

> the parties and their situation in the original position guarantees that ethical principles of justice have this general content. Inevitably, then, racial and sexual discrimination presupposes that some hold a favored place in the social system which they are willing to exploit to their advantage. From the standpoint of persons similarly situated in an initial situation which is fair, the principles of explicit racist doctrines are not only unjust. They are irrational.[182]

F. A. Hayek also provides an analysis compatible with the thesis developed here but adds the point that "laws" which make distinctions based on singling out specific groups of persons rather than general categories ordinarily do not comply with the rule of law at all.

> As a true law should not name any particulars, so it should especially not single out any specific persons or groups of persons. The requirement that the rules of true law be general does not mean that sometimes special rules may not apply to different classes of people if they refer to properties that only some people possess. There may be rules that can apply only to women or to the blind or to persons above a certain age.... Such distinctions will not be arbitrary, will not subject one group to the will of others, if they are equally recognized as justified by those inside and those outside the group.[183]

---

182. Rawls, John, *A Theory of Justice*, 1971, at 149.

Rawls' concept of rationality is based on a presupposition that a person would be ignorant about her special circumstances and characteristics. To that extent one might argue that his concept of rationality would allow for conclusions that differ from those set forth in this book. But I believe that a similar result is reached through the requirement that the spokesperson for the regime convince a disinterested outside observer of the rationality of the regime's differential treatment of those it favors as against those it disfavors. In the usual instance a per se distinction based on race or sex would no more convince the rational outsider than a per se distinction based on eye color. (But occasionally, distinctions based on race or sex might be rationally justified. If one is directing a movie about life in Sweden, he might be justified in rejecting the application of a Japanese actor for the lead role.)

183. Hayek, F.A., *The Constitution of Liberty*, 1960, at 153-5. Hayek's point that decrees distinguishing named groups of persons violate the rule of law is partly analogous to the difficulty we have in accepting bills of attainder as coming within the rule of law.

Hayek's notion that distinctions between groups have to be justifiable to those outside as well as inside the group favored by the distinctions is similar to my assertion that the concept 'the rule of law' implies that a regime's distinctions between groups can be rationally defended to neutral outsiders.

To return to the various ethical versions of the Golden Rule, one problem is that (with the exception of the Buddhist version) it does not protect the recipient of the action from the actor who would be willing to receive what he gives. The sadist who beats the masochist could respond to the critic, "but I enjoy being beaten (being the masochist) just as I enjoy beating (being the sadist)." If the recipient were, in fact, not a maso-sadist, then this response of the sado-masochist, while satisfying the Golden Rule, would not satisfy the recipient.

The Kantian ethic (though not the Categorical Imperative version set forth above) surmounts this difficulty by requiring the actor to consider the recipient's ends as well as his own. Under this ethic a sado-masochist could not beat the unwilling non-sadomasochist. Habermas' strong version of this ethic is that: "only those norms may claim to be valid that could meet with the consent of all affected in their role as participants in a practical discourse."[184]

But as Habermas himself recognizes in *Between Facts and Norms*, a legal system cannot function on the assumption that it requires the consent of everyone. Because self-interested people have different, conflicting needs and interests, these needs and interests cannot always be harmonized. A government that attempted Habermas' ethic would break down into anarchy. But even the weaker Kantian version of this ethic, one that takes into account the needs and interests of the recipient as well as the actor, could not always fit into a legal system. Sometimes a government that operates what would generally be considered a legal system has to ignore the perceived needs and interests of many of its citizens, as when it sends them off to battle to possibly die.

So the defense of the notion of a 'legal system' must by necessity employ the still weaker claim of treating similars similarly. But unlike the various ethical versions, a person applying the legal ideal is un-

184. Habermas, Jurgen, *Moral Consciousness and Communicative Action*, translated by Christian Lenhardt and Shierry Weber Nicholsen, 1991, at 197.

likely to be caught up in the difficulty posed above, namely, that these ethics cannot effectively respond to the sado-masochist. For the sadist in power, say, Hitler or Stalin, does not in fact inflict the same punishment on himself as he inflicts on others who are presumptively similar to himself. Once the totalitarian leader is unable to convince the rational disinterested outside observer that he is not similar to those whom he is killing, he has no additional effective argument to provide. The leader's response, "I too enjoy being tortured and killed," can be met with the incredulity it deserves since the totalitarian leader has chosen to do the torturing and killing rather than to be the recipient of these actions. His being alive is a sufficient refutation to the assertion that he is as much the masochist as he is the sadist.

But why should we make the assumption that human beings are similar? As noted more fully below, one source for making it comes from the human capacity to engage in applied logic or algebra. In these disciplines, each instance of a class is treated as similar to every other instance of that class. Likewise, in 'law' as a concept, one initially assumes that each person is a replicable instance of the class of humans, and then seeks to determine whether any purported differences among humans would justify treating them differently.

Another source, also explored below, is our capacity to feel empathy for other people (and for some of us sometimes other animals based on their being fellow sentient creatures). The source of this capacity to feel and empathize probably comes from a different part of the brain from that which produces our capacity for logic discussed in the last paragraph. One example of this capacity is the horror we feel when we see people being killed on television. The televised images in American living rooms of Vietnamese dying as a result of U.S. bombing and other military actions, for example, was a significant factor in turning U.S. public opinion against the Vietnamese War and ending our involvement there. Another example is the empathy kids and sometimes adults feel for the animals, talking or otherwise, created in Disney cartoons and other films.

Once one makes the assumption that all humans (and perhaps to some extent other animals) are relevantly similar in their ability to feel, this extends the requirement that similars be treated similarly from the way a regime treats its citizens to the way it treats any person living within its control. While this extension goes beyond the analysis provided by Hart, Rawls and Habermas who confine their parameters to citizens and/or precedent (cases), it is nontheless compatible with both the various ethical versions of treating similars similarily set forth above and our use of language and our way of thinking.

To make the case that the legal as well as moral logic of treating similars similarly extends beyond a country's in group (the elite and to whomever else the elite extends its protection), I turn to some examples. One example comes from Lewis Carroll's fable. When Alice encountered the Queen and King and was told that she violated rules that the royals had made up just two seconds before, the fact that Alice almost certainly was not a citizen of the royal realm did not lessen the legal absurdity of the royals' pronouncements.[185]

In addition, there are actual historical examples of a government's classifying people as not similar that are obviously irrational because the government acted inconsistently in its classification. Thus, these examples violate the rule of law as an ideal. One example comes from the U.S. Constitutional Convention and the Constitution itself. During the Convention representatives from Southern states sought to treat slaves as persons equal in status to white persons for the purpose of determining the number of members of the House of Representatives each state would obtain after each dicennial census.[186] The obvious rationale for this view was the self-interested one, namely, the more persons per Southern state, the more representatives in the House each state would have. However, Southern self-interest is not the same as legal rationality, for if slaves are fully persons when it suits one's interest, it is logically contradictory to argue that they are not when it does not suit one's interest.

The compromise worked out in the Constitution itself between Southerners and Northerners might well have been a triumph of pragmatism enabling the Convention to conclude in the drafting of a satisfactory Constitution, but it is a contradiction on its face and hence irrational. Article I, Section 2, Clause 2 states that "[r]epresentatives...shall be apportioned among the several States...according to their respective Numbers, which shall be determined by adding to the whole Number of free Persons...three fifths of all other Persons." Thus, African-Americans were regarded and treated as per-

185. *See* Carroll, Lewis, *Alice in Wonderland*, 1989, at 149-155. Some of the royals' pronouncements are set forth below in this text.

186. Collier, Christopher and Collier, James Lincoln, *Decision in Philadelphia*, 1992, at 142-3.

sons for the purpose of the census (albeit counting only as 3/5ths of whites), but despite this were allowed to be enslaved. Another logical absurdity in the early U. S.'s treatment of African-Americans was that it allowed them to be enslaved in some locales and accorded citizenship entitled to formal equality with whites in other locales.[187]

Another act of straight forward irrationality as well as a violation of the more specific ideal of legality comes from the Nazi inconsistent treatment of the Jew. For example, if the Jew was to be treated by the Nazis as subhuman, then one would not expect the Nazis to impliedly recognize any Jewish similarity to themselves when it suited their self interest. Yet they did. One way they did so was to use blood from Jewish concentration camp victims for transfusions to Germans needing it.[188] Another use of Jews slated for death was to put them in freezing conditions, forcing them "into a tank of ice water and [keeping them] there for seventy to ninty minutes, or as long as it took for them to lose consciousness."[189] The point of these experiments was to help Germans survive cold. Likewise, forcing Gypsies as well as Jews to drink sea water was designed to test whether German pilots could survive if shot down at sea.[190] In addition, concentration camp "doctors" performed various other gruesome experiments on Jewish prisoners.[191] These various experiments, which forced Jewish and Gypsy victims to undergo atrocious and sadisticly imposed conditions in order to help Germans faced with similar conditions in the future, seriously undercut the basic Nazi assumption that Jews and Gypsies were inherently different from and inferior to Germans.

Still another example of a violation of legality comes from the Nazi racial laws. As a result of Nazi racial law, Jews who had been German citizens were deprived of citizenship. They were also deprived of the right to engage in sexual relations with people of "German blood." "Sexual intercourse" was defined broadly so as to in-

---

187. One aspect of real equality did not arrive until 1967 in the U.S. Supreme Court's decision to declare unconstitutional as a violation of the 14th Amendment's Equal Protection Clause a state miscegenation law banning marriage between whites and blacks. *Loving v. Virginia*, 388 U.S. 1 (1967).

188. Lipton, Robert Jay, *The Nazi Doctors*, 1986, at 289.

189. Cohen, Nava, "Medical Experiments," *Encyclopedia of the Holocaust*, 1990, at 960.

190. *Id.* at 958.

191. Lipton, Robert Jay, *The Nazi Doctors, supra*, at 269-302.

clude a man's masturbation, his rebuffed attempt at sex and his becoming aroused while being given a massage by a German non-Jewish masseuse. If the Gestapo beat a confession out of a Jew that he engaged in the sort of "sexual relation" described above, that confession would be given more weight than its retraction at the "trial." The death sentence would sometimes be imposed.[192]

Once Germany occupied Czechoslovakia, non-Jewish Czechs were treated as though they were of "German blood" and regarded as though they had German citizenship as far as having sex with a Jew was concerned. Thus, hypothetically a Jewish male deprived of his German citizenship who had sex with a Czech woman who had been treated as though she had German citizenship could be prosecuted under Nazi law for "dishonoring the [German] race."[193] Does the fact that citizenship was taken away from the Jew or was provided in effect to the Czech in anyway change the nature of our understanding of this "law" and its application? I think not. The Nazi "law" treating people dissimilarly based on ethnicity (Jewishness as against Germanness) where no adequate basis for treating them differently is provided violates our ideal of what law appropriately contains based on our assumption of basic human similarity.

Elements of Due Process

As we have seen by virtue of my cataloguing many of the elements of 'the rule of law' in articulating the views of Fuller, Hart, Rawls and Habermas, I have also characterized elements of due process including publishing general rules in advance so that people have an opportunity to conform their behavior to them and determining guilt or innocence (or who wins the dispute) through a hearing where both

---

192. Muller, Ingo, *Hitler's Justice*, 1991, at 98-115.

193. *Id.* at 96-115.

194. Procedural justice in conflict resolution is...an impersonal value that everyone, whatever his positive moral ideals, may recognize and respect. It embodies the principle of hearing both sides of a disputed case, a principle that we are all bound to follow in our private reasonings.

> If we add to this [the principle] that public procedures of conflict resolution should always be customary, we have reached a universal minimum morality, a bedrock of fairness.

Hampshire, Stuart, "The Reason Why Not," *The New York Review of Books*, April 22, 1999, at 23. (Hampshire here is reviewing a book by T. M. Scanlon, *What We Owe to* sides are presented[194] before an impartial fact finder using what Hart called the secondary rules of adjudication (such as, rules of evidence) with reasons provided for the decision rather than, say, rendering "justice" through state sponsored forays of terror in the street.

But the mentioning of these characteristics of due process is not meant to be exhaustive. Their listing is not intended as either independently necessary conditions of legal procedure or even as collectively sufficient conditions. Rather, these characteristics are generally present to a greater or lesser extent when the rule of law is present. Thus, a regime can on occasion violate some of these characteristics and still be regarded as acting in accordance with law. It is not an all or nothing concept. As I have previously indicated, Fuller himself noted the lack of any firm boundary in the concept when he stated, "To me there is nothing shocking in saying that a dictatorship which clothes itself with a tinsel of legal form can *so far depart* from the morality of order, from the inner morality of law itself, that it ceases to be a legal system."[195] Fuller's statement implies that a regime's de-

---

Each Other. I believe that his reference to public procedures of conflict resolution refer to procedures that have been established and are not created ad hoc for this particular case.)

> [The] fact...that we can recognise procedures more easily than right results... enables us to agree on methods of settling disputes even if we cannot agree on a solution directly. As in other branches of philosophy, we can set up a "decison procedure" on whose validity we agree and about whose application there can be little doubt; and by means of such a decision procedure we can settle indirectly issues on which we could not reach agreement direct[ly].

Lucas, J. R., *The Principles of Politics*, 1966, at 13.

195. Fuller, "Positivism and Fidelity to Law—A Reply to Professor Hart," *Harv. L. Rev., supra*, at 660.

The positivist, Joseph Raz, asserts that one difference between himself and Lon Fuller is that he (Raz) would allow for a greater departure from the concept 'the rule of law' than Fuller would, that is, he would call a government institution a legal system even if there were a great degree of departure from the ideal of the rule of law.

> I have been treating the rule of law as an ideal, as a standard to which the law ought to conform but which it can and sometimes does violate most radically and systematically. Fuller, while allowing that deviations from the ideal of the rule of law can occur, denies that they can be radical or total...It is, of course, true that most of the principles enumerated [in Raz' enunciation of principles making up the ideal of the rule of law] cannot be violated altogether by any legal system.

Raz, Joseph, *The Authority of Law*, 1986, at 223.

This quotation suggests that Raz, the positivist, explicitly agrees with Fuller that there is an ideal, 'the rule of law,' against which the actual is to be measured. The difference parture from the idea of law in some contexts would not necessarily mean that the regime would be regarded as lacking legality in other contexts or lacking a legal system in general.[196] I would agree with this implication.

To support this thesis with an example, a paradigm instance of a regime's violation of the idea of law would be Nazi Germany's treatment of its Jews. But granting this would not necessarily mean that one would be forced to the conclusion that the regime lacked legality in other contexts, say, involving the marriages, divorces, contracts, property transactions and civil suits between non-retarded, heterosexual Aryan Germans in good political standing.

There is nothing particularly unusual about this approach. Indeed, it is quite consistent with the suggestion of Wittgenstein, who attempted to understand a linguistic concept in terms of the relationships of its uses rather than look for defining characteristics. As he put it, "the result of this examination is: we see a complicated network of similarities overlapping and criss-crossing: sometimes overall similarities, sometimes similarities of detail."[197]

The Rule of Law as Dealing with Behavior Rather than Status

Another aspect of a rational legal procedure is that it deals with activity or behavior rather than status. "[L]aw is defined as *a form of social organization through the systematic institution of supreme au-*

between them as to when the ideal has been breached by the actual becomes a matter of degree rather than kind.

But this analysis raises several questions: (1) How does Raz go about determining that there is such an ideal? And (2) isn't Raz asserting a natural law position which is difficult to square with his positivism?

196. "...Fuller does say that one would have to take a holistic assessment of his eight criteria, and apparently agrees that one deviation from legality would not be enough to undermine a legal system." Boyle, "Legal Realism and the Social Contract: Fuller's Public Jurisprudence of Form, Private Jurisprudence of Substance," 78 *Cornell L. Rev.*, 371, 391 (1993).

197. Wittgenstein, Ludwig, *Philosophical Investigations*, translated by G. E. M. Anscombe, 3rd ed., 1953, at 32e. Wittgenstein referred to the similarities in the various uses of a concept as family resemblances. He also provided this illuminating analogy: "[T]he strength of the thread does not reside in the fact that some one fibre runs through its whole length, but in the overlapping of many fibres." *Id.*

thoritative standards of conduct."[198] So far as the legal world remains a rational one, both criminal law and much of civil law must obviously deal with behavior rather than status. This is shown because of the terminology of the trial. When the verdict is rendered in a criminal case, the defendant is pronounced "guilty" or "not guilty." Presumably, the defendant is guilty of doing (or perhaps not doing) something. Except in an ironic sense, it does not sound appropriate in our use of legal language to say, "she was found guilty of just simply being."

Although implicit rather than explicit in civil cases, the law is imputing a behavioral violation to one of the parties in a dispute, e.g., "she committed a tort," "he breached the contract," "because he raided the company treasury, he is personally liable." And so far as civil law allows for an individual or several individuals to execute what might be called private legislation, say, writing a will or a trust, entering into a contract or a corporation, something is being done.

But there are situations where, what is widely regarded as a legal system, deals with what seems more like status than action. For example, because of one's status as a wealthy person, some of one's wealth will be taken by the state in taxes to be redistributed to the poor; or because of one's status as a minor, one cannot drink alcohol; or because of one's status as an old person, one must retire from one's job.

Several points can be made in partial response. One of these, as noted in the text above, is that the listing of characteristics of the concept 'law' does not preclude that in some instances, what is accepted as an appropriate example of a legal system will in some particulars violate some of these characteristics. That is to say, the notion of a 'legal system' does not have defining characteristics that always provide clear boundaries between what is to be included and what is not. To rephrase the point, what we regard as a legal system will generally have certain characteristics, but that does not mean that everything done by that system will always be describable as coming within these characteristics.

Also, there are degrees on the status-activity continuum. A paradigm example of a norm proscribing activity is a law that punishes X

198. Steven J. Burton, "Law as Practical Reason," 62 *So. Cal. L. Rev.* 747, 776 (1989).

(a person) for doing Y (say, committing murder). A paradigm example of a norm proscribing status is a regime's killing X (say, a Jew or Gypsy) for being X. While the examples given above involving wealthy persons, minors and old people regulate or proscribe status, they are not paradigm examples of proscribing status. This is because there is an element of activity involved. Assuming that X is about to do something that might result in the acquisition of wealth, she can expect that if she is successful the state will take some of it to be redistributed to the poor. Or if X (the minor or old person) does Y (drinks alcohol, hides the fact that she is at mandatory retirement age and tries to continue working as an airplane pilot), she is violating the law. Thus, because they involve elements of activity as well as status, these are closer to being borderline cases than to being paradigm examples of a regime's punishing status.

A behavioral element is implicit in other aspects of the rule of law that I have already noted. One of these is the requirement that general rules be published in advance of their being acted on. The point of such a requirement is that people have an opportunity to conform their behavior to them.[199] Another requirement is determining guilt or innocence through a hearing before an impartial fact finder using what Hart called the secondary rules of adjudication (such as, rules of evidence) rather than, say, rendering "justice" through state sponsored forays of terror in the street. The point of this requirement is that legality requires that a person's conduct be judged in accordance with the general rules rather than have the person be subject to irrational abuse unrelated to what she has done.

To summarize this section, the concept 'law' involves the public promulgation of general rules to be applied to a person's behavior rather than to her status prospectively and consistently, the treatment of similars similarly and an independent and impartial judiciary whose decisions are to be based on the terms of the rules to be enforced. In addition, 'rationality' is viewed as an element of 'law.' This concept includes using the accepted tools of deductive and inductive

---

199. One might argue that the American legal maxim that "ignorance of the law is no excuse" is inconsistent with the importance of the requirement that the legal rule be promulgated in advance so that a person could conform her conduct to it. But there is no inconsistence. Promulgation of the rule in advance does not necessarily lead to the person accused of violating it knowing in advance that he has violated it. Rather, it means only that theoretically she could learn the law in advance of her action.

logic, interpreting the texts taking into consideration how they are customarily understood and being open to counterexamples that might lead to changing both the legal rules and their application.

I close this section on the explication of the idea of legal procedure with the following observation. My focus in this book on the idea of legal procedure as distinct from substantive justice does not necessarily lead to perfect justice. It leaves open at least the theoretical possibility that a regime's adherence to the former might violate the latter. For example, if a regime were to treat shabbily the first hundred thousand people with whom it were to come in contact (assuming there was no initial violation of the requirement that similars be treated similarly), this would constitute no basis in substantive justice for treating the next similar case in the same shabby way. If the government were to continue to treat the next case the same, it would comply with the procedural requirement of treating similars similarly. But it would constitute a triumph of procedural natural law over substantive justice.[200] In general, I believe that applying the principles of procedural natural law in judging a regime's actions will produce a legal system that is fair, but it does not always produce perfect justice.

I have two arguments that mitigate the damage done by recognizing that adhering to procedural natural law does not necessarily lead to substantive justice. One is my assertion that a judgment about a regime's treating similars similarly be made outside the parameters of the regime's own asserted criteria of similarity, that is, be made by neutral observers from a trans-cultural perspective. Under such a perspective a regime would be required to justify its treatment of the others when it treats them differently from its own elite. Under virtually any effort to give content to the example in the last paragraph, which was assumed not to violate this principle, the regime would almost certainly violate the principle even though it were to treat similarly those with whom it came in contact.

The reason is that those running the government are not similar to those whom the government is treating shabbily. If others are treated shabbily, and the government's own elite is not, this constitutes a

200. "The legal order as a system of formality encounters [a] problem...which dominates modern legal thought[, namely] the struggle to escape from the dilemma of blind formalism and arbitrary, tyrannical equity...." Unger, Roberto Mangabeira, *Law in Modern Society*, 1976, at 209.

prima facie violation of the principle that similars are to be treated similarly.[201] The regime then has the burden of providing reasons that would satisfy the cross-cultural observer as to why its distinction between the two groups satisfies the principle of treating similars similarly, namely its own leadership and generally the elite on the one side and those whom it is treating shabbily on the other.

The second argument is to affirm once again that my concern here is not with perfect justice. Rather, my focus is on the following, as between two regimes (to the extent they can be otherwise similar), one of which adheres to the rule of law and the other of which doesn't, which one provides people living within its control greater protection against its arbitrariness, greater opportunity to live out their lives without unduly negative interference by the regime? The question is rhetorical. Since a regime complying with the ideal of the rule of law by definition acts more rationally and less arbitrarily and allows those living within its control more opportunities to plan their lives than a regime not complying with this ideal, it is to be preferred regardless of its degree of compliance with anyone's substantive ideal of justice.

201. I assert that the original difference in treatment between the regime's favoring its own elite (if it does so) and disfavoring the others (the people) needs adequate justification that would satisfy neutral outside observers. I also assume that this justification almost certainly could not be provided: "[t]he assumption is that equality needs no reasons, only inequality does so; that uniformity, regularity, similarity, symmetry…need not be specially counted for, whereas differences, unsystematic behaviour, change in conduct, need explanation and, as a rule, justification." Berlin, Isaiah, *Concepts and Categories*, 1979, at 84. By contrast, when the regime stops treating the others (the people) shabbily, this change can rather easily be justified to neutral outside observers.

8

Language As Justification for Procedural Natural Law

The justification for asserting the existence of procedural natural law is that it is embedded in our ordinary language. In attempting to justify procedural natural law by referring to how we use language, I will be following the approach taken by the philosopher, Ludwig Wittgenstein, who looked for the meaning of a concept through its use in language.[202] Habermas too emphasizes the importance of understanding our ordinary language when he states: "It is not surprising that ordinary language functions as the 'ultimate metalanguage'"[203] enabling members of specialized disciplines to understand each other. In what follows I will undertake an effort to understand how we use the concept 'law.'

Several examples will be provided that it is hoped will show that the term 'law' provides procedural contours which limit what a regime acting in compliance with it can do to those who interact with it. To put it another way, the descriptive language of 'state power' has broader application than the descriptive language of 'law.'[204] The thesis can be expressed in simple terms: in one sense of our use of language, to describe a government's use of its coercive power against those persons residing within its territorial control does not necessarily entail that, as we use language, it has exercised lawful authority over these persons. This does not, however, preclude the possibility of another use of the term 'law' which is co-extensive with state power.

To elucidate the thesis further, namely that, as we use language 'law' is not necessarily coextensive with 'state power,' assume that it is rejected. The rejection of the thesis entails that the ascription of the

---

202. Wittgenstein, *Philosophical Investigations, supra*, 3rd ed., § 139, at 54.

203. Habermas, *Between Facts and Norms, supra*, at 348.

204. Interestingly, the positivist, Hans Kelsen, recognizes that 'law' is not equivalent to 'state power.' He states that "[a] state is the political organization of a society," but that "[t]he legal system is only part of the norms constituting the political system. . . ." Raz, *The Authority of Law, supra*, at 100.

term 'lawful' to a regime's actions does not indicate that the regime's power to act has been limited in any way. Even though we would catch on soon enough as to how the term 'law' was being used in this sense, I think we would regard it as parasitic on its usual use, that is, it would be viewed as an attempt to take advantage of the positive connotation that the term 'lawful' ordinarily conveys. At any rate, if one rejects my thesis, then one is adopting the view that the term 'law' means whatever those in power do, that is, the term provides no definitional limits to a regime's power to act.

Since our use of language is the basis for supporting the thesis that an appropriate application of the term 'law' constitutes a descriptive limit on a regime's use of power, some examples are provided here.[205]

One example assumes that you are in a strange country. You are walking down a main street in the largest city. Suppose that you hear a siren and notice that it comes from a small truck coming toward you. The truck looks like a police van. The van stops in front of you

---

205. The examples in the text are developed from the author's imagination in an effort to convince the reader that we use and understand the legal language employed to criticize what is being done by a regime. But our public discourse contains similar examples. One such example is the report sent to the Polish Government-in-Exile during World War II by the Jewish Socialist Party in Poland, stating, "without a shadow of doubt, that the *criminal* German Government has begun to carry out Hitler's prophecy that in the last five minutes of the war — whatever its outcome, he will kill all the Jews in Europe." Gilbert, Martin, *Auschwitz and the Allies*, 1981, at 42 (emphasis added).

Another example is the statement of Christine Loh, a member of Hong Kong's Legislative Council, made just a few years before China's take-over of Hong Kong on the difference between China and Hong Kong.

> China is in some ways a medieval country. They are still trying to grow by edict. We are modern, professional, international. China now has no sense of its own moral values: nothing but get rich quick. We in Hong Kong do have a moral basis, the values of the *rule of law*.

Lewis, Anthony, "The Edge of the Wave," *New York Times (Int'l Ed.)*, July 19, 1993, at A15 (emphasis added).

One final example is the remark of Hanan Ashrawi, an articulate Palestinian leader, who chose to form a citizen's commission with the purpose of monitoring the proposed Palestinian government rather than join it.

> "It's not easy to establish a citizens' rights commission. Nobody wants a group of high-powered people with credibility telling them, '*This is illegal* and this is unjust.' But somebody has to have the guts to do it."

Dreifus, Claudia, "Hanan Ashrawi," *New York Times Magazine (Int'l Ed.*, June 26, 1994, at 24. (emphasis added).

and several uniformed men get out. Without notice to you, the men grab you, beat you into submission with their gun handles, drag you into the van and throw you onto the floor bound hand and foot with your mouth gagged. The van speeds off with the siren blaring and stops in front of a building that looks like a courthouse. You are dragged out of the van, and brought before someone who is dressed like a judge. The "judge" then informs you that you are undoubtedly guilty (without informing you of the charges) and that the punishment for your crime is death, but that you are still entitled to a trial before having the death sentence imposed. A burly looking gentleman who claims to be your lawyer then informs the "judge" that a trial isn't necessary because you are so obviously guilty. "Your lawyer" then smacks you a few times across the face with his gun handle, apparently for the sheer joy of it. Accepting the "lawyer's" assertion that no trial is necessary, the "judge" says, "very well, I am sentencing you to death by torture."

But before being dragged out of the "courtroom," the gag is removed from your mouth and you are allowed to utter a few choice thoughts. Let us assume that you try charm, flattery, bribery and threats, and nothing works. What would you say? Assuming you have embraced the legal positivist position that there is no necessary connection between law and morality, you could still attack what has happened to you on moral grounds.[206] You could call what was being done to you, "wicked, evil, indecent, immoral, barbarous and uncivilized."[207]

---

206. The positivist, Joseph Raz, explicates Hans Kelsen's, his fellow positivist's, moral position thusly:

> Kelsen's relativism does not preclude the possibility or necessity of assessing the law by moral standards. He simply insists that every evaluation is valid only relative to the particular moral norm used which in itself has no objective validity. Consequently moral criticism or justification of the law is a matter of personal or political judgment. It is not an objective scientific matter and does not concern the science of law.

Raz, *The Authority of Law*, supra at 131. The fact that Kelsen's morality is relativistic would not preclude other positivists taking an absolutist moral stance.

Hart also asserts that a legal system may be deserving of moral opprobrium: "If with the utilitarians we speak plainly, we say that laws may be law but too evil to be obeyed." Hart, H. L. A., "Positivism and the Separation of Law and Morals," Feinberg, Joel and Gross, Hyman, eds., *Philosophy of Law*, 1991, at 74.

207. You might also be tempted to use terms such as 'unjust' and 'unfair.' But these terms, unlike the ones given in the main body of the text, which indicate only moral

But suppose you realize from his sardonic smile that the "judge" obviously does not care one bit whether your moral sensibilities have been offended. In your rage you then seek to hurl an invective at the "judge" which, given the "judge's" so-called job description, might actually have some impact. So you scream, "you call this law? This isn't law. It's a mockery of everything that law stands for."[208]

If this verbal thrust seems understandable to you, you have entered into language of procedural natural law. What you are complaining about is the absence of the procedures of a trial in the sense that this term is used as a part of the notion of legality. In the example given there were apparently no published rules, certainly no notification of any alleged violation, no independent fact finder, no meaningful representation by counsel, no concern for the facts, no basing the decision on the facts, no justification for the decision and no effort to mete out a sentence that bore some proportionate relationship to the seriousness of the alleged crime. In short the "trial" was a total sham.

But to assert that this isn't law is to use language that transcends what logically can be said by someone who abides by the view that a descriptive definition of law is equivalent to whatever use of power a regime engages in. And even if you yourself would not use the language set forth in the example, if you would understand someone else using this language, then you are implicitly rejecting the view that our language only defines the term 'law' as coextensive with a regime's power to act.

So, the point of the example is to show that you are implicitly accepting that it makes sense to critique a regime's actions as unlawful using a standard of legality that exists outside of the regime's power

---

opprobrium, involve the combination of law and morality. Because these terms join together the two concepts 'law' and 'morality' that the text for heuristic reasons is attempting to separate, it would confuse the analysis to deal with them.

208. "On the gallows men would actually complain, in their 'last dying words', if they felt that in some particular the due forms of law had not been undergone." Thompson, E. P., *Whigs and Hunters*, 1975, at 268 (describing 18th Century British law).

At a later point in this book I will be asserting that totalitarian regimes also sometimes attempt to convey the impression that they comply with the notion of 'law' or 'legality' or 'the rule of law' in the sense described here. This attempt is illustrated by the Moscow show trials of the 1930s which Stalin used to justify getting rid of old communist comrades.

relationships. In effect, your acceptance of this example as making sense indicates that you have adopted the terminology of procedural natural law. Why? Because you are using an idea of what 'law' entails as the basis for asserting that the regime's apologists' claims that it is complying with 'legality' are false.

If by contrast you accept that the regime's description of what constitutes 'law' within its borders is the only basis for judging what the regime does under the name of 'law,' then there is no legitimate basis for you to reject what the "judge" has done in the name of 'law.' This view precludes an honest appeal[209] to the court of world public opinion to the effect that the regime's arbitrary and irrational "trial" had violated our common notion of 'legality.'

This would be the position of a pure positivist. But that by itself does not undercut the positivist's position. For under the positivist view one still can assert whatever moral (non-legal) arguments one believes are appropriate against what the regime has done. What does undercut the positivist's position, however, is your willingness to accept that, at least in some circumstances, how we use language is inconsistent with the positivist's assertion that the term 'law' is equivalent to the term 'state power.'

Here is another example designed to show that our use of language reflects that a regime's acting in accordance with law is not necessarily the same thing as its use of power. Assume that in the last example you miraculously escape from the clutches of the "law" through some sort of ruse. You now decide to cut short your visit to this strange country and instead visit a neighboring country. Taking a busperson's holiday, you decide to visit the country's one law school. You are given a tour of the law school's facilities and even get to meet the provost. You inform her that in your country you are a lawyer with a strong interest in comparative procedural law and you wonder if you could sit in on a civil or criminal procedure class. The provost informs you that at her law school there is no course on procedure or on anything that could be its functional equivalent. You ask, "don't

209. If you believe that the law is whatever the regime says it is, however, you are not prevented from making a dishonest appeal to the court of world public opinion. Thus, if you assume that others wrongly believe in the language of procedural natural law, you can still use that language as a rhetorical device to convince the gullible others that your verbal attack against the regime has merit.

your lawyers and officials need procedures for deciding what constitutes a violation of the law, for governing and judging adversarial proceedings, and for determining what rules to apply and how to change them?" The provost then informs you that, "we don't have rules or need for procedures in our country, for the Maximum Leader determines what is done by indicating his whim at that particular moment."[210]

The question to be asked here is, what would you think of such an approach to "law"? Would you think and presumably say, "how interesting, in our country we have something called procedure as part of our legal system, but in your country your legal system has managed to dispense with such a boring subject?" Or is it more likely that you would think (and presumably not say), "no matter what they call it, this can't be a legal system in any meaningful sense?" Again, if your unspoken response would be more a variant of the latter approach than the former, then you are treating the term 'law' as inconsistent with a definition that equates it with state power. Under this view you would think that it can't be a legal system because a legal system enables people to attempt to fashion their conduct to comply with what the government demands. Here there are no rules that would enable people to fashion their conduct, or even to know whether they would be judged based on their conduct. Nor were there rules to enable a judge to determine whether or not there has been a violation of some other unstated rule. Even if you yourself would not use this sort of language criticizing the regime's conduct as violative of legality but would understand someone else's using such language, you have accepted the discourse of procedural natural law.

For a final example, assume that, contrary to your better judgment, you decide to stay in this strange country. As a result you get to meet the Maximum Leader at a party at his presidential palace. At-

210. This approach has more or less already been tried:

> In effect,...the Revolutionary Tribunals [of the early USSR], from their foundation, operated as kangaroo courts, which sentenced defendants on the basis of a commonsensical impression of guilt.
>
> ...
>
> There were courts for ordinary crimes and for crimes against the state, but no laws to guide them; citizens were sentenced by judges lacking in professional qualifications for crimes which were nowhere defined.

Pipes, Richard, *The Russian Revolution*, 1990, at 798–799.

tempting to engage in small talk, you ask him how the law functions in his country. He tells you that he is the law. Further, he states that as part of his law he dispenses with the trial stage because, since everybody in his country is almost certainly guilty of something or other, it is a waste of time and money to bother with a trial. Rather than bothering with a trial, he proceeds directly to the punishment stage. Indeed, his legal judgments are meted out right here in the presidential palace. He then escorts you to a large sound proof room next door to the dining room where the prisoners are being tortured to death. He then says, "this is where I render the only legal judgments that matter in my country."[211] Presumably you would respond politely and quickly walk out of the room, take leave of the Maximum Leader and get out of the country.

---

211. Anybody familiar with the literature would be aware that the textual example of torture without benefit of a trial is not a figment of my imagination. But for those who would like a fairly similar factual account, here is a journalist's description of life in the Sudan.

> [O]utside the realm of the [Islamic] shari'a system, extralegal punishments have proliferated. The secret police pervade Khartoum.... [P]risoners of the secret police... have been whipped, sliced, burned, clubbed, shackled and hung by their wrists or ankles, mutilated, blinded, shocked and starved. They have been deprived of light, space, water, medicine, and sleep. They have been lowered into deep wells poisoned with animal carcasses.

Langewiesche, William, "Tarubi's Law," *The Atlantic Monthly*, Aug. 1994, at 32.

Another example is provided by Lenin's Soviet Union (and later continued under Stalin). As Lenin put it: "[t]he courts must not ban terror—to promise that would be deception or self-deception—but must... legalise [terror] as a principle.... Zile, Zigurds L., *Ideas and Forces in Soviet Legal History*, Lenin's Letter to Kursky, 1992, at 289. "The first step in the introduction of mass terror to Soviet Russia was the elimination of all legal restraint—indeed, of law itself—and its replacement by something labelled 'revolutionary conscience.'" Pipes, Richard, *The Russian Revolution*, 1990, at 796. Lenin's Commissar of Justice reported the following conversation with Lenin:

> It was difficult to argue with Lenin [with respect to his policy on terror] and we soon reached an impasse. We were discussing a harsh police measure with far-reaching terroristic potentialities. Lenin resented my opposition .... So I called out in exasperation, "Then why do we bother with a Commisariat of Justice? Let's call it frankly the *Commisariat for Social Extermination* and be done with it." Lenin's face suddenly brightened and he replied, "Well put... that's exactly what it should be... but we can't say that."

Id. at 795.

Later, the new Commissar of Justice, who was not inhibited by the old Commissar's scruples, stated: "[w]e must execute not only the guilty. Execution of the innocent will impress the masses even more." *Id.* at 822.

But what would you think about what you have seen? Undoubtedly, you would regard it as barbaric and sadistic. But wouldn't you also think that this was not law as you understood it? It was not law because it dispensed with rules determining what constituted a violation, dispensed with the requirement that one be guilty of violating some specified rule, treated people as irredeemably guilty regardless of what they had done or not done, dispensed with a trial altogether, tortured people and ignored any notion of proportionality in sentencing.

If you might think this, how could you justify to yourself this form of self-expression? If law is whatever those in power say it is or do, then what you have just witnessed is surely law. Even if you were inclined to accept what you had witnessed as law, though morally repugnant law, so long as you understood someone else's referring to what you had seen as a gross violation of the ideal of law you do not escape the realization that procedural natural law language is an appropriate part of our discourse. For as long as you understand this use of language, then you are admitting that in one sense the concept 'law' does not encompass just anything that a barbaric government might do to those living within its borders. The use of this version of the term 'law' would exclude a regime's extreme arbitrariness, brutality, irrationality, killing without rational justification, thuggery, torture and street violence.

This use of the concept 'law' produces contrasting judgments about democracies[212] and the more extreme dictatorships. The former

---

212. Even a democracy can violate 'legality.' A democracy that controls people who are not citizens (say, because they are of a different ethnic, racial or religious group) does not necessarily treat these subject people within the contours of the ideal of legality. Examples of such states would include the ante bellum United States (with respect to its African American slaves), the apartheid regimes in South Africa (with respect to its blacks, coloreds and other non-whites) and Israel's control of the West Bank and Gaza (with respect to the Arabs). One way of examining these states is to question the extent of their commitment to democracy. In the context of this article, the proposed way to examine these states is to view them as not extending the rule of law to the disfavored groups.

But in defense of some democratic governments that have not afforded the rule of law to hostile individuals or groups within their borders, it could be argued that another value, namely, the value of the survival of the state and the the society that supports it, is more important than the rule of law and therefore supersedes it. So, for example, Abraham Lincoln might have argued when he suspended habeas corpus during the Civil War or Israeli spokespeople could argue so long as there remains legitimate fear for the survival of the state.

Of course, in some instances this defense can be questioned on several bases. One is have legal systems while the latter, at least in part, do not. Thus, to use a paradigm example, Nazi Germany's treatment of its Jews (stripping them of citizenship and killing them) clearly violated this ideal. So did Stalin's Soviet Union where "enemies" were rounded up in the middle of the night and, without trial, shipped to camps in Siberia where they would be likely to die.

Perhaps the notion that the concept 'law' has an outer limit might be illuminated by way of an analogy with medicine. Suppose you were to go to a strange country, get sick while still at the hotel, and call the concierge requesting that a doctor be sent to your room. If a woman in a white hospital gown and a black bag were to come up to the room, the woman might look like a doctor. But when she takes a hatchet out of the bag and starts to swing it at you, you would decide soon enough that she wasn't performing as a doctor. Thus, the notion of a doctor has its limits. As one scholar put it, "A society in which doctors regularly poisoned their patients could not be said to have a medical system."[213]

Obviously, there are differences between medicine and law. Whereas medicine is advanced through the scientific method using empirical testing, law is not primarily empirically based.[214] By contrast with the use of the empirical methodology, a law is viewed as

---

whether a particular state is really in sufficient danger to justify its actions. Another is whether a particular state deserves to survive.

213. Summers, Robert S., *Lon L. Fuller*, 1984, at 39.

214. While not primarily empirically based, I believe there is some connection between 'law' and empirical evidence. As I will reiterate below, in determining what constitutes legality in creating legal rules and deciding cases, some connection with rationality is required. In turn, rationality includes being open to examples that falsify the legal thesis, that is, open to the empirical method.

Not all instances of a regime's acting contrary to the evidence, however, constitutes the sort of irrationality that involves its violating a commitment to legality. For example, Hitler's refusal to retreat at Stalingrad, thus allowing his troops to be encircled and captured, seems inconsistent with the evidence and thus irrational but does not come within the universe of 'law.' But if a regime generally and consistently ignores the empirical evidence involving an issue we would expect to come within the notion of 'law,' then it is acting irrationally, thereby violating the ideal of legality. If, for example, the Khymer Rouge summarily executed everyone wearing glasses as necessarily an enemy of the regime, then it acted irrationally in not considering empirical evidence that would have falsified this general thesis in specific instances and thereby violated the notion of 'law' as an ideal.

valid because it has been formulated in accordance with an authoritative norm. Also, there is a point to medicine, namely, curing the patient or at least not harming her. But it is an open question as to whether there is a point to law.[215]

Still, the relevance of the analogy also deserves mention. The concept 'medicine' has an outer limit. Its purpose is to cure or heal persons who are in need and curable.[216] It is implicitly entailed by this understanding of medicine that a doctor would not deliberately act to cause a patient undesired harm unrelated to any curative effort. Despite the fact that she is referred to as "Doctor," presumably we would agree that a more accurate descriptive term for the person in the example above would be that of hatchet murderess. For the woman would be acting beyond the outer limits of 'medicine.'

Similarly, I assert that in one sense the term 'law' also has an outer limit. Unlike 'medicine' this limit to 'law' is not analyzed by determining whether those practicing it use the empirical method to heal and cure and need not be analyzed by determining whether some purpose or goal implicit in the concept has been served. The examples above are designed to indicate that the outer limit of the term 'law' consists in its adherence to articulable procedures. If the regime grossly violates what are regarded as appropriate procedural constraints, then what is being done by the regime is not law.[217] If the ex-

---

215. Philosophers of law who believe in substantive natural law, such as, Aquinas, Finnis and Fuller (the latter adhering to both a substantive and a procedural natural law position), also believe that law contains a purposive element, namely, to facilitate human activity. (By contrast, positivists who believe that law has no necessary moral element, such as, Austin, Hart, Kelsen and Raz, reject the notion that law contains a purposive element.) As one who adopts a purely procedural natural law position, it isn't necessary for me to deal with this question.

216. If a patient is not curable, then traditionally the purpose of medicine has been to reduce pain and needless suffering. If assisted suicide were to become generally accepted, then the purpose of medicine would be expanded to include helping a terminally ill patient die with dignity.

217. Although not my position, some commentators have drawn a similar conclusion from a substantive law perspective rather than the procedural perspective that I adopt, namely, that unless the state adheres to certain purposive substantive values, it ceases to comply with the rule of law. Here are several examples.

"[A] purported legal system that purposefully systematically deeply diminished the well-being of those living within its borders might be said to lose not only its legitimacy, but also its title as law." Summers, *Lon L. Fuller, supra*, at 40.

amples above are persuasive, there is a sense in which we use the term 'law' that limits what a government can do in its name and still come within it.

> [T]hose [natural law] principles justify the exercise of authority in community. They require . . . that authority be exercised . . . with due respect for the human rights which embody the requirements of justice, and for the purpose of promoting a common good . . . [A]ttention to the principles . . . justifies regarding certain positive laws as radically defective, *precisely as laws*, for want of conformity to those principles.

Finnis, *Natural Law and Natural Rights, supra*, at 23.

9

Procedural Natural Law in Literature

The idea of legal procedure exists not only in our language and in the writings of philosophers. It also exists in some of our great literature. One example is that of Franz Kafka, another that of Lewis Carroll, a third Arthur Koestler and a fourth Wole Soyinke.

Franz Kafka was trained in the law. Although it can be read in several different ways, one way of reading his *The Trial* is as an allegory about a state's "legal system" that violates the essential elements of what we think of as the rule of law. Here are some excerpts uttered either by or to the accused, one K, or by the narrator.

> (by K) And the significance of this great [judicial] organization, gentlemen? It consists in this, that innocent persons are accused of guilt, and senseless proceedings are put in motion against them, mostly without effect, it is true, as in my own case. But considering the senselessness of the whole, how is it possible for the higher ranks to prevent gross corruption in their agents? It is impossible. Even the highest judge in this organization cannot resist it.[218]

> (by K) ... [I]t is an essential part of the justice dispensed here that you should be condemned not only in innocence but also in ignorance.[219]

> (to K) "What you say sounds reasonable enough,' said the man, 'but I refuse to be bribed. I am here to whip people, and whip them I shall."[220]

> (narrator) They wanted to eliminate defending counsel as much as possible; the whole onus of the Defense must be laid on the accused himself. [N]othing could be more erroneous than to deduce from this that the accused persons had no need of defending counsel when appearing before this Court. For the proceedings were not only kept secret

218. Kafka, Franz, *The Trial*, 1964, at 57-8.
219. *Id.* at 62.
220. *Id.* at 107.

> from the public, but from the accused as well.... For even the accused had no access to the Court records.[221]
>
> (narrator) The case had simply reached the stage where further assistance was ruled out, it was being conducted in remote, inaccessible Courts, where even the accused was beyond the reach of a lawyer. Then you might come home some day and find on your table all the countless pleas relating to the case, which you had drawn up with such pains and such flattering hopes; they had been returned to you because in the new stage of the trial they were not admitted as relevant; they were mere waste paper.[222]
>
> (to K) [T]he Court, once it has brought a charge against someone, is firmly convinced of the guilt of the accused and... can never be dislodged from that conviction.[223]
>
> (to K) [I]n these proceedings things are always coming up for discussion that are simply beyond reason, people are too tired and distracted to think and so they take refuge in superstition. [O]ne of the superstitions is that you're supposed to tell from a man's face, especially the line of his lips, how his case is going to turn out. Well, people declared that judging from the expression of your lips you would be found guilty, and in the near future too.[224]
>
> (to K) "[I]t is not necessary to accept everything as true, one must only accept it as necessary." "A melancholy conclusion," said K, "it turns lying into a universal principle."[225]
>
> (narrator on the end result of K's struggle with the law) But one of the hands of the partners was already at K's throat, while the other thrust the knife deep into his heart and turned it there twice.[226]

Instead of providing us with the elements of the rule of law, Kafka can be read as providing its obverse: not informing the defendant (K) of the nature of the charges, willingly condemning him to death de-

---

221. *Id.* at 145-6.
222. *Id.* at 154.
223. *Id.* at 187.
224. *Id.* at 217-8.
225. *Id.* at 276.
226. *Id.* at 286.

spite his innocence, corruption, whipping as a sadistic form of punishment, not allowing the defendant to have counsel, not providing the defendant with the records of the proceeding, judges not having open minds, using superstition rather than reason to determine guilt, lying and killing the defendant on the street without his having the benefit of a formal verdict of death read to him in the courtroom.

A second example of the absence of the rule of law is provided by Lewis Carroll. Again, although one can read Lewis Carroll in several ways, one way to do so is to view him as making the point that law reguires rationality or non-arbitrariness. This 19th Century novelist was, after all, also a logician by vocation.

> At this moment the King...called out, "Silence!" and read from his book, "Rule Forty-two. *All persons more than a mile high to leave the court.*"
>
> Everyone looked at Alice.
>
> "*I'm* not a mile high," said Alice.
>
> "You are," said the King.
>
> "Nearly two miles high," added the Queen.
>
> "Well, I shan't go, at any rate," said Alice; "besides, that's not a regular rule: you invented it just now."
>
> "It's the oldest rule in the book," said the King.
>
> "Then it ought to be Number One," said Alice.
>
> The King turned pale and shut his notebook....
>
> "Let the jury consider their verdict," the King said, for about the twentieth time that day.
>
> "No, no!" said the Queen. "Sentence first —verdict afterwards."
>
> "Stuff and nonsense!" said Alice loudly. "The idea of having the sentence first!"
>
> "Hold your tongue!" said the Queen, turning purple.
>
> "I won't!" said Alice.
>
> "Off with her head!" the Queen shouted at the top of her voice.[227]

227. Carroll, Lewis, *Alice in Wonderland*, 1989, at 149-155.

As with Kafka, Carroll can be read as demonstrating the obverse of the notion of the rule of law. Here are some of the elements that violate the rule of law: separation of those who have the power to determine what constitutes a violation of the law from those who judge whether there has been, in fact, a violation, a deliberate rejection of the empirical method in refusing to judge accurately the fact of Alice's size, making up the rules as the "trial" goes along, dispensing with the sentence before the verdict and generally acting irrationally. As to the last item, the positivist, Joseph Raz, agrees with Lewis Carroll's seeming demonstration that a legal system necessarily limits arbitrariness. As Raz puts it, there is a "difference between law and a system of absolute discretion.... It is a necessary feature of all legal systems...that they have limits.... [W]hy is it necessary that legal systems have limits? The answer is that the only alternative...is a system of absolute discretion.[228]

Raz' notion of the rule of law as distinct from absolute arbitrariness would preclude a ruler's constant changing his edicts whenever it suited the ruler's purpose. This constant change of the "law" is also a feature of Alice's interaction with royalty and distinguishes it from the rule of law.

A third example of literature demonstrating the absence of the rule of law comes from the pen of Arthur Koestler based on his experience as a Communist agent in the 1930s and on the actual Soviet show trial of some of the leading Communist officials, particularly Nicholas Bukharin. At one point before his arrest the central figure of the story, Rubashov, mused: "[t]he Party knew only one crime: to swerve from the course laid out; and only one punishment: death.... [Death] was the logical solution to political divergences.[229]" After his

---

228. Raz, Joseph, *The Authority of Law*, 1979, at 113, 115. Raz's reasoning here is circular: a system of law is distinguished from a system of absolute discretion because if it weren't distinguished it would be a system of absolute discretion. Still, this language of Raz is useful as an assertion that a government's use of absolute discretion is inconsistent with the concept 'law.'

But later Raz appears to undercut this assertion by stating: "The rule of law is often rightly contrasted with arbitrary power. Arbitrary power is broader than the rule of law." *Id.* at 219. If (contrary to my view of his overall position) this statement can be interpreted as an assertion that the rule of law is a subset of the larger universe of absolute discretion, then he is disagreeing with what I am asserting and what he himself had previously been quoted as asserting.

229. Koestler, Arthur, *Darkness at Noon*, 1941, at 57.

arrest Rubashov wrote in his diary about what can be taken for a comment on the absence of the rule of law: "[w]e were the first to replace the ninteenth century's liberal ethics of "fair play" by the revolutionary ethics of the twentieth century."[230] He went on to write that "[h]istory has taught us that often lies serve her better than the truth; for man is sluggish and has to be led...."[231] He added that "[w]e resembled the great Inquisitors in that we persecuted the seeds of evil not only in men's deeds, but in their thoughts."[232] Once arrested he was charged with belonging to the organized opposition. One piece of "evidence" against him was that he had failed to denounce his loyal (and innocent) secretary until forced to by the Party late in the proceedings against her. He was also charged with seeking to attempt to assassinate the Maximum Leader. The "proof" was a "confession" of a rather dim-witted person who alleged that Rubashov was the leader of the assassination plot.

But Rubashov did not need to be tortured in order to "confess." He "confessed" out of loyalty to the Party that he had served for so many years: "I plead guilty to having rated the question of guilt and innocence higher than that of utility and harmfulness. Finally, I plead guilty to having placed the idea of man above the idea of mankind...."[233] But the Party wanted more, it wanted a "confession" at a public "trial" of Rubashov's alleged attempted assassination of the Maximum Leader. Rubashov gave what the Party wanted, a "confession" at a public "trial." His "punishment" was the death sentence.

Although Rubashav was not tortured into making a false confession, he felt forced to do so because of his loyalty to the goals of the Party and the fact that he had used the same tactics on others that the Party interrogators were using on him. It goes without saying that the confession was false, that he did not plot to attempt to assassinate the Maximum Leader and that he had not joined any organized opposition. It also goes without saying that the death sentence was almost certainly determined by the Party before the "trial" began and not after "evidence" was found. Also, no concern for finding evidence was manifested at the "trial," no effort was made to cross-examine

230. *Id.* at 73.
231. *Id.* at 74.
232. *Id.* at 75.
233. *Id.* at 136.

Rubashov's accuser or to determine whether his "confession" was psychologically coerced, no legal defense was provided and there were no lawyers present who honestly represented the defendant. This story certainly is not reflective of a trial or the rule of law as we understand these terms, but rather its obverse.

The fourth example of literature demonstrating the absence of the rule of law, while less rich in content than the previous three, is especially useful because it comes from a non-Western context. As such, it indicates what seems intuitively obvious but which has been denied by some radical scholars, namely, that regardless of culture people share the same values in terms of how they want their governments to treat them. The writer is the winner of the Nobel Prize for Literature, Wole Soyinka. Here he is quoting one of the earlier followers of Idi Amin's Uganda.

> At the start...you more or less knew what to do and what to avoid if you wanted to stay alive. You knew when to speak, when to shut up and what to say or not say. What saved you yesterday turns out to be your death-warrant today. I have no friends, no colleagues left. They are all dead or escaped. But mostly dead.[234]

What Soyinka is pointing out is the lack of consistency in the rules of the country, the lack of published rules, the lack of separation of power between Amin's deciding what the rule is (acting as legislator) and his applying it in an individual case (acting as judge), and the total arbitrariness of the momentary whims of Amin.

234. Soyinka, Wole, *A Play of Giants*, 1984, at x (quoting Robert Serumaga).

10

Why Procedural Natural Law Is Important

So far, I have suggested that we have an idea of law as involving certain procedural elements that have been fleshed out above (including rationality, treating similars similarly, Fuller's eight procedural principles,[235] Hart's rules of adjudication and his other secondary rules).[236] Further, when government violates this procedural ideal, it makes sense to criticize the government as violating a moral norm.

But this description of the rule of law does not explicate why the rule of law is important. I will suggest that the rule of law is important for a number of reasons: (1) in states that apply the concept, people can plan their lives more easily and with less fear that their plans will go awry due to bureaucratic interference; (2) in states that apply the concept generally, there is a basis for criticism whenever the concept is abrogated; (3) in states that apply the concept generally but not to some disfavored outgroup, there is a basis for criticism for the state's creating an exception for this outgroup; (4) in states that apply the concept, sometimes the the concept is applied even to protect an outgroup; (5) totalitarian states that do not apply the concept sometimes pay homage to the power of the concept by attempting to fool the public into believing that the concept is being applied; (6) it is important because the international community has come to regard it as important.

---

235. These principles are that law must be: (1) sufficiently general; (2) publicly promulgated; (3) sufficiently prospective; (4) clear and intelligible; (5) free of contradictions; (6) sufficiently constant through time so people can order their relations accordingly; (7) does not require the impossible; and (8) administered in a way sufficiently congruent with its wording so people can abide by it.

236. Hart's other secondary rules are rules of recognition (rules that enable one to determine which rules to apply) and rules of change (rules that determine how to change the rules).

It Is Important Because it Reduces Fear and Enables People to Plan Their Lives

By providing some minimal protection to persons against government irrationality and arbitrariness,[237] a regime that applies the rule of law enables people to plan their lives with a greater sense of security. This assumes that if people are rational, that is, if they intelligently pursue their own self interest, then they would believe that it would be desirable to have these protections against government. And it is not just that these protections are desirable, but that people would regard them as morally worth having.[238] *(cont. on page 96)*

---

237. This understanding provides a partial response to the critique of Duncan Kennedy. Professor Kennedy distinguishes between rules and standards and emphasizes the value of the latter in judicial decision making. He refers to 'the rule of law' model of decision making "as the deduction of legal rules from first principles, and the mechanical application of the rules to fact situations." Kennedy, Duncan, "Form and Substance in Private Law Adjudication," 89 *Harv. L. Rev.* 1685, 1754 (1976). Under this vision of the rule of law the "system, defined in terms of some point in the past, has the qualities of internal consistency necessary to allow the judge to distinguish between usurpation and the simple extension of existing principles." *Id.* at 1762. By contrast, under a regime of standards "every case would require a detailed, open-ended factual investigation *and* a direct appeal to values or purposes." *Id.* at 1752.

While I agree with Kennedy that sometimes a judicial application of standards is appropriate because it provides for more just decison making, the result is less consistency and less opportunity for future reliance. To explicate this further, my view is that the concept the rule of law includes general rules that are often applicable and applied in individual instances. Many of these instances of application occur in a mechanical fashion at the administrative level, say by police officers and clerks, without there being any need for judicial resolution. But once a case does arise that requires a judicial resolution, I do not suggest that these rules can be applied in a straight forward deductive fashion or be applied mechanically. Nor do I intend to suggest that, as part of the concept 'the rule of law,' judges would necessarily ignore either political preferences (policies) or what Kennedy calls the application of a standard, that is, the individualized case-by-case analysis in an attempt to reach a just decision. But what would be rejected by an approach that did not follow the rule of law is the refusal to consider applying general rules, ignoring them in favor of ad hoc decision making that makes no effort at providing consistent application or the basis for future reliance either by the public or by officials of the regime.

238. While I would not have expected it prior to working on this book, there is a certain ironic congruence between the thesis developed in the text and some of the statements made by the positivist, Joseph Raz: "That the test [for the content and determination of the existence of the law] is *capable* of being described in value-neutral terms does not mean that no value or deontic conclusions are entailed by it." Raz, *The Authority of*

Law, supra, at 40. Raz goes on to affirm, as a matter of fact, a core value that I also assert as the central, morally desirable feature of procedural natural law: "[we value the rule of law because w]e value the ability to choose styles and forms of life, to fix long term goals and effectively direct one's life towards them." *Id.* at 220.

Thus, Raz is making two relevant assertions: (1) his value neutral descriptive analysis of law does not preclude value laden conclusions entailed by the description; (2) the value laden conclusion that he draws from his description is that we humans desire a regime's adherence to the rule of law because, as a result, we can plan our lives more easily.

But against an arguably similar position taken by Lon Fuller, the point has been made that Fuller's internal morality of the law provides people with strategic principles for following the law rather than moral reasons. Wueste, Daniel E., "Book Review: Fuller's Processual Philosophy of Law," 71 *Cornell L. Rev.* 1205, at 1216 (1986).

I disagree with Wueste's assertion that only pragmatic values are involved in people's preference for a government following the rule of law and not also moral ones. The basis for this disagreement is perhaps best expressed by the observation of Robert Summers.

> Admittedly, the choice may be a choice to obey an evil law, but the citizen will at least have had a fair chance to decide whether to do so or not, and to act accordingly. This is in itself moral, even though, overall, what the state happens to be doing to the citizen through the substance of the law is immoral. Observe that if the principles of legality were violated, there could be a dual moral objection: the citizen could be subjected to an evil law *and* could lack any fair opportunity to know of it in advance and act accordingly. Indeed, to punish or sanction a citizen for not following an evil (or even a beneficent) law that is unfollowable is also unjust. And injustice is indisputably immoral.

Summers, Robert S., "Summer's Primer on Fuller's Jurisprudence —A Wholly Disinterested Assessment of the Reviews by Professors Wueste and Lebel," 71 *Cornell L. Rev.* 1231, at 1234 (1986).

Raz also rejects the assertion that there is a necessary connection between legal procedure and morality: "Fuller's attempt to establish a necessary connection between law and morality fails." Raz, Joseph, *The Authority of Law, supra*, at 224. But it is not clear to me why Raz believes that Fuller's attempt to establish a necessary connection between law and morality fails.

On the one hand Raz's assertion that the rule of law deserves no moral merit is flawed. For him the rule of law is designed to minimize the danger of arbitrary power. His argument goes as follows. By virtue of his definition of the concept 'law,' namely, as involving generality, clarity, and prospectivity, the law cannot bring about evils which altogether violate these values. Thus, according to Raz, since "the law cannot sanction arbitrary force or violations of freedom and dignity through [the] total absence of generality, prospectivity, or clarity," the law deserves no moral credit for not bringing about those evils including arbitrariness which as a matter of definition it could not bring about. *Id.* at 224.

If I am adequately presenting what Raz is asserting, one weakness of his position is that the moral issue is not, as he suggests, whether a government operating under the rule of law could commit evils that, as a matter of one's definition (Raz', Fuller's or

Law, thus, has a necessary moral element because rational, self-interested persons would believe that government morally ought to provide them with such protection.[239]

---

mine), it cannot commit. The moral issue is whether the rule of law, if followed by a government, restrains the degree of government arbitrariness and irrationality. It is government arbitrariness and irrationality that the rule of law restrains. So, for Raz to assert that there can be no moral merit in the law's adherence to principles which, by definition, it cannot violate is to miss the point: it is government's adherence to the rule of law rather than the law's adherence that has, to use Raz's terminology, moral merit because government could violate the rule of law. If, as I have argued here, the notion that a government's adherence to the rule of law restrains its arbitrariness and irrationality, then contrary to Raz's view it is appropriate to assert both that there is a necessary connection between the rule of law and morality and that a government which follows the rule of law can be viewed by those who deal with it as morally desirable.

Another point worth making is that the argument presented here is not, as Raz would make it, that something called 'the law' (Raz's terminology) or 'rule of law' deserves moral credit. The issue is whether, from the perspective of the person who has to deal with the government, the government's adherence to the rule of law is morally desirable. The argument is that it is because the result of the government's self restraint is that the person can more easily plan her life. And she would regard this as morally desirable.

On the other hand, while Raz insists that law and the rule of law deserve no moral credit, he also states that the rule of law does have a moral value: "...the rule of law is not merely a moral virtue." *Id.* at 225. "The special status of the rule law does not mean that conformity with it is of no moral importance." *Id.* at 226. While I could attempt to articulate Raz's position in fuller detail, I still wind up wishing that he had been more careful in explicating his easy dismissal of Fuller's view.

239. "Some reasons for wishing officials to be faithful to the law are grounded on moral considerations. Considerations of fairness and autonomy, for example, argue against penalizing people for doing what they had no reason to believe would be punishable."

Lyons, David, *Ethics and the Rule of Law*, at 201.

The positivist, Joseph Raz, makes a point that might be confused with the argument that is put forth here.

> It may be a necessary truth that all legal systems conform to some moral values and that a system which violates these values cannot be a legal system. My claim is merely that if this is indeed the case then these necessary moral features of law are derivative characteristics of law. If the legal system necessarily possesses certain moral characteristics they possess them as a result of the fact that they have other properties which are necessary for them to fulfill their unique social role.

Raz, *The Authority of Law, supra,* at 104.

From the context of this statement (which I don't reproduce here) I gather that Raz is asserting that any existing legal system would need to have achieved a certain level of

In the next few paragraphs I will illustrate this thesis by looking at specific aspects of the concept 'law.' One such aspect is the publication of general rules in advance and the changing of these rules only through some recognized and published procedure. Thus, a legal system contains some constancy through time. This aspect of the concept enables people to govern and plan their lives according to some structure insuring that their expectations will not be arbitrarily thwarted.[240] If the government bureaucracy can be thought of as a

---

acquiescence by the population it controls, and that this might not be achievable without the system's having certain moral features. But this is a derivative, social fact about a legal system.

By contrast, the argument I put forth in the text is that the moral component of any legal system is not derivative, but rather consists in its being a necessary feature of a legal system. A legal system, any legal system, definitionally has certain contours that circumscribes what government can do and thereby limits government arbitrariness and irrationality. Because of this, persons who might interact with government can plan their lives more easily. The reliance factor resulting from the legal limits on government power is self evidently morally desirable, at least when contrasted with its obverse.

While Raz does not assert that the concept 'law' contains a necessary moral element, he does indicate that it enables people to plan their lives. As he puts it: "Legal systems... do provide guidance to individuals." *Id.* at 112.

240. A criticism of Fuller's inner morality of law is that his allowance of some legal retroactivity is inconsistent with the supposed morality involved in enabling people to plan their lives in accordance with the existing laws.

> [I]t is hard to see how compliance with a set of principles that does not completely disallow retroactivity — because, as Fuller says, retroactive laws "may actually be essential to advance the cause of legality"...necessarily guarantees that citizens have a fair opportunity to obey the law. Because lawmakers do not necessarily run afoul of Fuller's principles by enacting retroactive laws and because there can be no fair opportunity to obey such laws,...[w]e shall have to rest content with the weaker but plausible claim that compliance with Fuller's principles tends to secure this opportunity for citizens.

Wueste, *Book Review: Fuller's Processual Philosophy of Law*, *supra*, at 1209.

I agree with Wueste's point that Fuller's application of his own concept 'law' does not always, in fact, enable people to comply with all of its specific requirements. Regardless of Fuller's view, I regard any instance of a retroactive "law" as inconsistent with a core aspect of the concept of 'legality.' Because a paradigm or core aspect of legality is its providing those people governed by it with a theoretical opportunity to comply with its requirements, a retroactive "law" violates this aspect of the concept.

But this does not mean that a government's occasional use of retroactivity renders the concept of 'legality' inapplicable to its actions in general. For the argument presented here as to what constitutes a government's adherence to the rule of law does not require that the government adhere to every aspect of legality in each instance of its actions. Indeed, there might be justifiable non-legal reasons for a government's violation of the maze that could engulf the unwary, then having a government complying with the requirement of publication of general rules that can be changed only through recognized and public procedures provides the person with a blueprint of how to get through the maze:

> The rule of law plays such a central and abiding role in the theories of liberal thinkers because they judge it to be an indispensable mechanism for securing the dominant value cherished by their tradition—individual liberty...The law is an indispensable mechanism for regulating public and private power in a way that effectively helps to prevent the oppression and domination of the individual by other individuals and by institutions.[241]

Because paradigm examples of law going back to Aristotle treat similars similarly,[242] we generally take for granted that under the rule of law everyone similarly situated will be treated the same. One essential difference between some legal philosophers' explication of treating similars similarly, however, and mine as expressed in this

---

principle of non-retroactivity. Israel's trial of Adolph Eichmann comes to mind. (One reason why Israel's trial of Adolph Eichmann does not seem much of a stretch of this aspect of the rule of law is that no reasonably intelligent person in Eichmann's position could have relied on not being punished if Germany had lost the war.) But if the number and character of the government's use of retroactivity increases to the extent that people cannot generally plan their lives with the expectation that their compliance with government laws will secure them protection from its sanctions, then the concept of 'legality' would be violated.

241. Altman, Andrew, *Critical Legal Studies*, 1993, at 13.

Some feminists argue that the notion of liberty or autonomy is a masculine value rather than a feminine one. According to this theory, women value connectedness and intimacy rather than independence. *See* West, Robin, "Jurisprudence and Gender," 55 *U. Chi. L. Rev.* 1 (1988). But regardless of the strength of this argument, I believe that women as well as men would prefer not to needlessly suffer the embrace of governmental Big Brother any more than necessary.

242. This idea has been traced back to Aristotle.

> The essential idea of distributive justice Aristotle defined as that of *treating equals equally*. In this sense, the principle of distributive justice served to constitute the state as a form of human association whose members were bound together as equals under a system of publicly defined rules and laws. From this principle of distributive justice Aristotle derived, albeit provisionally, many of the principles that were taken by later theorists to be implicit in the very concept of the rule of law.

Covell, Charles, *The Defence of Natural Law*, 1992, at 5.

book is that I do not limit the state's legal obligation to those whom the state might regard as appropriate for similar treatment. Rather, if the state controls the person, whether or not it regards the person as its citizen or deserving of coming within the ambit of those treated more favorably, it must either treat the person similarly to what a rational outsider would regard as its relevantly similar citizens or else be able satisfactorily to explain to the rational outsider why it is not doing so.[243] This understanding does not require that the resident alien be treated similar to the citizen. Rather, it requires the regime's spokesperson to justify the difference to the rational outsider. Because paradigm examples of law include being able to provide reasons that explain to a disinterested outside observer why one person is similar and another is dissimilar, the government cannot comply with the concept "law" when it arbitrarily singles one out from others for irrationally disparate treatment.

And because paradigm examples of law involve determining the outcome of disputes through an impartial fact finder examining the evidence presented and relying on recognized and published procedures for deciding cases in accordance with published rules and recognized standards, people are somewhat protected against being arbitrarily deprived of their liberty or property.

So, the importance of procedural natural law, to the extent governments actually comply with it, is that it reduces people's fear that they will be arbitrarily singled out for unfavorable treatment. This in turn allows people to plan their lives with the expectation that they can comply with government's stated rules and thereby escape sanc-

---

243. One critic of the notion of equal treatment, Peter Westen, has written that the concept is empty of content, that it is circular. Because it depends for its force on there being an external substantive right to which the persons seeking equal treatment are comparing themselves, what is really being demanded is that the person be given her due in accordance with that right. As Westen puts it: what this comes to is that "people who by a rule should be treated alike should by the rule be treated alike." Gottlieb, Stephen E., *Jurisprudence*, Westen, Peter, *The Empty Idea of Equality* 1993, at 493.

A response to this thesis is that it does not seem to be an empty idea to ask of the regime to justify to the neutral outsider how it distinguishes between those people whom it favors and those whom it disfavors by providing articulable, rational reasons for the distinction. Since what is at issue is whether the regime's basis for distinguishing between some favored ones and others is rational, requiring the regime's spokesperson to explain the basis for the distinction in language that actually explains the distinction rather than simply repeats it is not circular. And when it is actually applied, it is not empty.

tion. I cannot easily imagine that a civilized society could operate without making a good faith effort to comply with the rule of law.

The Existence of the Concept 'The Rule of Law' Is Important in a State That Generally Applies the Concept Because It Provides a Basis for Criticizing the State Whenever It Abrogates an Aspect of It

Another reason why the concept is important is because a government that attempts to comply with it might be stung by criticism that, in a particular instance, it is not doing so. This leads to the possibility of a correction in the legal process to the benefit of those caught up in its web. For example, the existence of a procedure (writ of habeas corpus) for enabling people in jail to get a court to determine the justification for the jailing constituted a basis for criticizing President Abraham Lincoln when he suspended that writ during the Civil War.[244]

Regimes That Generally Apply the Rule of Law Can Be Criticized When They Do Not Apply It to Disfavored Outgroups

'The rule of law' concept can be used to criticize some democracies not only for abrograting a law here and there but rather for going much further, namely, while applying the rule of law to the in-group, these democracies regard some people within their control as unworthy of coming within the concept. This occurs when a democracy controls people to whom it does not provide the advantages of citizenship (say, because they are of a different ethnic, racial or religious group). In such instances the democracy does not treat these subject people within the contours of the ideal of legality. Examples of such states would include the ante bellum United States (with respect to its African American slaves), the Confederacy during the Civil War, the apartheid regime of South Africa (with respect to its blacks, coloreds and Indians) and Israel's treatment of the Arab people living in the West Bank and Gaza.

244. In this instance, however, the criticism emanating from the Supreme Court did not force Lincoln to change his suspension. Donald, David Herbert, *Lincoln*, 1995, at 299-304.

The Israeli government, until recently including its Supreme Court, has condoned what it calls "moderate physical pressure"[245] as applied to perhaps 5,000 Palestinians per year.[246] As used on one detainee, this "pressure" included his being kept without sleep "in contorted and excruciating positions with a stinking bag over his head"[247] for some 17 days. During that time he was shaken violently. As a result his head flopped uncontrollably and his spine and neck hurt terribly. At least one such detainee died as a result of this torture.[248] I would like to think that this sort of violation of the rule of law will recede and ultimately cease as a result of the recent Israeli Supreme Court's pronouncement against it especially when and if the Palestinian Authority takes full control over most of its own people. But this is less than certain since the Palestinian Authority also engages in torture.[249]

One way of examining these democratic states that do not extend the rule of law to all of the people under their control is to question the extent of their commitment to democracy. But in the context of this book dealing with the rule of law, I confine myself to viewing such regimes as not extending the rule of law to the disfavored groups. Implicit in this description is a criticism for this failure.

But in defense of some democratic governments that did not afford the rule of law to members of hostile subordinated groups within their borders, it could be argued that another incommensurate value might be regarded as taking precedence. For example, it could be argued that the value of the survival of the state and the society that supported it was more important than the rule of law and therefore superseded it. Thus, I am not making the claim in this book that the

---

245. Segal, Maomi, "High Court in Israel to Hear Petitions on 'Shaking' Prisoners," *Jewish Telegraphic Agency*, May 19, 1998, *Westlaw*, at 1; but see Sontag, Deborah, "Israel Court Bans Most Use of Force in Interrogations," *The New York Times*, Sept. 7, 1999, at A1.

246. Schmemann, Serge, "Israel Seeks to Justify Physical Coercion of Prisoners," *The New York Times*, May 11, 1997, *Westlaw*, at 4.

247. Lewis, Anthony, "The Calloused Torturer and the Corrupted Society He Represents," *Id.*, May 14, 1997, *Westlaw*, at 2.

248. "Israeli Officians Defend Use of Force in Interrogations They Told a U.N. Panel," *Id.*, May 8, 1997, *Westlaw*, at 1.

249. Schmemann, Serge, "Israel Seeks to Justify Physical Coercion of Prisoners," *Id.*, May 11, 1997, *Westlaw*, at 1.

rule of law is the only relevant value or necessarily the most important one.[250]

For example, if the relevant state officials thought that a recently captured prisoner who was demonstrably hostile to the state knew the particulars about an attempt to smuggle atomic weapons into the state's largest city in order to kill as many people as possible, would not these state officials be justified in torturing the prisoner in order to obtain the necessary information to prevent the mass deaths? Would not these officials be justified in torturing the prisoner even though this would constitute a violation of the rule of law?

This is not just a hypothetical problem. In fact, this is not so far from the argument used by Abraham Lincoln when he suspended habeas corpus during the Civil War. Article I, Section 9 (2) of the U.S. Constitution provides that "[t]he privilege of the Writ of Habeas Corpus shall not be suspended, unless when in Cases of Rebellion or Invasion the public Safety may require it." This indicates that it was constitutional for the writ of habeas corpus to be suspended during the Civil War, but the Constitution puts the authorization for its suspension in Article I, the article granting Congress authority, rather than in Article II, the article granting the President authority.

Acting without congressional authorization, President Lincoln suspended the writ of habeas corpus along the route between Washington and Philadelphia on April 27, 1961. One John Merryman, a lieutenant in a successionist drill company, was imprisoned and secured a writ of habeas corpus from the U.S. Supreme Court Chief Justice, Taney. The writ ordered that Merryman be tried by a regular court or released. Lincoln had the arresting officer ignore Taney's ruling, and when Taney later ruled that Lincoln acted unlawfully Lincoln ignored this ruling as well. Later, in his July 4th message to the special session of Congress, Lincoln defended his action, asserting both that he had

---

250. I am indebted to Isaiah Berlin for making this point, albeit at a purely abstract level:

> Again and again... Berlin warns us against the deep error of supposing that all goods, all virtues, all ideals are compatible, and that what is desirable can ultimately be united into a harmonious whole without loss.... It is... that we have no coherent conception of a world without loss, that goods conflict by their very nature, and that there can be no incontestable scheme for harmonising them.

Williams, Bernard, *Introduction*, Berlin, Isaiah, *Concepts and Categories*, 1979, at xvi.

not violated the law, and that "'such extreme tenderness of the citizen's liberty' as Taney had shown could lead to the danger of allowing 'all the laws *but one* to go unexecuted, and the government itself go to pieces, lest that one be violated.'"[251] Chief Justice William Rehnquist has referred to this action by Lincoln as well as other actions taken by the United States government during wartime as *inter arma silent leges* (during war the laws are silent, during war the law does not apply).[252]

A similar argument might be made by a spokesperson for the state of Israel to justify its use of torture on Palestinian prisoners, namely, legal niceties must be subordinated to the need for physical survival of Israeli citizens so long as there remained a legitimate fear for the survival of the state. If "moderate" physical torture of prisoners is needed to pry open information that they might have about terror attacks upon citizens of Israel, then survival takes precedence over legality.

Of course, in some instances this defense could be questioned on several bases. One is whether a particular state is really in sufficient danger to justify its extra-legal actions. Another is whether a particular state deserves to survive.[253] One example where many of us would agree that the state's survival was not justified was the Confederacy during the Civil War. Another would be the apartheid regime of South Africa.

But regardless of whether or not a democratic state's violation of the principle of procedural natural law as applied to those whom its dominant element regard as outsiders can be justified on the ground that it is necessary for the state's survival, such a state can be criti-

251. Donald, *Lincoln, supra,* at 299, 303-4.

In later war years Lincoln often suspended the writ of habeas corpus, twice suspending it throughout the country. *Id.* at 304.

252. Using Lincoln's language in his title, Supreme Court Chief Justice William Rehnquist has written a book exploring the suspension of ordinary legal rights during wartime. While discussing other historical events including Lincoln's suspension of habeas corpus during the Civil War, the book, titled *All the Laws but One: Civil Liberties in Wartime*, is most controversial when it defends part of the Supreme Court's decision affirming the internment of Japanese during the Second World War, specifically, that part dealing with Japanese aliens. As the reader might guess. I don't agree with Rehnquist's view on this point.

253. For the record I think that Israel deserves to survive.

cized by enlightened public opinion abroad (and sometimes at home) for violating an important value. The fact that the Union forces could be mobilized to defeat the Confederacy can be ascribed, in part, to the outrage created by the institution of slavery, a violation of procedural legality as well as substantive natural law theory and morality. And the fact that the apartheid regime in South Africa no longer exists can be ascribed, in part, to the outrage created by the institutional mistreatment by the politically dominant whites against blacks, coloreds and Indians. The criticism of apartheid too was based on procedural natural law grounds as well as substantive natural law theory and morality. Finally, Israel also has had to respond to criticism and has reduced its control over Arab non-citizens. So, procedural natural law theory, while obviously not the only basis for criticizing democratic regimes' practices in violating the rule of law, has played a positive role.

Sometimes the Rule of Law Triumphs Over Xenophobia and Is Applied to Outsiders

Another indication of the importance of the rule of law (as well as various understandings of substantive natural law and substantive natural rights) is the willingness of the U.S. military to apply the concept of treating similars similarly as part of its Code of Military Justice. The U.S. Code of Military Justice provides a basis for trying U.S. servicemen who have wantonly killed civilians while engaged in combat in foreign countries. And the U.S. military has actually tried such individuals. One example of the concept's application is the Kinder case where a serviceman killed a Korean civilian during the Korean War at the apparent request of his superior officer. Kinder's assertion that he was following orders was regarded as no defense and he was found guilty, court martialed and sentenced to life imprisonment.[254]

The military's court martial, conviction and sentence to life imprisonment of Lieutenant Calley for murdering civilians at My Lai (or Xom Lang) during the Vietnamese war is another example of the application of this concept.[255] Here again the United States government

254. *United States v. Kinder*, 14 C.M.R. 742 (ACM 7321) (1954).

255. Hammer, Richard, *The Court-Martial of Lt. Calley*, 1971. The fact that President Nixon later commuted Calley's sentence does not take away from the military's initial recognition and application of the concept of treating similars similarly.

and its military recognize that there is no relevant difference between the defenseless U. S. citizen and the defenseless stranger: through its positive law the U. S. military has been willing to try a soldier for the unjustified killing of a civilian stranger in the stranger's own country on more or less the same basis as it would try a soldier's unjustified killing of a U. S. citizen on American soil. In both instances the justification for the trial is to punish murder.

Even during the period Israel used "moderate" torture on Arab prisoners,[256] at least in theory, it recognized the value of procedural (and substantive) natural law as informing its positive law seemingly even as applied to Arab non-citizens. The President of the Supreme Court of the state, Aharon Barak, noted that there exists "judicial review of statutes which unlawfully infringe upon constitutionally protected human rights..."[257] He went on to state:

> "The requirement that any infringement upon a Human Right be prescribed by statute, reflects the requirement of legality...this principle is not of a purely formal character." Hence, an infringement prescribed by statute means that the law should be general, public, known and publicised.
>
> The statute must be accessible (in its meaning) and certain (as to the scope of its application).
>
> Consequently, vague criminal statutes cannot fulfill the requirements of the limitation clause.[258]

It Is Important Because Totalitarian States Attempt to Use Its Positive Image in Order to Convince a Hoped for Gullible Public of Their Decency

One might argue that this minimal procedural morality entailed by the concept 'law' does not, in fact, provide persons much protection against government arbitrariness and irrationality. It has been ar-

256. *See* Greenberg, Joel, "Israel Court Weighs Legality of What Many Call Torture," *The New York Times International*, Jan. 25, 1999, at A10.

257. Barak, Aharon, "The Constitutionalization of the Israeli Legal System as a Result of the Basic Laws and its Effect on Procedural and Substantive Criminal Law," *Is. L. Rev.*, Vol. 31, Nos. 1-3, 1997, at 3.

258. *Id.* at 13 (footnote from the text is omitted).

gued, for example, that Nazi Germany acted in accordance with Fuller's eight procedural principles with the exception to some extent that the law be promulgated.[259] But this is much too cribbed an application of Fuller's procedural views. Among Fuller's principles is the requirement that people can comply with the state's promulgated rules with the inference that if they do so they will survive. Obviously, Nazi Germany violated this principle in treating the Jews as exterminable based on their status rather than judging them based on their individual behavior in relation to published rules. But apart from the specifics of Fuller's eight principles, his procedural morality also excluded the use of government thugs to engage in forays of terror in the streets. Again, in the case of the Jews, this principle was violated on Kristalinacht (when their property and synagogues were destroyed) as well as when they were rounded up to be deported to the concentration camps.

In addition, the Nazis violated the principle that similar cases be treated similarly.[260] While the Nazis could (and did) argue that Jews, Gypsies, the retarded, communists and homosexuals whom they killed were not similar to those protected by the regime,[261] under the

259. Wolfgang Friedmann, *Legal Theory*, 1967, at 18-19.

260. Fuller stated that justice requires that like cases be treated alike. Summers, *Lon L. Fuller, supra*, 1984, at 28. Fuller also scornfully referred to Hart's positivistic limitation on this principle. Hart viewed the principle as being limited to the administration of the law rather than as part of the concept 'law' itself. Hart, H.L.A. "Positivism and the Separation of Law and Morals," Feinberg, Joel and Gross, Hyman, eds. *Philosophy of Law*, 4th ed., 1991, at 624. Fuller's response was that "[Hart] does make brief mention of 'justice in the administration of the law,' which consists in the like treatment of like cases, by whatever...perverted standards the word 'like' may be defined." Fuller, Lon, "Positivism and Fidelity to Law— A Reply to Professor Hart," 71 *Harv. L. Rev.* 630, 645-46, 1958 . Thus, Fuller seemed to accept the view of legality that includes a requirement that real similars be treated similarly, and not just deference to the government apparatus' determination of who is similar and who is not.

At any rate, this is the view I have developed in this book. This requirement entails a standard of rationality that excludes the arbitrary and perverted distinctions that might be created and defended by the regime itself.

In contrast, the positivist, Joseph Raz (like Hart) explicitly disagrees with this characterization of the rule of law: "Racial, religious, and all manner of discrimination are not only compatible [with] but often institutionalized by general rules" which accord with the rule of law. Raz, *The Authority of Law, supra*, at 216.

261. These primarily consisted of "politically correct," normally intelligent, Aryan heterosexuals.

analysis developed here this argument would satisfy the requirement only if the regime's spokespeople could persuade the disinterested neutral outside observer that the alleged dissimilarity was sufficiently rationally based.[262]

If, for example, the Nazis' argument rested, at least in part, on the assertion that every Jew was "a parasite, a bacillus and a vampire, bleeding all nations to death and corrupting all that was noble and healthy in 'Aryan' and German life,"[263] then the burden would be on the Nazis to provide evidence to the neutral disinterested outside observer that there was sufficient rational evidence to support this claim. Simply the assertion by Hitler that this was so, while it would satisfy the regime's apologists,[264] would not be sufficient to satisfy the rational outside observer. Indeed, it is difficult to imagine how the regime could even begin to satisfy this assertion about every member of the disfavored groups.

---

262. One writer, commenting on the notion of legal objectivity within a society, states that the only objectivity that he can accept in the law "which makes a clear claim about the nature of the reality it seeks to explain" is its being available for public criticism and evaluation. Reynolds, Noel B., "The Concept of Objectivity in Legal Reasoning," 14 *W. Ontario L. Rev.* 1, 24 n. 74 (1975). If what Reynolds means here by "objectivity" is the inter-subjective agreement provided by neutral observers when they engage in a public evaluation of an alleged legal system and how it is applied outside the constraints imposed by a particular regime and culture, then I am in agreement with his comment.

If I understand him correctly, Jurgen Habermas also suggests the possibility of a cross-cultural appeal to a consensus in public discourse:

> [W]e may assume that the know-how informing argumentative practices represents a point of convergence where participants, however diverse their backgrounds, can at least intuitively meet in their efforts to reach an understanding. In all languages and in every language community, such concepts as truth, rationalaity, justification, and consensus, even if interpreted differently and applied according to different criteria, play *the same grammatical role*. At any rate, this is true for modern societies that, with positive law, secularized politics, and a principled morality, have made the shift to a postconventional level of justification and expect their members to take a reflexive attitude toward their own respective cultural traditions.

Habermas, Jurgen, *Between Facts and Norms*, 1996, at 311-2.

263. Gilbert, Martin, *Auschwitz and the Allies*, 1981, at 13.

264. The willingness of a significant portion of the legal elite to identify with the Nazi regime has been viewed by one commentator as an ongoing German trait. "Muller identifies a disturbing trait that, in his view, runs through the German judiciary more or less uninterrupted from the late nineteenth century until today: "loyalty to 'state leadership'... and a feeling of obligation to 'government authority'...." Dubber, Markus Dirk, "Hitler's Justice: The Courts of the Third Reich by Ingo Muller," 93 *Colum. L. Rev.* 1807, 1823 (1993).

Assuming that the regime's spokespeople could not otherwise satisfy the outside judge that its actions came within the notion of legality, the spokespeople might attempt the following ploy:

> You (Americans, Western Europeans, Japanese) use the term 'legality' to include certain procedural requirements. In our country we use the same terminology in a more honest way to describe what is really occurring. To put it simply, the elite of every country uses its governmental apparatus to favor those whom it wants to favor and to oppress and destroy those whom it seeks to harm. In some countries (yours for example) a phony distinction is drawn between the government's use of power to achieve its ends by whatever means and its use of certain so-called legal procedures to achieve the same ends. But this distinction is artificial because "Western legality" is the disguised use of pure power. In our country, therefore, we have decided to collapse this phony distinction between power and legality and just use the one term, 'legality' to refer to everything that government does.

This hypothetical response is inspired by the language used by apologists for the former Soviet regime. When questioned about the lack of democracy and legality in the Soviet Union, the response was that the nation had a superior form of democracy and legality; namely, Soviet democracy and Soviet legality. One purported reason why Soviet legality was superior was because, unlike Western law which pretended to transcend the interests of the dominant bourgeois class, the Soviet version was honestly based on the dominant class' interest, namely, that of the proletariat. Here, for example, are the remarks of the Procurator (Prosecutor) of the USSR, Andrei Vyshinsky:

> Right is the ensemble of the rules of behavior, which expresses the will of the ruling class and is fixed in a legislative way.... The application of these rules is sanctioned by means of the coercive power of the state for the purpose of the security, stabilization, and development of social relations and conditions that are satisfying and advantageous to the ruling class.[265]

---

265. Bloch, Ernst, *Natural Law and Human Dignity*, translated by Schmidt, Dennis J., 1987, at 224.

Thus, the Marxists or deconstructionists argue that the concept of law is always an instrument of the strong, that is, those in power. Thus, any protection the weak think they might obtain from the existence of legal procedures is either illusory or a sop provided by those in power so as to make them acquiesce in the existing status quo power relationships.

Still, even if this critique of legal procedure resonates with you, it can be accommodated within the thesis I develop here. Even if the rule of law reflects and reinforces the political status quo, it nonetheless provides some desirable protection against the power elite's more irrational and arbitrary use of its dominating power. One can assume that wealthy, heterosexual, white males dominate a particular society. Still, despite their subordinated status, poor, lesbian, African-American females are more fully able to maximize whatever opportunities are available to them if the government dominated by the male power elite adheres to the rule of law.

What I am asserting is that the procedural requirements of law provide an argument on behalf of the weak against the strong that the latter are violating a widely accepted conceptual norm.[266] Contrary to a substantive natural law criticism of procedural natural law,[267] this is a powerful verbal weapon in the hands of those appeal-

---

266. In support of this assertion, though it seems self evident to me, I turn to one commentator's critique of the Nazi regime's willingness to ignore its own rules as written (the existing positive law) when it suited the regime's purposes:

> Indeed...in face of concrete circumstances a "positivistic" sticking to the letter of the law in applying the legal rules can be the ultimate device in helping the oppressed, as opposed to a "liberal" interpretation designed to further the nefarious spirit of the legislator. Not surprisingly, the Grand Criminal Panel of the Nazi Supreme Court exhorted German judges to recall that "the judiciary...can fuflill the task imposed on it by the Third Reich only if it does not remain glued to the letter of the law, but rather penetrates to its innermost spirit...."

Englard, Izhak, "Nazi Criticism Against the Normativist Theory of Hans Kelsen: Its Intellectual Basis and Post-Modern Tendencies," *Isr. L. Rev*. Vol 32, No. 2, 183, 188 (1998).

267. Here is one substantive natural law philosopher's critique of Hart's positivist version of treating similars similarly. (Remember, Hart requires that similars be treated similarly but limits the requirement to the administration of the law within a particular legal system.):

> Nor are the requirements of justice in my account restricted (like Hart's) to what can be drawn from the principle "Treat like cases alike and different cases

ing to enlightened world opinion on behalf of the disfavored. For, if a regime cannot rationally explain to the outsider why it treats its disfavored differently than its favored, then to that extent the regime's use of power to achieve its aims violates the limits imposed by the concept of legality.

Even if the regime's leadership does not care that the regime is violating this concept, enlightened world opinion often does care. The unanswered assertion that the regime has violated 'legality' becomes a useful verbal weapon on behalf of the regime's victims in mobilizing enlightened world public opinion (and perhaps action) against the regime. Indeed, this might be virtually the only weapon the weak and defenseless have at their command against the regime's guns.

In fact, however, totalitarian regimes sometimes indicate that they understand that violating the concept 'legality' constitutes an indictment of their regimes and attempt to demonstrate that they are applying the concept. These regimes often think complying with some semblance of the form of law is important in order to assuage possibly hostile public opinion both at home and abroad. That is, totali-

---

> differently." My theory includes principles for asserting how one person ought to treat another (or how one person has a right to be treated), regardless of whether or not others are being so treated, a principle forbidding torture in ALL cases is a principle of justice.

Finnis, John, *Natural Law and Natural Rights*, 1980, at 163-64.

By contrast to Hart, my argument is not subject to this criticism. One reason is that the concept 'the rule of law' seems inconsistent with the use of torture either as a means of obtaining evidence or as a basis for punishing someone for having committed a legal violation. (Even Hart could make that argument for he emphasized the value that society's punishment for voluntary offenses should be proportionate to the crime and torture as a form of punishment it is rarely, is ever, proportionate to any crime. *See* Hart, H.L.A., *Punishment and Responsibility*, 1968, at 161–70.

I would also argue that the application of torture could not, in fact, be done consistent with the principle of treating similar cases similarly. In order to satisfy this criterion as I assert it must be imposed under the rule of law as an ideal, the regime's leadership could not just simply explain that all those who had committed the offense were similarly tortured. Rather, it would have to be able in good faith to convince outside judges that its membership would agree to be tortured if they were engaged in a similar violation of the law. Unless that leadership were capable of sufficient masochism to honestly apply the same principle to itself and convince neutral outsiders that this was so, that leadership would be in a poor position to argue convincingly to enlightened world opinion that similars were being treated similarly. Thus, contrary to Finnis' understanding of Hart, torture almost certainly could not be justified under my version of the principle of treating similars similarly.

tarian regimes sometimes attempt to convey the impression that they comply with the notion of law or legality or the rule of law in the sense described here. This constitutes a kind of tribute that vice pays to virtue.

Thus, whereas the spokesperson for a totalitarian regime might argue that the critic who attacks the regime for violating moral norms is attempting to apply an inapplicable, relativistic morality (for example, "bourgeoisie morality"), the very same spokesperson might attempt to respond to the critic of the regime's so-called "legality" with an effort to show that the regime does, in fact, comply with the critic's concept of legality. The regime's spokesperson might regard it as important to appear to respect legality even though the very same spokesperson might regard the critic's morality as unworthy of notice.

Before illustrating this point I should point out a related ploy of totalitarian regimes, namely, to attempt to confuse the public by using the term 'law' to refer to raw state power. The term 'law' has been used by the Soviet (or Nazi) spokesperson in order to confuse two different (though related) concepts. It is done to take advantage of the positive connotation of the term 'law' or 'legality' by using the same term to denote a different concept which, if properly understood, would have a negative connotation, namely, the use of raw state power to harm the regime's leaders' perceived enemies. Once this ploy is understood as a deliberate effort to confuse the issue by using the term with the positive connotation ('law' meaning the rule of law or legality) to refer to a different concept ('law' meaning raw governmental power), the term 'law' has no more persuasive value than if the regime's spokesperson had used the more explicit terminology of brute power to refer to the regime's activities.

Perhaps a sports analogy might be helpful. Assume that one goes to a strange country and asks the hotel concierge whether baseball is played in her country. She says, "yes," and shows you a man in a broom closet using a paddle to hit a ball against the wall. The fact that she informs you that "here we have a baseball game in progress" does not mean that you are witnessing baseball as you understand the term. Rather, she is using a term familiar to you to refer to some other activity.

But the more persuasive ploy of totalitarian regimes is to don the mask of legality without actually complying with its substance. An illustration of this attempt to come within the widely respected umbrella of legality is Stalin's use of show trials in the 1930s where he attempted to justify getting rid of old communist comrades. One distinguished writer, Robert Conquest, made the following observation:

> The trial [of Zinoviev and Kamenev] had on the whole been a success for Stalin.... [T]he outside world, whose representatives he had allowed in to authenticate it... was at least inclined not to reject it outright, from the start, as a fabrication... The allegations were examined in detail. They were found convincing by various British lawyers, Western journalists, and so forth [though they] were thought incredible by others.[268]

Thus, whereas the spokesperson for a totalitarian regime might argue that the critic who attacks the regime for violating moral norms is attempting to apply an inapplicable, relativistic morality (for example, "bourgeoisie morality"), the very same spokesperson might attempt to respond to the critic of the regime's so-called "legality" with an effort to show that the regime does, in fact, comply with the critic's concept of legality. The regime's spokesperson might regard it as important to appear to respect legality even though the very same spokesperson might regard the critic's morality as unworthy of notice.

This is illustrated not only by the show trials of Stalin's Soviet Union but also some of the Nazi "trials" and more recently the trial by the Khymer Rouge of Pol Pot. One of the famous Nazi trials was the Katzenberger case that took place on March 13, 1942. This was the case made famous because it was depicted in the movie, *Judgment at Nurenberg*. Lehmann Israel Katzenberger, a German Jew, was charged with having had sexual intercourse with a married German gentile woman, Irene Seiler, committing "racial pollution" in violation of Nazi law. Seiler was charged with sitting on Katzenberger's lap and Katzenberger, "in order to achieve sexual satisfaction," caressed and patted her. While they admitted kissing each other and that she sat on his lap, they denied any sort of sexual involvement. Despite their denials, the trial court found that Katzenberger, a merchant, having lent money to Seiler, received sexual favors in return. One reason for this view was that Katzenberger, who was approxi-

268. Conquest, Robert, *The Great Terror*, 1990, at 105.

mately 69 years old at the time of the trial, admitted that he was still capable of sexual intercourse. Although the judge believed that Katzenberger engaged in actual intercourse with Seiler, he reasoned that "[e]ven if the Jew had only done these so-called [acts of petting] in lieu of actual intercourse] with Seiler, it would have been sufficient to charge him with racial pollution in the full sense of the law." As a result Katzenberger was subject to the death penalty and Seiler, who was found to have committed perjury in denying sexual intercourse with Katzenberger, was sentenced for two years of hard labor.[269]

Using hindsight to look at the "trial," it is pretty obvious that any evidence of the defendant's innocence was irrelevant. Indeed, the "judge" was determined to covict regardless of the evidence. In addition, the "judge" interpreted the statute's reference to sexual intercourse so as to include petting, which no reasonable outside observer would regard as coming within the perameters of the text (though the precedents might support the "judge's" conclusion). In addition, it would be difficult for any neutral outside observe to regard the death penalty (or indeed any penalty) as appropriate to the "crime."

Since European Jewry had begun to be deported to death camps at the time the trial took place)[270] regardless of whether or not they committed any act in violation of Nazi law (other than continuing to live), the "trial" seems a waste of precious wartime German judicial energy and time. So, why did the "trial" occur at all? It is difficult for me to understand this case except as a tool for reinforcing some of the political values of the Nazi regime both internally with its own bureaucracy and with the German people. For one thing the trial took place in the city of Nuremberg.[271] It was a public trial, that is, not one held in secret.[272] Even before the trial some 535 Jews had been deported from Nuremberg and ten days after the trial 650 more were deported.[273] Thus, it is reasonable to assume that the trial was

---

269. D'Amato, Anthony and Jacobson, Arthur, *Justice and the Legal System*, 1992, at 312-318.

270. *Id.* at 312. March 13th and 14th, 1942 were the dates of the trial.

271. Muller, Ingo, *Hitler's Justice*, 1991, at 113.

272. *Id.* at 114.

273. Gutman, Israel, *Nuremberg, Encyclopedia of the Holocaust*, Vol. 3, 1990, at 1075. After one more similar deportation in the fall of 1942, the Nazi newspapers boasted that Nuremberg was now free of Jews. The trial of Katzenberger took place on March 13th and 14th, 1942. Muller, *Hitler's Justice, supra*, at 113.

one of many propaganda efforts to help the Germans living in Nuremberg not to be troubled by the disappearance of the Jews. More broadly, I assume the trial helped to reinforce the Nazi regime's message that the racial laws, with their stridently-anti-Jewish content, were a normal and acceptable part of the social order, and indeed something worth fighting World War II for. It did so by associating the application of these laws with something as traditionally acceptable as a criminal trial involving a defendant's violation of the law.

A Nazi non-trial illustrates the same point. One Herschel Grynszpan killed a German diplomat, Ernst vom Rath, stationed in France in 1938. Upon arrest Grynszpan indicated the reason for the killing was the expulsion of his parents from Germany to their native Poland as well as other Nazi barbarities. The Nazis planned to put Grynszpan on "trial" as representing "World Jewry['s]" effort to draw the West into war with Germany. Everything was planned in advance, including the defense lawyer who was actually serving the prosecution and, of course, the verdict. However, the trial never took place, at least in part because Grynszpan changed his justification for the murder from the political one that would have fit the Nazi propaganda effort to a personal one, namely, he did it because of a gay lovers' quarrel involving a gay Nazi official. Once the Nazis could not so easily use Grynszpan to "educate" the German people about the threat from "World Jewry," the whole trial idea was dropped.[274]

One final example of a totalitarian group's use of a "trial" is that of the Khmer Rouge's putting its former leader, Pol Pot, on trial in 1997 for his crimes against humanity. Pol Pot's regime was depicted in the movie, *The Killing Field*. When Pol Pot's troops captured the capital, Phnom Penh, everyone including the elderly, the blind, the sick and infants were resettled in the countryside. Tens of thousands died within a few weeks of this resettlement. Most of the people were turned into slaves. Husbands and wives were separated from each other, people were told whom to marry, and children who did not inform on their parents were killed. Religion was outlawed and Buddhist monks were murdered. Pol Pot used slave labor to farm the fields. Thousands died from malnutrition, thousands more died from overwork, and other thousands died as a result of torture. People who were not Cambodian by ethnic background (Chinese, Muslims,

---

274. Kirchheimer, Otto, *Political Justice*, 1961, at 101-4.

Chams, Vietnamese, Thais) were also killed even when their ancestors had lived in the country for generations.[275] Perhaps three million people were killed as a result of Pol Pot's rule.[276]

Pol Pot's trial was widely regarded as a sham, a show trial. It consisted of people still in the Khmer Rouge going up to a microphone and shouting at Pol Pot while onlooker members of the group jeered him. He was sentenced to life imprisonment,[277] and put under house arrest. He has since died.

The question to be asked of this "trial" as with the others discussed here is, what purpose does it serve? As one Cambodian survivor living int the U.S. put it, "[i]t's like having Hitler being tried by the nazis...."[278] Obviously, when a regime or a group as brutal and indifferent to the deaths of others as the Khmer Rouge decides to hold a "trial" of its former leader rather than just kill the person outright, there must be some reason for doing so. My guess is that the "trial" serves several related purposes. First, the Khmer Rouge was expecting to be forced to compete for the hearts, minds and votes of ordinary Cambodians in future elections, so that putting Pol Pot on "trial" for his "excesses" might improve the group's image among the people. And secondly, the group probably was also trying to gain a more favorable image in international public opinion. But regardless, this is another instance in which a regime or a group attempts to use the moral status of the institution of legality to attempt to boost its own status, its own image either among its own people or among foreigners.

It Is Important Because the International Community Has Come to Regard It as Important

Perhaps the most important reflection of the development of the concept 'procedural natural law' (as well as its substantive sibling) is the recognition of dominant elements in the international community

---

275. Mydans, Seth, "Pol Pot, Brutal Dictator Who Forced Cambodians to Killing Fields, Dies at 73." *The New York Times International*, April 17, 1998, at A12.

276. "Trial of Pol Pot," *Nightline, American Broadcasting Company*, July 29, 1997, *Westlaw*, at 2.

277. Becker, Elizabeth, "Videotape Shows Pol Pot Facing Khymer Rouge Justice," *The New York Times*, July 29, 1997, at 6.

278. *Nightline, American Broadcasting Company, Westlaw, supra* at 5.

(Western Europe, the U. S., and well educated elites elsewhere) that leaders of regimes who wantonly kill innocents without sufficient justification, whether they are killing citizens or aliens, must be tried in accordance with recognized legal procedures. Even though these leaders may well have acted in accordance with the positive law of the states that they controlled (thus coming within what their own countries set forth as the positive law), they cannot assume that their rationalizations about the differences between themselves and those whom they slaughtered would be accepted by the judges of an international tribunal. Although the tribunal, such as that at Nurenberg and the Japanese War Crimes Trials following World War II as well as current efforts to examine criminal activity in the former Yugoslavia by Slobodan Milosevic and others,[279] would probably refer to a substantive doctrine as the basis for its conviction, such as, Crimes against Humanity, the basis also fits comfortably within the procedural idea that what they had done violated our notion of legality, one of the rocks upon which civilization is founded. The violation of legality includes such concepts as taking life only for published crimes of behavior rather than status, taking life only after a conviction through a trial based on evidence of a violation of published rules presented before an impartial fact finder with an attorney representing the defendant and treating relevant similars similarly.

---

279. To respond to mass atrocity with legal prosecutions is to embrace the rule of law. This common phrase combines several elements. First, there is a commitment to redress harms with the application of general, preexisting norms. Second, the rule of law calls for administration by a formal system itself committed to fairness and opportunities for individuals to be heard both in accusation and in defense. Further, a government proceeding under the rule of law aims to treat each individual person in light of particular demonstrated evidence. In the Western liberal legal tradition, the rule of law also entails the presumption of innocence, litigation under the adversay system, and the ideal of a government of law, rather than by persons. No one is above or outside the law, and no one should be legally condemned or sanctioned outside legal procedures.... To bring these ideas to state-sponsored or state-countenanced mass murders, tortures, and deprivations of human rights requires a belief that even these massive horrors can and should be treated as punishable criminal offenses perpetrated by identifiable individuals....

A trial in the aftermath of mass atrocity...cools vengeance into retribution, slows judgment with procedure, and interrupts, with documents, cross-examination, and the presumption of innocence, the vicious cycle of blame and feud.

Minow, Martha, *Between Vengeance and Forgiveness*, 1998, at 25-26.

To summarize material from this section, the institution of the rule of law is important because we treat it as important in our use of language and thinking. People who live in a state where the rule of law is employed can rest more easily that they can escape government arbitrariness and irrationality and can plan their lives with the expectation that their expectations will be fulfilled.

Further, where the rule of law is generally applied as a concept, we can criticize a government for any specific violation and have some reason to think this criticism will resonate and possibly be corrected. In addition, sometimes the in-group in partially democratic countries can be criticized for violating the concept of procedural natural law in their treatment of members of races or ethnic out-groups, and sometimes this criticism has an impact. Also, the notion of legality has seeped into the existing legal structure of some democratic countries as applied to their dealings with outsiders. One example is the U.S. military's dealing with local people in its more recent Asian wars.[280] Another is the Israeli Supreme Court's recognition that there are basic human rights theoretically applicable to Palestinians within their control.

Procedural natural law is also important because sometimes the very regimes whom we are likely to criticize because of their abuse (or lack) of procedural legality demonstrate its importance by attempting to hide their misdeeds under the veneer of applying this very legality. These regimes attempt to use the moral cachet which this concept embodies by attempting a sham version of its outward form, namely, a show trial. Finally, the growing willingness of powerful elements within the international community to view totalitarian leaders as appropriately subject, when caught, to trials for their crimes against innocent people reflects an acceptance of procedural (and substantive) natural law concepts cross culturally.

280. This is not to suggest that the U.S. government's record always fits this ideal. For example, its treatment of aliens has not always complied with the ideal of legality.

11

Where Does the Concept 'Law' Come From?

What I am asserting is that we have a concept called 'law' that can be applied to certain activities of government, but not necessarily to all activities of government. Thus, not every act of governmental power necessarily comes within the concept 'law' as defined in terms of procedural natural law. This concept, if used in the way discussed, protects persons against some of the more extreme forms of government arbitrariness and irrationality because it provides procedures that persons can rely on and follow in an attempt to live their lives without becoming enmeshed in the government bureaucracy. From the person's perspective these legal procedures that government complies with constitute a morally desired limitation on government power.

But where does this concept 'law' come from? What is the epistemological basis of the concept? Did I make it up? Is it something that developed as part of Western civilization and has no relevance outside of that context? Is the concept some sort of floating universal, a Platonic ideal[281] or Justice Holmes' "brooding omnipresence in the sky?"[282] *(cont. on page 121)*

---

281. Essentialism... has a history stretching back to Plato's notion of ideal universals, namely, the notion that every class or group of things has an essential or fundamental nature, common to every member of the class, and that the process of defining consists in isolating and identifying this common nature or intrinsic property. In this way, to define a class expression, such as "law," is to state an inherent fact about the world as it is.

Freeman, M. D. A., *Lloyd's Introduction to Jurisprudence*, Sixth Edition, 1994, at 48.

Having to respond to the accusation of adopting a Platonic ideal ought to confront anyone defending a natural law position, my procedural version as well as the various substantive ones. But the need for a response is not limited to someone taking the natural law position. It also confronts any positivist who appears to be asserting that the concept 'law' has describable defining characteristics who does not limit these descriptive characteristics to what has been observed thus far. To the extent that the positivist makes a claim that his articulated descriptive characteristics extends beyond specific empirically observed legal systems, how can this claim be justified? Thus, when, for example, the positivist, Hans Kelsen, asserts that his pure theory of law is "objectivistic and universalistic," he too can be asked, "on what basis can you assert this?" Kelsen, Hans, *Pure Theory of Law*, translated by Max Knight, 1989, at 191. Indeed, his reference to his concept as universalistic suggests more a Platonic ideal than an empirical study.

Indeed, even a positivist as empirically cautious as H. L. A. Hart seems to be making an assertion about a concept that transcends any particular national culture:

> Most educated people have the idea that the laws in England form some sort of system, and that in France or the United States or Soviet Russia and, indeed, in almost every part of the world which is thought of as a separate 'country' there are legal systems which are broadly similar in structure in spite of important differences. Indeed, an education would have seriously failed if it left people in ignorance of these facts....

Hart, H. L. A., *The Concept of Law*, 1961, at 2-3.

If this were truly an empirical statement, Hart would have amassed a good deal of evidence to support his position that virtually every country's legal system had similar features. This he does not do. He also would be willing to amend his analysis if newly studied countries were, by chance, to have entirely different legal structures. This too he appears unwilling to do. Thus, Hart seems to be asserting that his descriptive characteristics for the concept 'law' has (nearly?) universal application.

Hart also observes that the positivist John Austin was not content to make empirical assertions about the nature of law. Rather, his concept of law reads like a universal claim: "The theory does not merely state that there are *some* societies where a sovereign subject to no legal limits is to be found, but that everywhere the existence of law implies the existence of such a sovereign." *Id.* at 65.

Joseph Raz is less clear. At one point he seems conscious of the possible dilemma created by attempting to give a descriptive analysis to a concept that appears to have universal application, and specifically rejects the idea that his descriptive analysis has any universal application: "It is not part of the argument that a similar conception of legal systems is to be found in all cultures and in all periods." Raz, Joseph, *The Authority of Law*, 1986, at 50.

In this passage Raz seems to be asserting that the conception of a legal system can change, depending on the culture, that is, it is culturally relative. But elsewhere he adopts the view that his analysis of law does have universal application.

> The first [assumption I wish to mention] is the assumption of universality according to which it is a criterion of adequacy of a legal theory that it is true of all the intuitively clear instances of municipal legal systems. Since a legal theory must be true of all legal systems the identifying features by which it characterizes them must of necessity be very general and abstract. It must disregard those features which some legal systems fulfill in some societies because of the special social, economic, or cultural conditions of those societies. It must fasten only on those features of legal systems which they must possess regardless of the special circumstances of the societies in which they are in force. This is the difference between legal philosophy and sociology of law. The latter is concerned with the contingent and with the particular, the former with the necessary and the universal....Legal philosophy has to be content with those few features which all legal systems necessarily possess. *(cont. on next page)*

The easiest of these questions to answer is that I did not make up the concept 'law.' Rather, I am employing a concept used in our society and others as well as explicated by such legal thinkers as Lon Fuller[283] and H. L. A. Hart[284] among others.[285]

The concept originated from what we would call Western antecedents, particularly Greece and Rome.[286] And today it is a concept

---

Id. at 104-05.

Raz also makes what appears to be universal claims for what he calls the social functions of law. These claims are beyond what could be expected from a cautious descriptive empirical account of the legal institutions that he has so far examined.

> It seems to me that all legal systems necessarily perform, at least to a minimal degree,...social functions of all the types to be mentioned, and that these are all the main types of social functions they perform....There are four primary functions.
>
> (a) *Preventing Undesirable Behavior and Securing Desirable Behavior...*
>
> (b) *Providing Facilities for Private Arrangements Between Individuals...*
>
> (c) *The Provision of Services and the Redistribution of Goods...*
>
> (d) *Settling Unregulated Disputes*

Id. at 167, 169, 171-72.

But Raz goes even further than this in adopting a universal notion of the concept of or ideal of the rule of law. He illustrates "the fruitfulness of the formal conception of the rule of law" by presenting a list of eight principles which he regards as "similar" to Fuller's own list. *Id.* at 218 n.7. These principles are: (1) all laws should be prospective, open and clear; (2) laws should be relatively stable; (3) particular legal orders should be guided by open, stable, clear and general rules; (4) the independence of the judiciary must be guaranteed; (5) the principles of natural justice must be observed; (6) the courts should have review powers over the implementation of the other principles; (7) the courts should be easily accessible; and (8) the discretion of the crime-preventing agencies should not be allowed to pervert the law. *Id.* at 211-19.

Raz uses the verbal form 'should' in setting forth several of these principles. On its face it is not clear whether he means by the use of this verbal form a. that it is desirable for a legal system to comply with the principle set forth or b. that in order for there to be a legal system it must comply with this principle. If the latter, then Raz is setting forth a necessary feature of law that seems more like Platonic essentialism than an empirically based analysis.

282. Lloyd, Lord and Freeman, M. D. A., *Lloyd's Introduction to Jurisprudence*, 6th ed., 1985, at 226.

283. *See* Fuller, Lon, *The Morality of Law*, 1964, particularly at 33-94.

284. *See* Hart, H. L. A., *The Concept of Law*, 1961.

285. *See* Kelsen, Hans, *Pure Theory of Law*, translated by Max Knight, 1989; Raz, Joseph, *The Concept of a Legal System*, 1980.

286. Lloyd, *Lloyd's Introduction to Jurisprudence*, *supra*, at 93–94; Weinreb, Lloyd L., *Natural Law and Justice*, 1987, at 15-46.

arguably most extensively employed in countries that would be viewed as the heirs of Greece, Rome and the Judeo-Christian world views. These countries would particularly include the democracies of Western Europe, North America, Australia, New Zealand, and Israel.[287] If this is so, then what value does the concept 'law' have except that it happens to be employed by persons in the countries of the West?[288]

I will here provide four possible bases for the concept, 'the rule of law.'[289] I will call the first basis for this concept the conventionality basis, the second the pragmatic basis, the third the rationality basis and the last the empathetic basis. The first two bases make no assumptions about the concept's being universal in the sense of being innate to the human species, whereas the last two do.

The Conventionality Basis

The first basis for the rule of law is the legal conventionality basis. This basis assumes that the concept is culturally bound. Here no assumption is made that we could find substantial empirical evidence that the concept's use has spread from users of Western languages to human speakers around the world. Rather, under this approach, the relevant speakers are those within the various legal communities in the world who share the Western sense of legality.[290] Assuming that

---

287. This list is not meant to exclude other countries, such as, Japan and India, whose history has interacted with the West but cannot so easily be described as heirs of Greece, Rome and Judeo-Christianity.

288. "Only the Occident has witnessed the fully developed administration of justice of the folk community...and only the West has known 'Natural Law.'" Weber, Max, *Economy and Society* in Lloyd, *Lloyd's Introduction to Jurisprudence*, *supra*, at 552.

289. These bases are not intended as necessarily exhaustive.

290. "Wittgenstein's solution to the skeptical paradox [that is, the question of determining whether someone is following a rule of the language] is crucially framed in terms of a community of language users." Chomsky, Noam, *Knowledge of Language*, 1986, at 224.

There is nothing in Wittgenstein's approach that precludes the community of language users from being specialists in a particular discipline, such as, the Western concept of law, rather than speakers of a natural language, such as, English or Urdu. Here, for example, is one writer's description of language use in terms of those within a discipline rather than in terms of users of a particular natural language: "We can read [Thomas] Kuhn [in *The Structure of Scientific Revolution*] as showing the ways in which scientific one can determine which legal communities use legal terminology in the Western sense,[291] then one can determine whether the actions of the governments where those legal communities exist are complying with this terminology.

A problem with this approach is that it is tautological. If one accepts the definition of legality provided by Western legal scholars, then all one is asserting is that certain actions of various governments comply or do not comply with this definition. There is no effort to show that the concept has universal applicability, only that it is applied where it is applied. What is the value of such an approach?

A response is that it has rhetorical value. A reference to the absence of legality in the Western sense can be used as the basis of a verbal attack on a regime that asserts it is acting legally. In itself, this has value. It has value because the regime that violates the Western sense of legality while at the same time its spokespeople assert that it is acting in accordance with this very same notion of legality is attempting to confuse (gullible) public opinion by trading in on the positive connotation that is associated with the Western use of the term 'legality.'[292] The clearing up of linguistic confusion serves a useful purpose in itself. But in this case the value in clearing up the confusion is substantially greater. This is because, even if one assumes that the concept 'law' in the Western sense of legality does not have cross-cultural application, it seems to be widely perceived by many educated people around the world as a positive value, and its absence as a negative value.[293] Thus, the clearing up of a linguistic confusion has the addi-

innovations change *the language of scientists*." Ramberg, Bjorn T., *Donald Davidson's Philosophy of Language*, 1989, at 132 (emphasis added).

291. Both the analysis of procedural natural law provided by Fuller in the text above and that of the positivists discussed below provide a good guide to what is included within this terminology.

292. [A] critique of the ideological co-option of language would also have to involve an account of incommensurability. It must be a critique that shows how a discrepancy between linguistic conventions and the meaning of what is said serves to disguise certain social facts. It should demonstrate how linguistic conventions have been manipulated, that is, how the production of meaning *via* a language has actually served to obscure linguistic understanding, and how this has served particular interests or social institutions.

Ramberg, *Philosophy of Language, supra,* at 133.

293. This observation is based in part on the staying power of such organizations as Amnesty International and the perceived importance of the U.S. State Department's annual list of countries that engage in human rights abuses.

tional important effect of casting regimes that pretend to be acting in accordance with the rule of law in the Western sense in a negative light for many. The rhetorical effect is not based on sophistry; that is, making an argument for the sake of arguing, but rather because the person making it (or on whose behalf it is being made) is in desperate need of help and thinks that this appeal will resonate.

The Pragmatic Basis

The second basis for the concept 'the rule of law,' the pragmatic basis, is related to the first. It assumes arguendo that what is being discussed is a concept that developed in the West[294] and is employed in the West. Even if so, this would not negate the concept's value. This is because, regardless of its source or origin, the concept has utilitarian value that can appeal to people across cultural boundaries.

294. An issue that is not discussed here is whether, regardless of how one explains the origin of the concept 'the rule of law,' it can be subject to substantial, further modifications in the future. The primary reason why this issue is not discussed is that, I am not so sure of my answer as to explicate it in depth.

But it seems reasonable to say this much. If one adopts a rationalist approach, then presumably once the contours of the concept 'the rule of law' are known, then the concept would not change in its essentials. (This view would not prevent people from using the same conceptual terminology, 'the rule of law,' to come to refer to some very different concept, such as, 'the whims of the ruling elite.') Alternatively, if one takes an empiricist approach, then the concept would change with the circumstances of language use. Thus, if one accepts the empiricist approach, what is described in this book is a concept whose meaning can be explicated as of the present time, but that is subject to change in the future. (But even under an empiricist approach, as the terminology 'the rule of law' radically changed what it was referring to, one would be expected to accept that the same term was now referring to something descriptively different.)

For what it is worth, the positivists discussed below, with the exception of Raz, seem to assume that the concept 'law' has a certain fixed meaning.

The difficulty of determining the degree to which the concept 'the rule of law' can remain the same concept even though its referent changes has its corollary in the philosophic literature discussing scientific concepts. Here are the examples of two inconsistent views. "In the sciences, at least, disciplines are regarded as conveniences...and their boundaries shift or disappear as knowledge and understanding advance." Chomsky, Noam, *Knowledge of Language*, 1986, at 35. "Katz insists that disciplines such as chemistry, biology, and so forth have inherent, conceptually determined boundaries. Indeed, he regards the claim as uncontroversial, the alternative being a form of 'nihilism' that 'would turn the spectrum of well-focused academic disciplines into chaos.'" *Id.* n. 22 at 49 (quoting Katz, J., *Language and Other Abstract Objects*, 1981, at 79-80).

This view is exemplified in part by the fact that a number of articles in the United Nations' Universal Declaration of Human Rights provide human beings with specific legal protections that are consistent with the procedural natural law protections discussed in this book. Here are some examples:

> Article 7. All are equal before the law and are entitled without any discrimination to equal protection of the law. All are entitled to equal protection against any discrimination in violation of this declaration and against any incitement to such discrimination.
>
> Article 8. Everyone has the right to an effective remedy by the competent national tribunals for acts violating the fundamental rights granted him by the constitution or by law.
>
> Article 9. No one shall be subjected to arbitrary arrest, detention, or exile.
>
> Article 10. Everyone is entitled in full equality to a fair and public hearing by an independent and impartial tribunal in the determination of his rights and obligations and of any criminal charge against him.
>
> Article 11. 1. Everyone charged with a penal offense has the right to be presumed innocent until proved guilty according to law in a public trial at which he has had all the guarantees necessary for his defense. 2. No one shall be held guilty of any penal offense on account of any act or omission which did not constitute a penal offense, under national or international law, at the time when it was committed. Nor shall a heavier penalty be imposed than the one that was applicable at the time the penal offense was committed.[295]

Because the U.N.'s Declaration of Human Rights reflects the view of many member states or at least their shared acquiescence, it suggests that what it contains is desired by people in many different cul-

295. Gottlieb, Stephen E., "United Nations, A Universal Declaration of Human Rights," *Jurisprudence*, 1993, at 153.

tures. Thus, the notion that people are provided some protection against a regime's irrationality and arbitrariness through that regime's maintaining procedural safeguards that come within the concept of the rule of law would seem desirable to people regardless of their backgrounds.[296] I call this the pragmatic basis because those persons, regardless of culture, needing a verbal tool to defend themselves against government irrationality and arbitrariness, would find the concept 'the rule of law' useful.[297] The fact that the origins of this verbal tool are Western is irrelevant to the fact that it is available for use by people put in extreme positions by their government and likely to be thought by them as worth using. Unlike the conventionality basis, the rule of law would be thought worth using not simply as a rhetorical device to persuade people but because the utterer believed in its usefulness.[298]

To the extent that the basis for the rule of law is a pragmatic one, it is like other concepts that have transcended their cultural origins because they are perceived to have cross-cultural value. Indeed,

---

296. For example, here is a description of the use of what can be regarded as a British import to one of its colonies, namely, the use of the rule of law by Indian leaders against their colonial masters:

> For this law has found its way to a good many parts of the globe. But even here the rules and rhetoric have imposed some inhibitions upon the imperial power. If the rhetoric was a mask, it was a mask which Gandhi and Nehru were to borrow, at the head of a million masked supporters.

Thompson, E. P., *Whigs and Hunters*, 1975, at 266.

297. "[T]he principles of legality, which [Fuller] terms 'the inner morality of the law' were urged by [the positivist] Bentham on his contemporaries in the name of utility." Hart, H. L. A., *Essays in Jurisprudence and Philosophy*, 1985, at 357.

298. One critic of traditional natural law theory does suggest the possibility that there might be shared conventional values:

> In most cases, rules will have plain meanings not because men believe in intelligible essences, but because their common interests lead them to categorize the world and to subsume facts under the categories, in similar ways. Rules and the acts by which they are applied to particular situations can then be viewed as the working out of a common vision of the world, based on agreed-upon values. The convergence of values might in turn be explained, though it could not be justified, as the product of a particular form of social organization.

Unger, Roberto Mangabeira, "Liberal Political Theory," Hutchinson, Allan C. ed., *Critical Legal Studies*, 1986, at 34.

'democracy' itself would be an analogous concept having crossed beyond its cultural origins. Other analogous concepts might include 'monotheism,' 'philosophy' and 'public opinion polling.'

Human Rationality

Another possible response to the question, "where did the concept "law" come from?" is to suggest the possibility that it comes from human rationality. I call this the rationality basis. The concept of rationality I use here is not to be confused with the concept of rationality used in several other ways. Earlier in the book I referred to rationality as an aspect of the concept 'law.' In the earlier use of the term 'rationality,' I was distinguishing it from irrationality and arbitrariness. As applied there the concept 'law' as an ideal requires that the government, that seeks to come within its domain, apply its legal procedures in a way consonant with such principle as treating similars similarly. The effect of rationality in this sense is that government power is channeled and controlled and arbitrariness and irrationality are reduced.

As applied here, however, the concept refers to the epistemological basis of knowledge. In contrast to empiricism which posits that all human knowledge comes from the senses (the mind or brain being a tabla rasa), the assumption underlying rationalism is that while humans need external stimulation through the five senses to spark brain processes, the information received from the senses is processed and formed through the structure of the brain. Thus, rationalism is a theory of how humans come to know what they know and its obverse is empiricism, whereas when the word 'rationality' was used earlier in conjunction with law it referred to limits on governmental power.

However humans come to the concept 'the rule of law,' whether through how their brains are structured or some other epistemological source, I assert that they regard it as in their rational self interest to seek its implementation on the ground that the concept has value for them. Thus, I am using the concept 'rationality' in a third sense, namely, as a reflection of an intelligent pursuit of self interest as distinct from the two other senses previously discussed, that is, as a part of what the rule of law means and as the source of how we come to an awareness of the rule of law.

Returning to the use of rationalism as the source of our knowledge of the rule of law (an epistemological basis that goes back to Kant,[299] Leibniz and earlier philosophers[300] and extends forward in our time to Chomsky[301]), the assumption is that, regardless of culture, rational

299. "Kant argued that all subjective experience of the natural world was governed by certain so-called *categories of the understanding*. For Kant, these categories were basic and original forms of human thought, which possessed a universal or *a priori* validity." Covell, Charles, *The Defence of Natural Law*, 1992, at 35.

Kant's Categorical Imperative, which required that one's actions could be justified only if they were universalizable, came from man's rationality which was part of the basic human structure. Thus, Kant went on to assert that the Categorical Imperative: "... must...hold for all rational beings (to which alone an imperative can apply), and only for that reason can it be a law for all human wills." Immanuel Kant, *Grundlegung Zur Metaphysik Der Sitten*, reprinted in part in Gottlieb, Stephen E., *Jurisprudence*, 1993, at 448.

Kant asserted that by virtue of his rationality, man is to be treated as an end by others and not simply as a means:

> Now I say, man, and, in general, every rational being exists as an end in himself and not merely as a means to be arbitrarily used by this or that will...Such a being is thus an object of respect and, so far, restricts all (arbitrary) choice.... The practical imperative, therefore, is the following: [a]ct so that you treat humanity, whether in your own person or in that of another, always as an end and never as a means only.

Id.

Kant's analysis differs from that taken by me in this book in several respects. (1) Kant is referring to how humans ought to treat other humans, while the book deals with the concept 'the rule of law' as a concept that, if applied, does limit governmental arbitrariness and irrationality.

(2) I am following Kant in treating rationality as an epistemological source of 'legality' or 'the rule of law.' As with Kant, because of the way the human brain is structured, regardless of a person's culture, if given the opportunity, he or she would come to recognize the concept 'the rule of law' as limiting governmental power. But I am making the additional argument that, regardless of the epistemological source of a person's coming to recognize the concept, from each person's perspective there is a rational desire (based on self interest) that government come within the parameters of the concept so as to limit its arbitrariness and irrationality. Nonetheless, the end result in both Kant's approach and mine is a moral argument against the arbitrary treatment of one person by another person (in Kant's analysis of morality) or by government (in my analysis of procedural legal morality).

300. "Plato's answer [to the question of how we come to know what we know] was that much of what we know is inborn...Leibnitz argued that the idea is basically correct.... Much of our knowledge is innate, he held..." Chomsky, Noam, *Knowledge of Language*, 1986, at 263.

301. Rationalism...makes the unobjectionable claim that some mental capacities come as part of the start-up kit of the mind. One of the best formulations of

humans[302] process information in certain common ways because their thinking mechanisms function in similar ways.[303]

---

rationalism is by Leibniz, who compares the mind to "a block of marble which has veins," and who says that learning is essentially a "labor to discover these veins, to clear them by polishing, and by cutting away what prevents them from appearing.... For Chomsky, in his starkest formulation of rationalism, one of these genetic veins in the marble of our minds enables us to grow a language.

...

It might be, as Chomsky suggests... that the relevant innate endowment of humans [which includes the] cognitive properties which guide the growth of vision also guide the growth of language.... Or it might be... that the language faculty is itself a highly specific mental organ with its own special and independent character, that such things as noun and verb and sentence are not just in the data, but genetically prewired into the brain. But, in either case, rationalism is a necessary part of the explanation....

Harris, Randy Allen, *The Linguistic Wars*, 1993, at 66-7.

302. There are differences among us, but these generally concern the faculty with which we grasp the import of an argument. Some people are unable to follow abstract reasoning at all, but this is a deficiency in mental capacity, not a matter of exclusion from a select group who are endowed with inexplicable moral insight.

Lyons, David, *Ethics and the Rule of Law*, 1984, at 191.

The point I am making here relies on the same faculty for grasping an argument as Lyons mentions in this sentence or a related faculty for rationally understanding what is in one's own self interest. But whereas Lyons may be implying that moral insight does not depend on the faculty of reasoning (whether for grasping an argument or for grasping what is in one's interest), my suggestion at this point is that this faculty might itself be the basis for people's grasping the value of a government acting in accordance with a form of legal morality I call procedural natural law. The reason why the faculty of reasoning might be the the basis for recognizing the value of procedural natural law is that it might be through this faculty that one recognizes that procedural natural law protects oneself (as well as others) against government arbitrariness and excess. If this is so, then a person deficient in the ability to reason will not be able to grasp the value of this form of protection.

303. "It is important to bear in mind that the study of one language may provide crucial evidence concerning the structure of some other language, if we continue to accept the plausible assumption that the capacity to acquire language, the subject matter of [universal grammar], is common across the species." Chomsky, *Knowledge of Language, supra*, at 37.

One commentator presents Chomsky's views simply as a deduction "from the way we make sentences [to] our ability to communicate through language [inferring that both are] rooted in the brain's basic wiring." He goes on to state: "[t]his once controversial idea has been verified by neurobiologists...." Papert, Seymour, "Noam Chomsky," *Time*, March 29, 1999, at 107.

While people in a particular culture, such as those who wrested the Magna Carta from King John at Runnymede, might have been the first to express an awareness of a concept, that does not necessarily mean that the concept is culturally dependant. The fact that specific humans in a specific time and place are the first to verbalize the processing of information about the external world (the world lying beyond themselves) in a novel but valuable way does not detract from this novel processing of information having cross-cultural appeal. To use an analogy from science, the fact that Archimedes was the first who articulated and verbalized the notion of specific gravity does not mean that use of the concept is limited to those living in ancient Greece.

What is required for rationality (in the sense of knowledge based on how our brains are structured) to be the basis for procedural natural law is not just that humans, regardless of culture, commonly use language in similar ways, including indicating past and future tenses and using nouns and verbs, but also that they share certain ways of looking at the world.[304] This would indicate that they use certain concepts in common or, if they had not become familiar with some such concept, they would use this concept once they became familiar with it. Under this view one such concept would be the rule of law.[305]

---

304. Chomsky makes the following point:

> We are also assuming another idealization. That the property of mind described by [Universal Grammar] is a species characteristic, common to all humans. We thus abstract from possible variations among humans in the language faculty. It is possible to suppose that apart from pathology..., such variations as there may be is marginal and can be safely ignored across a broad range of linguistic investigations.

Chomsky, *Knowledge of Language, supra*, at 18.

305. Here is how one Chomsky supporter puts it: "So what are the modules of the human mind?.... Being a bit foolhardy myself, I will venture a guess as to what kinds of modules, or families of instincts, might eventually pass [the] tests [of what is determined by the various relevant scientific disciplines].... [Included in the list would be] [j]ustice, [and a] sense of rights, obligations, and deserts." Pinker, Steven, *The Language Instinct*, 1994, 419-20.

While Pinker's terminology seems more consistent with a substantive natural law position than the procedural one enunciated here, it does suggest that the desirability of being governed under the rule of law might also be included under what Pinker calls an "instinct."

Interestingly, the positivist, Joseph Raz, as part of his defense of a version of the con-

Again, even assuming that people in some totalitarian country had never been exposed to the rule of law, if they were to be exposed to this concept they would accept it. The reason for this optimistic assessment of the cross-cultural appeal of this concept is that it offers people protection against the arbitrariness of their rulers. In short, what's not to like about a concept that protects people against a governmental bureaucracy run amuk? Once exposed to the concept, its acceptance is a no brainer.

The Capacity to Empathize

A fourth epistemological basis for the rule of law is the capacity to empathize. First I will articulate this capacity as a basis for morality before turning to its moral-legal correlate. A recognition of this source of the capacity to empathize as a basis for morality goes back to Thomas Hobbes, David Hume and Adam Smith.

Hobbes put it as follows:

> Pity is imagination or fiction of future calamity to ourselves, proceeding from the sense of another man's calamity. But when it lighteth on such as we think have not deserved the same, the compassion is greater, because there appeareath more probability that the same may happen to us, for the evil that happeneth to an innocent man may happen to every man.[306]

Hume stated that it was not reason or the connection of ideas but rather our sentiments which give rise to the sense of justice.[307] While he referred to self interest as a basis for justice, he also mentioned the pleasure "men receive... from the view of such actions as tend to the peace of society, and an uneasiness from as such are contrary to it."[308] Elsewhere he stated: "[e]xtinguish all the warm feelings and

cept 'the rule of law,' notes that "it is *universally* believed that it is wrong to use public powers for private ends..." (emphasis added). Raz, Joseph, *The Authority of Law*, 1986, at 220. Assuming that he is right, where does this universal belief come from? This certainly is not an empirical observation on Raz's part. Could it come from our common ability to reason about legal-moral issues?

306. Hobbes, Thomas, *The Elements of Law: Natural and Politic, Of the Passions of the Mind*, 1969, at 40.

307. Hume, David, *A Treatise of Human Nature*, 1888, at 496.

308. *Id.* at 533.

prepossions in favor of virtue, and all disgust or aversion...and morality is no longer a practical study, nor has any tendency to regulate our lives and actions."[309]

As Smith put it:

> By the imagination we place ourselves in [the] situation [of our brother upon the rack], we conceive ourselves enduring all the same torments, we enter as it were into his body, and become in some measure the same person with him, and thence form some idea of his sensations, and even feel something which, though weaker in degree, is not altogether unlike them. His agonies, when they are thus brought home to ourselves, when we have thus adopted and made them our own, begin at last to affect us, and we then tremble and shudder at the thought of what he feels. For us to be in pain or distress of any kind excites the most excessive sorrow, so to conceive or to imagine that we are in it, excites some degree of the same emotion....[310]

This ability to put ourselves in another person's shoes (President Clinton's famous "I feel your pain") sometimes gives rise to our awareness that certain treatment of others by others would, if it were directed at ourselves, be unfair. As a result we direct a feeling of empathy toward the unfortunate other.

I would guess that this capacity to empathize even transcends the human species and explains a recent action by a female gorilla at the Brookfield Zoo outside of Chicago. This gorilla picked up a three year old boy who fell 18 feet into the primate exhibit at the Zoo. The gorilla cradled the boy in her arms and carried him out of the reach of the other gorillas and to the zookeepers' gate where help could be obtained.[311] I cannot imagine any other plausible explanation for this

---

309. Hume, David, *Enquires Concerning Human Underestanding and Concerning the Principles of Morals*, 1902, at 172.

Annette Baier points out that for Hume a person's morality is based on feeling for one's fellows rather than a Kantian universalizable rule based on reason. Baier, Annette C., *Moral Prejudices*, 1994, at 54-56.

310. Smith, Adam, *The Theory of Moral Sentiments*, 1976, at 9.

311. Likens, Terri, "Brookfield Gorilla Grabs World's Eye with Rescue," *Peoria Journal Star*, Aug. 20, 1996.

Of course, this assumes that the female gorilla who saved the boy believed that her fellow gorillas might have lacked the empathy that she displayed.

action. Whether or not you agree that the Brookfield gorilla exemplified empathy as a source of morality, nevertheless, as Hobbes, Hume and Smith observed, this capacity almost certainly plays a critical role as a source of morality among humans.

And it probably also constitutes a source of the moral-legal idea of the rule of law. Based on my own fear of government mistreatment, I empathize when it mistreats others. Just as I would want government to give me the opportunity to conform to its requirements by coming within stated rules, so would I want government to give others similar opportunities. Otherwise how could I be sure that in the future government would not mistreat me?

Analogy to Child Rearing

The closest analogy to the notion of the rule of law that comes to mind is the notion that child rearing involves nurturing. Each parent starts as a novice, and yet one guesses that most parents, at least in theory, recognize that the task of child rearing includes attempting to inculcate the child's self-acceptance and self-love so that the child could later function adequately in the world.[312] The fact that the nurturing parent need not have read about nurturing a child in some expert's book on child rearing suggests that this insight is intuitively grasped by the typical parent regardless of the culture.

---

312. The firm establishment of enduring patterns for the solution of the nuclear conflict of basic trust versus basic mistrust in mere existence is the first task of the ego, and thus first of all a task for maternal care.... [T]he amount of trust derived from earliest infantile experience... [depends] on the quality of the maternal relationship. Mothers create a sense of trust in their children by that kind of administration which in its quality combines sensitive care of the baby's individual needs and a firm sense of personal trustworthiness within the trusted framework of their culture's life style. This forms the basis in the child for a sense of identity which will later combine a sense of being "all right," or being oneself and of becoming what other people trust one will become.

Erikson, Erik H., *Childhood and Society*, 1993, at 249.

When a mother is perceptive of her child's signals and responds promptly and appropriately to them her child thrives and the relationship develops happily. It is when she is not perceptive or not responsive, or when she gives him not what he wants but something else instead, that things go wrong.

Bowlby, John, *Attachment*, 1969, at 357.

The arguable similarity of nurturing applied to child rearing compared to the value of the concept of legality lies in the fact that people across cultural divides would be likely to recognize in theory that the application of each concept is desirable.

12

Why Do Regimes Violate the Rule of Law?

If people across various cultural divides would be likely to recognize that the application of the concept 'the rule of law' is desirable, why then do regimes often violate the concept? The reason is suggested by focusing on where the analogy between the two concepts of nurturing children and the rule of law breaks down. At least on the surface conscious level, in child rearing the interest of the parent is perceived by the parent as the same as that of the children.[313] Thus, the parent believes that it is part of his or her role to help nurture the child. And if, contrary to fact, the child were mature enough to articulate her views, she presumably would agree that she needed to be nurtured.

But there is no similar theoretical assurance that a regime's rulers will regard it as in their interest to provide those living within their control with protection against their own irrationality and arbitrariness. The perceived self-interest of the regime's leaders, like that of King John at Runnymede before the signing of the Magna Carta, might be in opposition to the subjects' interests.[314] Thus, whereas it might be comparatively easy to provide empirical support for the notion that nurturing children is widely perceived as a positive value regardless of the cultural, a similar cross-cultural effort on behalf of the notion of legality runs up against the fact that those who have the guns (the regime's leaders) often perceive it as in their interest to ignore the concept that their subjects presumably would want implemented. Since there is no good way to poll the subjects of a totalitarian regime as to whether they would want the regime to honestly implement the notion of the rule of law, it might seem that the concept has little cross-cultural appeal.

---

313. After Freud we are aware that unconscious parental motivation is often more complicated than this simple theoretical model indicates.

314. "In form a donation, a grant of franchises freely made by [King John], in reality a treaty extorted from him by the confederate estates of the realm, a treaty which threatens him with the loss of his land if he will not abide by its terms." Pollock, Sir Frederick, & Maitland, Frederic William, *The History of English Law, Vol. 1*, 1968, at 171.

But from the perspective of the regime's subjects, just as from the perspective of the inarticulate children dealing with child rearing, it seems obvious that they would prefer to be treated better rather than worse and, therefore, would prefer the implementation of a concept that promised to treat them better. Just as Alice in Wonderland preferred the rule of law to the Queen's whims, so would rational subjects prefer the rule of law so that they could more easily plan their activities, govern their lives and attempt to comply with the government bureaucracy.

The argument I am attempting to address is, if the rule of law can be so easily and universally accepted, why do so many political leaders also reject it? I could name a rouges gallery of political leaders who have rejected the rule of law. The list would include Hitler, Stalin, Lenin, Trotsky, Mao, Idi Amin, Pol Pot, Saddem Hussein, Slobodan Milosevic and many others less well known. Why have they rejected it?

As I mentioned above, part of the explanation is that it is not necessarily in the interest of the leader to accept the rule of law. The reason why it is not in his interest is because at some point it can be used against him. It is a verbal tool available to the weak to be hurled against the strong when there is nothing else more powerful available for use. So, why would the leader want to help out his potential enemies by agreeing with them that there is such a thing as the rule of law that he is violating?

Another part of the explanation is that the sort of person who becomes the leader of a country, particularly a country with a totalitarian or authoritarian tradition, is himself likely to be very ruthless. Otherwise he would not get to the top.[315] This very quality of ruth-

---

315. Those who "climb... to the top of the greasy pole," (Kaplan, Justin, *Bartlett's Familiar Quotations*, 16th ed., 1992, at 435) (quoting Benjamin Disraeli)) particularly in totalitarian and authoritarian countries, must, by necessity, be at least as ruthless as their opponents.

This offers a key to understanding how a concept arguably can have cross-cultural appeal even though the leadership in some regimes does not abide by it or even recognize it. The same key to understanding is suggested by Habermas' use of the developmental psychology of moral consciousness developed by Kohlberg (and discussed briefly above) as indirect confirmation of Habermas' own moral philosophy. What Kohlberg suggests is that as the person goes through stages of physical and emotional development, he achieves higher levels of moral judgment. For Kohlberg, the highest stage of moral judgment is that of universal ethical principles. Habermas, Jurgen, *Moral Consciousness and Communicative Action*, translated by Christian Lenhardt Shierry Weber Nicholsen, lessness would seemingly be inconsistent with a highly developed moral consciousness. Thus, the leadership in such countries would be inclined to maximize their power with a minimal concern for self restraint based on moral or other concerns. This would explain why they often ignore the rule of law. Such people have not gotten where they are by observing ethical niceties, including such moral-legal niceties as the rule of law.

Another group that doesn't seem to grasp the concept of the rule of law is that element in a society which is benefitted by a ruthless leader's rejection of it. For such people learning where one's bread is buttered also requires learning the likes and dislikes of the leader who does the buttering. Since the ruthless leader has nothing to gain by accepting the rule of law (at least while he remains in power) and much to lose, understandably his underlings will almost certainly adopt the same posture.

But what about the masses who often seem to adopt to the ruthless leader's demands? Many followers are willing to do the totalitarian or authoritarian leader's bidding either because of sadism (or what the Germans call schadenfreude), herd instinct or easily aroused latent fear (whether justified or not) in many of us. Part of what I am referring to is illustrated by Stanley Milgram's famed experiment. Milgrim obtained the services of male adults from various occupations in the New Haven and Bridgeport Connecticut areas. Their ages were between 20 and 50. The subjects were told that they were taking part in a memory experiment whereby they would be told by the experimenter to administer (phony) "shock treatments" to people in the next room who got the answer wrong. The more wrong answers that were given, the higher the experimenter told the subjects to administer the "shock treatment." The person in the next room could be heard by the subject complaining about the discomfort and pain caused by the "shock treatment." Yet at the behest of the experimenter, the subject was willing to administer ever more powerful "shock treatments." Here is Milgram's take on the experiment:

1991, at 119-33. My argument rests on the assumption that those who seek power and are ruthless enough to obtain it, particularly in a totalitarian state, would not be as likely to have achieved a higher level of moral judgment for otherwise he would be constrained by his conscience. Under this view ordinary people would have a better chance of developing an understanding of the concept 'the rule of law' than their ruthless leader.

> Subjects often expressed deep disapproval of shocking a man in the face of his objections, and others denounced it as senseless and stupid. Yet many subjects complied even while they protested. The proportion of obedient subjects greatly exceeded the expectations of the experimenter and his colleagues. At the outset, we had conjectured that subjects would not, in general, go above the level of "Strong Shock." In practice, many subjects were willing to administer the most extreme shocks available when commanded by the experimenter. For some subjects the experiment provides an occasion for aggressive release. And for others it demonstrates the extent to which obedient dispositions are deeply ingrained....
>
> ...
>
> With numbing regularity good people were seen to knuckle under the demands of authority and to perform actions that were callous and severe.
>
> ...
>
> The results...raise the possibility that human nature... cannot be counted on to insulate the citizens from brutality and inhumane treatment at the direction of malevolent authority.[316]

---

316. Milgram, Stanley, *Some Conditions of Obedience and Disobedience to Authority*, Bishin, William R. and Stone, Christopher D., *Law, Language, and Ethics*, 1972, at 76-7.

Daniel Goldhagen argues that at the time Hitler arrived on the scene the average German was already predisposed by antisemitism to accept Hitler's extermination orders:

> My explanation...is that the perpetrators, "ordinary Germans," were animated by antisemitism...that led them to conclude that the Jews *ought to die*.... Simply put, the perpetrators, having consulted their own convictions and morality and having judged the mass annihilation of Jews to be right, did not *want* to say "no."
>
> ...
>
> Hitler leaped across the moral chasm that ordinary Germans on their own could not cross....By bringing people harboring an eliminationist mind-set with exterminationist potential into institutions of killing, by sanctioning their actions by orders, hence the blessings, of a charismatic, beloved leader, the German state was able, easily to enlist ordinary Germans in the program of extermination, even though, prior to its implementation, most of them had certainly never

This is a chilling commentary on the willing availability of ordinary people to become possible accomplices to a ruthless leader's schemes.

But while this might explain why many totalitarian and authoritarian leaders and their immediate subordinates can obtain supporters to assist them in violating the rule of law, it does not explain why some people become such leaders and their immediate subordinates. I am ultimately left with only one explanation, namely, there is something missing in how they were nurtured or there is some innate defect in their ability to care about the fate of others. (By analogy one might wonder whether the rottweiler who kills an unprovoking stranger was raised to be overly aggressive or has been bred to genetically reflect that trait.) If the defect turns out to be innate, perhaps one can analogize it to autism. For whatever reason such leaders as Lenin, Stalin, Hitler, Mao, Pol Pot and Idi Amin have demonstrated a very strong sadistic streak. My guess is that if we could learn about their infancy and early childhood, we would find that they were not adequately loved by their parents or other primary child rearers. Without such love it is hard to emphasize with others, care whether others are being harmed or killed by one's actions or able and willing to control that sadistic element which constitutes one of the darker elements in the human psyche.[317] And yet, a lot of people with poor childhoods never aspire to become sadistic leaders or their immediate subordinates.

Earlier in the text I referred to a person's capacity to empathize as a basis for morality and moral-legality, that is, as a basis for accept-

---

imagined that they would be mass executioners.

Goldhagen, Daniel Jonah, *Hitler's Willing Executioners*, 1996, at 14, 447.

317. I write this while thinking of my own childhood. The movies I saw as a kid virtually always featured a cartoon where one character (the smaller and weaker) was able to triumph over a another character (the larger and stronger). After the larger character unsuccessfully attempted to inflict physical harm on the smaller one, the larger character wound up being hurt or killed. The Hollywood people who developed these cartoons expected children to identify with the smaller and weaker characters and laugh at the pain inflicted on the larger and stronger ones. Such was the level of humor promoted in my childhood. Although there was an element of "justice" involved (the larger character "deserved" it), there also seemed an element of sadism (the children laughing at the travail of the larger character). I don't think humor has changed much. As a matter of fact, a lot of humor reflects this sadistic characteristic, as when we are expected to laugh when a stuffed shirt falls on a banana peel. As I mentioned in the text, the Germans call it schadenfreude (pleasure in someone else's pain).

ing the rule of law. And here I am asserting that the ruthless leader's inability to feel anything for the others whom he has ordered to be killed reflects his lack of something we expect to be part of each human being's make up. Yet I have also admitted that many ordinary people are willing to carry out the ruthless leader's bidding. Doesn't my admission that ordinary people can be induced to carry out the sadistic policies of the ruthless leader contradict my expectation that ordinary people can be expected to empathize with the plight of others?

I don't think so. The ruthless leader who lacks any feeling for his fellow human needs to be explained. That is, his behavior seems aberrational. Whereas the person who demonstrates feeling for his fellow humans does not need to be explained as some freak of human nature. Such a person seems normal.

Also, I think that ordinary people are complicated. Thus, they feel for their fellow humans particularly those whom they perceive as similar to themselves. But people have more difficulty empathizing with people who do not seem similar to themselves, such as the ethnic, racial, religious, alien. Also this feeling of empathy can easily be overcome by a ruthless leader who lacks it. For some people it is overcome because they also enjoy seeing others suffer. Others have a strong desire to do what is acceptable to their superiors and peers (the herd instinct we often ascribe to wolves but applies to humans as well). For others still there is a fear of not doing what is expected. For some people the willingness to follow orders might be explainable based on more than one of these reasons or based on some other reasons altogether.

13

Procedural Natural Law Theory Does Not Derive an Ought from an Is

As noted above, David Hume asserted that it was a logical fallacy to derive an ought from an is.[318] In the past substantive natural law theories seemingly have committed this fallacy, thereby illustrating Hume's point. Thomas Aquinas, for example, asserted that certain aspects of human nature gave rise to corresponding natural laws. These aspects constituted the following:

> [T]he order of the precepts of the natural law is according to the order of natural inclinations. For there is in man, first of all, an inclination to good in accordance with the nature which he has in common with all substances, inasmuch, namely, as every substance seeks the preservation of its own being, according to its nature.... Secondly, there is in man an inclination to things...*which nature has taught to all animals*, such as, sexual intercourse, the education of offspring and so forth. Thirdly, there is in man an inclination to good according to the nature of his reason, which nature is proper to him. Thus man has a natural inclination to know the truth about God, and to live in society,... to shun ignorance, to avoid offending those among whom one has to live....[319]

---

318. Hume, David, *A Treatise of Human Nature, Book III*, Pt. 1, § 1, 1888, at 469. William Frankena, a 20th century philosopher of ethics, puts the general consensus as follows: "ethics does not depend *logically* on facts about man and the world, empirical or nonempirical, scientific or theological." Frankena, William, *Ethics*, 1963, at 84. John Finnis refers to the standard interpretation of Hume "as announcing the logical truth, widely emphasized since the latter part of the nineteenth century, that no set of non-moral (or, more generally, non-evaluative) premises can entail a moral (or evaluative) conclusion." Finnis, John, *Natural Law and Natural Rights*, 1980, at 37. Hans Kelsen puts the thesis thus: "Nobody can assert that from the statement that something is, follows a statement that something ought to be, or vica versa." Kelsen, Hans, *Pure Theory of Law*, translated by Max Knight, 1989, at 6.

319. Saint Thomas Aquinas, "Concerning the Nature of Law," Feinberg, Joel, and Gross, Hyman, eds., *Philosophy of Law*, 4th ed., 1991, at 19.

In general terms the argument goes: man has a certain nature and therefore law ought to comply with that nature. The reason why this is perceived as a fallacy is that even if one concedes that humans have the nature that Aquinas (or later Finnis) ascribed to them, it is not at all clear why law ought to comply with this nature. Suppose the dictator interested in his own survival were to say:

> I do not wish to make my legal system conform to human nature, for this would put my regime in danger. Rather, what I want is to keep my subjects in fear. The way for me to keep my subjects in fear is to be arbitrary, capricious and irrational. If I act in this way, it would keep my subjects from revolting and therefore better secure the continued existence of my regime and my own personal survival. This is all I care about.

It is difficult to see how an analysis of human nature responds to the dictator's thrust. For what secures the dictator's regime's stability is an empirical question as to which he can be right or wrong, and not a question either about human nature or what ought to follow from it.[320]

---

320. Several defenders of natural law theory have made an effort to respond to Hume's is/ought dichotomy. One such effort was undertaken by Lon Fuller who:

> [i]nterpreted [the doctrine that an ought cannot be derived from an is]...to the effect that facts cannot tell lawyers, legislators, and judges what they ought to do....[H]e flatly repudiated any such notion [that we could not derive an ought from an is]. The existence of purposes is factual, and from given purposes we may readily argue that we ought to have one rule rather than another.

Summers, Robert F., *Lon Fuller*, 1984, at 70.

John Finnis also defends himself as well as Thomas Aquinas against a reading of Hume to the effect that they are engaging in a logical fallacy. As Finnis puts it:

> For Aquinas...what is decisive, in discerning the content of the natural law, is one's understanding of the basic forms of (not-yet-moral) human well-being as desirable and potentially realizable ends or opportunities and thus as to be pursued and realized in one's action, action to which one is already beginning to direct oneself in this very act of practical understanding....Aquinas would deplore... Hume's failure to see that reason is an "active principle" because one is motivated according to one's *understanding* of the goodness and desirability of human opportunities, including the opportunity of extending intelligence and reasonableness into one's choices and actions. Aquinas would reject the assumption...that the primary and self-evident principles of natural law are moral principles (in the modern sense of "moral") or that they are initially grasped as principles concerned with self-evident relations of conformity or dis-conformity to human nature.

Finnis, *Natural Law and Natural Rights, supra*, at 45, 47–48. *(cont. on next page)*

By contrast, the defense of procedural natural law undertaken in this book does not rest on human nature,[321] human purposes or human opportunities. And it does not derive an ought from an is. The argument begins with an empirically based premise as to how language is used to describe an institution rather than, as Aquinas, Finnis and Fuller would have it, how humans are or what their purposes or opportunities are. It asserts that we describe an institution called law as containing certain procedural features. If government does not follow these features, then in one use of our language government is not operating under the rule of law. But if government does, in fact, follow these procedural features, then to some extent the governed are protected against aspects of governmental power used in arbitrary and irrational ways. Under this use of our language the rule of law is not necessarily coextensive with what government does with its power, that is, the former concept cannot correctly be applied regardless of how arbitrarily and irrationally government uses its power.

Further, as we use language, we understand that the presence of the procedural limitations embodied in legality as a restraint imposed on the use of governmental power have some moral value. The rea-

---

If I understand Fuller and Finnis (and I might not), they are asserting that one ought to act to promote one's purposes (Fuller) or opportunities (Finnis). They are not troubled by the apparent jump from an is (one's purposes or opportunities) to an ought, whether the ought is viewed as moral or non-moral (what one ought to promote). If this is what is being said, this still does not explain why law ought to promote a person's purposes or opportunities. Whether or not what is being referred to is human nature or something else (say, Finnis' human opportunities or Fuller's human purposes), is it not a logical fallacy to assert (as they seem to be doing) that law ought to comply?

Suppose the totalitarian leader were to assert that "I seek to protect myself rather than my subject's purposes and opportunities and my governmental structure, which deliberately keeps my subjects enslaved, is designed for this purpose." The assertions of Fuller and Finnis are not responsive to the leader's point.

Another response of Fuller is that law itself is purposive, that is, it exists in order to fulfill human purposes. But this does not seem self evidently so. To the contrary, I assume that the dictator could argue that the purpose of his "legal system" was to promote his own ends even if it meant thwarting those of all of his subjects.

321. My version of natural law does not go from how we humans are supposed to be to how law ought to be. But it does conclude that we humans, by virtue of our presumed preference for being treated better rather than worse, would prefer a government that complied with the rule of law to a government that did not.

son why these procedural features of a legal institution are morally as well as pragmatically desirable is because they enable us to plan our lives with greater certainty. It is not (as Fuller would seem to contend) that the purpose of governmental legality is to enable us to plan our lives more easily. Rather, regardless of government's purpose or lack thereof in cohering to procedural legality, we can, in fact, plan our lives more easily.[322] Thus, if we do what the government has indicated that it requires, we can more easily survive and sometimes even prosper. Since the government's acting in accordance with legality fulfills a desired expectancy interest on the part of those who have to interact with it, it has a moral dimension for these people.

This argument does not go from an is to an ought but rather stays purely on the level of is. If government acts in accordance with certain procedures, such as, providing us with published rules to which it adheres, sanctioning behavior rather than status, allowing a person accused of a violation of a governmental rule an opportunity to present evidence on her own behalf before an independent fact finder, etc., then it follows that the government is acting within the rule of law. Further, if a government provides for the features coming within our notion of the rule of law, it provides us with some desired moral protection. That you and I believe that government ought to provide us with this protection (an ought), while an implicit assumption underlying the reason for writing this book, is not needed and is not used as an explicit conclusion from a premise about states of affairs in the world (an is).

---

322. In his dispute with H.L.A. Hart, Lon Fuller asserted:

> I have insisted that law be viewed as a purposeful enterprise, dependent for its success on the energy, insight, intelligence, and conscientiousness of those who conduct it.... In opposition to this view it is insisted that law must be treated as a manifested fact of social authority or power, to be studied for what it is and does, and not for what it is trying to do or become.

Fuller, *The Morality of Law, supra*, at 145.

In contrast to Fuller's position in his dispute with Hart, which concerns whether law is purposive or not, my point is that the notion of law, whether viewed as purposive or not, enables people to plan their lives according to its requirements. The difference can be exemplified by the following. Suppose a particular statute appears not to have any understandable purpose. In my view it would still exemplify the concept 'law' if it were clear enough so that it became interpretable in a way whereby it could be followed. In contrast with Fuller's view that such a law would in some sense be unsuccessful (and therefore less of a law?), I would emphasize that a person could plan her life in accordance with it.

An analogy might be helpful. Suppose one is asked whether he or she has been a parent. The question is ambiguous. Does it mean, "did you become a parent"[323] or does it mean, "have you raised and nurtured a child?" If the question involves the latter, then a positive response accurately describing what one has done also involves the normative element of what we believe ought to be done, namely, raising and nurturing the child. This analogy, like the discussion of legality in this book, has two alternative descriptive references, only one of which also contains a normative element. Here, parenting either refers to giving birth or involves nurturing. It is only the latter that we view as having positive normative content. Similarly, one alternative description of the concept 'law' is simply whatever a regime does. The other alternative contains certain procedural protections that we view as having normative content. But in neither the parent analogy nor in using the concept 'law' are we going from an is to an ought. Rather, as we use the term, 'parenting,' it descriptively does involve nurturing. Nurturing is included in the very notion of parenting. Likewise, procedural regularity is included in the very notion of legality. And that the applications of the terms 'parent' in the sense of one's being a nurturer and 'law' in the sense of legality are viewed by us as morally desirable is also a fact.

Of course, I believe that a parent in the biological sense ought to be a parent in the nurturing sense. This is implicit in my motive for undertaking a discussion of parenting. But that my ought motive is the reason why I undertake a factual analysis of one of the uses of this concept, namely, 'parenting as nurturing,' does not mean that this motive is explicitly a part of this factual analysis.

For those with a little knowledge of both German and Yiddish, admittedly a small subset of English speakers, another analogy might be helpful. If one refers to someone as a mensch, one might be using the German word 'mensch,' which in English is translated to mean man. Alternatively, one might be using the Yiddish word 'mensch,' which means responsible (male?) adult. If I am undertaking an analysis of the Yiddish usage of the word, then the descriptive term 'mensch' already contains a prescriptive element, that is, one is describing a (male?) person as having what is regarded as the positive characteristic of being a decent, responsible, morally upright adult. Under this

323. This would occur either by participating in giving birth or by adoption.

usage, it would be unnecessary and useless to add, "then he ought to become a responsible adult!" This is because, while remaining purely at the descriptive *is* level, we bring to the descriptive *is* an understanding that being a mensch in this sense is desirable, that is, it implicitly contains the prescriptive *ought*. Similarly, to state that a government is complying with the features of the rule of law is to remain on the descriptive level even though one's motive for such a description might well be prescriptive, namely, that this is the sort of government that I ought to live under.

14

Positivist Acceptance of Procedural Natural Law Dissolves Some of the Conflict Between Positivism and Natural Law

It was the positivists, Jeremy Bentham and John Austin, who laid down the gauntlet to natural law theory. Bentham, proffering utilitarianism, rejected natural law theory as "nothing but a phrase."[324] Austin put it, "as opposed to [natural law]... every law properly so called is a positive law.... The *science of jurisprudence*... is concerned with positive laws, or with laws strictly so-called, as considered without regard to their goodness or badness."[325] "The existence of law is one thing its merit or demerit is another."[326] More recently, the positivist Hans Kelsen reiterated the same theme:

> The Pure Theory of Law is a theory of positive law. It is a theory of positive law in general, not of specific legal order.... The theory attempts to answer the question what and how the law is, not how it ought to be.... It is called a pure theory of law because it only describes the law and attempts to eliminate from the object of this description everything that is not strictly law[, such as,]... psychology, sociology, ethics and political theory.[327]

Thus, according to the positivists, their task is to provide a complete descriptive analysis of the concept of law without referring to any necessary moral element.

---

324. Freeman, M.D.A., *Lloyd's Introduction to Jurisprudence*, 6th ed., 1994, at 229.
325. *Id.* at 255.
326. *Id.* at 260.
327. Kelsen, Hans, *Pure Theory of Law*, translated by Max Knight, 1989, at 1. Hart also posits a similar separation of law and morals as one of his definitions of positivism, namely, as "the contention that there is no necessary connection between law and morals or law as it is and ought to be...." Hart, H.L.A., "Positivism and the Separation of Law and Morals," 71 *Harv.L.Rev.* 593, n. 601, 1958.

In this book I have rejected the positivists' claim. But in addition, in the pages that follow I also will make the claim that, at least to some extent, the positivists themselves, by providing their descriptive analyses, are setting forth a concept of law that undoes their very claim. For the positivists, here specifically including Austin, Kelsen, Hart and Raz, attempt to describe law by articulating a concept that is not coextensive with a regime's use of power. Although the descriptive analysis of each positivist is not always in agreement with the descriptive analysis of the others, each of them provides an analysis which, to a greater or lesser extent, if adopted, would limit the ability of a regime to use its raw power on those living under its control. This limitation on a government's arbitrariness and irrationality, as I have argued above, constitutes a moral element built into the concept 'law.' Indeed, under the analysis I provided above, each positivist's descriptive analysis of the concept 'law,' because it is more limited than that of governmental power, inferentially contains necessary moral protection for those living within the regime described. I will survey and summarize some of the strands of the description of law set forth by each of the positivist thinkers (Austin, Kelsen, Hart and Raz) to make this point more clearly.

John Austin

I begin with Austin. Austin's descriptive analysis of law is designated as having a universal quality, that is, as applying cross-culturally.[328] So far as this is so, he is not engaging in a simple descriptive exercise based on empirical evidence gleaned from the studies of various legal systems, for that would be too vast a task for one person. Rather, he is implicitly stating that the features he describes have a prescriptive character, that is, they ought to apply if what he is describing can be called a legal system.

In addition, Austin's descriptive analysis of law implicitly provides some limitations on the proper use of the concept. Austin stated, for example, that a "law... may be said to be a rule laid down for the guidance of an intelligent being by an intelligent being having power over him."[329] This statement implies several limits on a regime's use

328. Raz, Joseph, *The Concept of a Legal System*, 1980, at 25.

329. Austin, John, "A Positivist Conception of Law," Feinberg, Joel, and Gross, Hyman, eds., *Philosophy of Law*, 1991, at 27.

of power. First, that the law has some element of rationality or else the requirement that the rule be laid down by a being who is intelligent would seem to be an unnecessary addition to the description.

And second, it implies that law is concerned with conduct rather than status for otherwise there would be no need for a requirement that the law be laid down for the guidance of an intelligent being.[330] The assertion that law requires conduct is explicitly asserted elsewhere. "[A] law is a command which obliges a person or persons to a course of conduct."[331] Also, "[b]y every command, the party to whom it is directed is obliged to do or to forbear."[332] If, as I suggest, Austin viewed law as requiring conduct rather than status, this would rule as outside the concept the Nazis killing of Jews and Gypsies for who they were rather than for what they had done.

Austin also distinguished between "laws and occasional commands."[333] "Now where it obliges *generally* to acts or forbearances of a *class*, a command is a law or rule."[334] "If uttered by an absolute monarch, without deliberation or ceremony, it would scarcely be confounded with acts of legislation, and would be styled an arbitrary command."[335] Here Austin seemed to be providing several descriptive limitations on law. One of these is that a law exists through time and is not constantly changed as an arbitrary command might be. This

---

330. These implications are strengthened by other assertions of Austin. One of these is that "where *intelligence* is not, or where it is too bounded to take the name of *reason*, and therefore is too bounded to conceive the purpose of a law, there is not the *will* which law can work on, or which duty can incite or restrain." *Id.* at 28. "[A] law is a command which obliges a person or persons to a *course* of conduct." *Id.* at 32.

Also, Joseph Raz summarizes this part of Austin's thesis as: "A desires some other persons to behave in a certain way." Raz, *The Concept of a Legal System, supra*, at 11.

331. Austin, John, *The Province of Jurisprudence Determined*, Lecture I, 1832, at 15.

332. *Id.*

333. Austin, John, "A Positivist Conception of Law," Feinberg and Gross, eds., *Philosophy of Law, supra*, at 31.

334. Austin, *Province of Jurisprudence, supra*, at 10.

335. Austin might not mean for this criterion to be an absolutely necessary condition for law, for as he puts it:

> As issued by a sovereign legislature, and as wearing the form of a law, the order which I have now imagined would probably be *called* a law. And hence the difficulty of drawing a distinct boundary between laws and occasional commands.

Id.

would seem to rule out of the domain of "law" the Queen's commands to Alice in Wonderland. Also, the use of descriptive terminology that is the obverse of being arbitrary, such as, the reference to deliberation, would again associate law with rational thought. In addition, it could be argued that the notion of ceremony associated with law might suggest that law involves a public process or procedure. The view that Austin's understanding of the concept 'law' involved publication so that those whom it governed could, in theory, attempt to comply with it is strengthened by his statement that "[a legal] command . . . is a signification of desire."[336] A "signification of desire" indicates that the desire is to be made public. This understanding of Austin is also supported by his assertion that the term 'command' (which is a necessary component of law) includes "[an] expression or intimation of the wish by words or other signs . . . The expression or intimation of the wish [or command is] presented *prominently* to my hearer."[337]

To summarize Austin, he asserted that the concept 'law' is limited in that it involves rationality. It involves publication so that its recipients can learn what it contains and attempt to comply with it. It also involves rules that persist through time and do not constantly change and it commands conduct (the doing of something or its forbearance) rather than status. All of these are descriptive elements in Austin's theory of law. Unlike the sovereign's use of raw power, if a sovereign were to comply with Austin's notion of law, he would be constrained.[338] And as compared with the sovereign's use of raw power, his subjects would find these limits on the sovereign's power morally desirable.

336. Raz, *The Concept of a Legal System, supra*, at 11. Supporting this understanding, Raz summarizes Austin's thought as including the two following propositions: "[A] has expressed [his] desire [that some other persons behave in a certain way] and [the law] expresses the content of his desire." *Id.* Again, to the same point, Raz summarizes Austin as asserting that "a command is law only if it is *addressed to* people who are likely to suffer the prescribed sanction." *Id.* at 15 (emphasis added). Also, "[o]beying a command involves knowing it." *Id.*

337. Austin, *Province of Jurisprudence, supra*, at 9.

338. Austin did add, however, that "[s]upreme power limited by positive law is a flat contradiction in terms." Lloyd, Lord and Freeman, M.D.A., *Lloyd's Introduction to Jurisprudence, supra*, at 263. But this does not mean that law means whatever the sovereign decides to do, only that a sovereign need not act in accordance with law.

Hans Kelsen

Like John Austin, Hans Kelsen attempted to develop an understanding of the concept of law independent of any moral element. The very title of his classic work, *Pure Theory of Law*, indicates the seriousness of his effort to cleanse all extraneous material, including a discussion of morality, from his analysis of law. To repeat Kelsen's description of what he was up to: "[i]t is called a "pure" theory of law, because it only describes the law and attempts to eliminate from the object of this description everything that is not strictly law[;] [i]ts aim is to free the science of law from alien elements," such as, "psychology, sociology, ethics, and political theory."[339]

But if one applies the basis of analysis I have adopted in this book, namely, determine that Kelsen's attempted descriptive definition of law limits what a regime can do under its name, then Kelsen too provides some limitation on this concept's appropriate use. Thus, if I can show that a regime complying with Kelsen's analysis of law is limited in what it can do to people living under its control, then these people are protected against some of the regime's potential but unrealized excesses.

One example of Kelsen's limiting law more than what a regime, using all the power at its disposal could do to people is Kelsen's assertion that "[t]he legal order... is a normative order [commanding, permitting, forbidding or authorizing] human behavior."[340] In a similar vein Kelsen asserted that law precluded contradiction. Thus, Kelsen accepted a version of the logical law of the excluded middle: "The two norms: "a ought to be" and "a ought not to be" exclude each other insofar as they cannot be both obeyed or applied by the same individual at the same time; only one can be valid."[341] "Two legal norms are contradictory and can therefore not both be valid at the same time, if the two rules of law that describe them are contradic-

339. Kelsen, Hans, *Pure Theory of Law*, translated by Max Knight, 1989, at 1.

340. *Id.* at 4, 5, 10. Also, "[i]t is a legal norm only if it purports to regulate human behaviour." Raz, *The Concept of a Legal System*, 1980, at 113, (quoting Kelsen, Hans, *General Theory of Law and State*, 1945, at 123). Raz elsewhere puts Kelsen's theory "of the nature of norms" as "divided into two groups." The first group explains the nature of norms as *guiding and justifying behaviour*. The second group is concerned with the nature of norms as *justified standards* of behaviour. *Id.* at 122.

341. Kelsen, Hans, *Pure Theory of Law, supra*, at 25.

tory...."[342] From his insistence on the application of the law of the excluded middle, I gather that Kelsen's concept of law requires that the state only demands of the (juristic) person one of two obverse possibilities, that is, to some extent the state cannot ask the behaviorally impossible. If this defining characteristic were strictly applied by Kelsen, which it was not, it would determine that government edicts dealing with a person's status rather than her behavior were not laws.[343] *(cont. on page 155)*

---

342. *Id.* at 74. "[A] legal order may be described in rules of law that do not contradict each other." *Id.* 205. "[T]he principle of non-contradiction must be posited in the idea of law, since without it the notion of legality would be destroyed." Raz, *The Concept of a Legal System, supra*, at 78 (quoting Kelsen, *General Theory of Law and State, supra*, at 406).

343. As I will suggest below in this footnote, the overall impression created by Kelsen's writings is that he believed that a legal entity could do whatever it wanted to someone based on her status, including killing her. Still, at several points he did recognize the status/behavior distinction and indicated that a legal entity could sanction someone based only on her behavior, not her status. For example, "[f]or the content of legal norms is not individuals, but their behavior; it is not human beings, but a certain human behavior." Kelsen, *Pure Theory of Law, supra*, at 165. Elsewhere, he stated:

> A legal order — like any normative social order — can command only specific acts or omissions of acts; therefore, no legal order can limit the freedom of an individual with respect to the totality of his external and internal behavior, that is, his acting, wishing, thinking or feeling.... [A] minimum of freedom, that is, a sphere of human existence not interfered by command or prohibition, always remains reserved.

Id. at 43. Another indication that his notion of law regulates behavior is that he applied the concept of imputation, a normative relationship of behavior deserving (in the sense of a legal ought) a reward or punishment. *Id.* at 89-99.

But in various ways Kelsen did not strictly apply this limiting defining characteristic. For example, he stated that "[c]ollective liability is a characteristic element of primitive legal orders." *Id.* at 119. Nonetheless, it appears from his analysis that when collective liability is applied, it is applied because of the behavior of someone else whom the legal order determines is related to the person liable.

At another point, however, he stated:

> [T]he condition for the deprivation of liberty is not a definite behavior of the individual, but the suspicion of such a behavior.... The legal order of totalitarian states authorizes their governments to confine in concentration camps persons whose opinions, religion, or race they do not like, to force them to perform any kind of labor; even to kill them. Such measures may morally be... condemned, but they cannot be considered as taking place outside the legal order of those states.

Id. at 40.

He attempted to reconcile this view with his requirement that law deals with behavior by asserting that here the law "is a reaction against a delict [illegality] that has not even been committed yet, but is expected in the future as a possibility,...a socially undesired behavior of which...in the opinion of the legal authorities [the undesired persons] are considered capable." *Id.* at 41.

Seemingly, statements such as these would suggest that Kelsen believed that, while a person could be committed to an institution or even killed because of the state's fear of what she would do in the future or could be found liable for what a relative had done, a person could not be legally enslaved or killed simply because of who she was rather than what was feared she would do or to whom she was related. Also, if a person was killed because of her status, contrary to Kelsen's assertion above, the law would have eliminated all of the dead person's "wishing, thinking and feeling." *Id.* at 43. Thus, killing someone solely based on her status unrelated to past or future action would seemingly be a violation of Kelsen's concept of law.

So far, the summary of Kelsen's views seems consistent with the assertion that he would have denied the notion of legality to a regime that killed people based purely on their status. The obvious example is Nazi Germany where Jews, Gypsies, homosexuals and "the mentally challenged" were killed. While Kelsen's analysis would accommodate some of what the Nazis did to the Jews and the others under the notion of legality, based say on the fear of what they would do in the future, it would not be able to accommodate all the killing the Nazis engaged in.

But Kelsen went further in his attempt to accommodate the Nazi regime and other such regimes within his understanding of legality. He did so by asserting that the law would determine who a person was. If the law determined that someone was not a person, then that non-person could be enslaved or killed:

> [E]ven the so-called physical person is an artificial construction of jurisprudence — that even the so-called physical person is actually only a "juristic" person.... Slaves are not "persons," they have no legal personality....The so-called physical person, then, is not a human being, but the personified unity of the legal norms that obligate or authorize one and the same human being. It is not a natural reality, but a legal construction created by the science of law — an auxiliary concept in the presentation of legally relevant facts. In this sense a physical person is a juristic person.

Id. at 172, 174.

So, by virtue of his determination that the state could legally decide who is a person and who is not, Kelsen could reject the thesis asserted in the text that legality involves behavior rather than status.

Another even more central thesis that Kelsen seemed in part to reject is the insistence that state power is broader than legality: "the dualism of state and law is abolished," for "every state is governed by law." *Id.* at 318, 313. Thus, applying Kelsen's terminology, if the state kills a person, then it would necessarily follow that the state's legal system is killing her; but if the state does not regard what is killed as a juristic person, then what is being done is not the killing of a person by the state's legal system.

Thus, for Kelsen whether the state has killed a person would depend on whether the state gave that person legal or juristic status before she was killed. "The question whether an individual belongs to a state is...a legal question" *(cont. on next page)* determined by the state's legal system. *Id.* at 288. If the state regards the human being as a juristic person, the state's legal system can sanction her behavior or sanction her because of her relative's behavior but presumably not her status unless the state fears that the person will engage in undesired behavior in the future. Obviously, Kelsen's analysis offers the person virtually no protection against the state's arbitrariness and irrationality. "A relatively centralized, autocratic coercive order which, if its flexibility is unlimited, offers no legal security [and yet] is a legal order too." *Id.* at 319. The bottom line is that if the state decides that the person does not belong to the state, then the state's killing the person purely because of her status (and not fear of her future conduct) cannot be described as the state's legal system killing a juristic person.

Assuming that this is an accurate summary of Kelsen's views, one's agreement with it depends on one's acceptance of two important points: (1) that who is and who is not a person is a juristic concept determined solely by the state; and (2) as far as a human being is concerned as distinct from Kelsen's juristic person, a state can deal with her as it wishes and still not violate the concept 'law.'

For me, to restate these points is to indicate Kelsen's inadequacy. Indeed, Kelsen seems to be pulling a sleight of hand in order to avoid the problems created by his position. This is because earlier in the text he indicated that he is engaging in an ordinary language descriptive analysis of 'law.'

> To arrive at a definition of law, it is convenient to start from the *usage of language*...Our task will be to examine whether the social phenomena described by [the English "law," and the German, French and Italian equivalent,] have common characteristics by which they can be distinguished from similar phenomena, and whether these characteristics are significant enough to serve as elements for a concept of social-scientific cognition. The result of such an investigation could conceivably be that the word "law" and its equivalents in other languages designates so many different objects that they cannot be comprehended in one concept. However, this is not so. Because, when we compare the objects that have been designated by the word "law" by different peoples at different times, we see that all these objects turn out to be *orders of human behavior.* (emphasis added in first italics) *Id.* at 30-31.

Thus, Kelsen was presumably using an ordinary language analysis to assert that the concept 'law' determines who is a person (as well as that it concerns behavior). If this is what Kelsen was asserting, it is from our ordinary language understanding that we learn personhood is a juristic concept rather than an ordinary language or biologic concept. (This technique has its analogue in the United States Supreme Court's use of the term 'person' as a legal concept so as to exclude a fetus from constitutional protection in Roe v. Wade, 410 U.S. 113 (1973).) But regardless of Kelsen's alleged descriptive survey of legal systems, contrary to Kelsen's position a legal person retains an ordinary language usage which is not manipulable by a government to exclude from the concept whomever the government wishes to exclude.

Kelsen concluded that the dualism between law and the state was abolished. But if state power is equivalent to state legality, then on what basis does he write a 356 page book purporting to provide a descriptive analysis solely devoted to explicating the concept 'law'? He could have stated in a page or less that law is whatever a state apparatus in control of people within a geographic territory says it is. *(cont. on next page)*

Also, Kelsen's normative order gains its validity by having been authorized by a higher norm. The higher norm in turn is authorized by a higher norm. This authorization process extends upward through a hierarchy of valid norms.[344] At the apex of this hierarchy lies the basic norm, which is presupposed rather than authorized by a higher

---

I would guess that the reason why he wrote a book describing the nature of law rather than a page monograph is that he did not believe that law is equivalent to state power. But if he did not believe it, then why did he not aritulate his belief more clearly? Perhaps the reason is because he was acutely conscious of the natural law position that he was attempting to leave out of his analysis and was determined not to provide any support for that position. *See id.* at 319.

One further difficulty with an attempt to comply with Kelsen's terminology is that its application provides no adequate way to describe what the state's legal apparatus is doing. For example, if the state were to kill a biologic person who had not achieved juristic personhood, how could the killing be accurately described? It would not be a sufficiently informative description to assert that it was killing a thing, or killing a non-person, or killing organic matter or disposing of a person-like creature or a non-juristic physical person. By virtue of Kelsen's assertion that law was equivalent to state power and his effort to treat the state as determining who was a person, he not only violated his own effort to use language in its ordinary sense, but also made it difficult to understand descriptively what was going on when the totalitarian state killed human beings not recognized by it as juristic persons simply because it did not like them. In attempting to escape his self-created dilemma (that is, defining law as dealing with human behavior in some sense rather than pure status but regarding a government acting in accordance with the rule of law as not constrained by this fact), he created more problems than he solved.

344. "[L]aw...is not a single norm, but a system of norms; and a particular norm may be regarded as a legal norm only as a part of such a system" *Id.* at 47. "The norm which represents the reason for the validity of another norm is called...the "higher" norm." *Id.* at 194. "[T]he structure of the legal order is a hierarchy of higher and lower norms, whereby the higher norm determines the creation of the lower one." *Id.* at 206.

> To the question, why the individual norm is valid as part of a definite legal order, the answer is: because it has been created in conformity with a criminal statute. The statute, finally, receives its validity from the constitution, since it has been established by the competent organ in the way the constitution prescribes.

Raz, *The Concept of a Legal System, supra*, at 97 (quoting Kelsen, Hans, *General Theory of Law and State*, 1945, at 115).

345. The presupposed highest norm is referred to...as [the] basic norm. All norms whose validity can be traced back to one and the same basic norm constitute a system of norms....The basic norm is the common source for the validity of all norms that belong to the same order — it is their common reason of validity.

Kelsen, *Pure Theory of Law, supra*, 1989, at 195. *(cont. on next page)* norm.[345] Thus, in the United States it is the Constitution which constitutes the basic norm, for the American people presuppose that they ought to follow as that document directs. In Nazi Germany the orders of Hitler constituted the basic norm, for it was his wishes that the German people presupposed they ought to follow. But even though this analysis by Kelsen provides people with very little protection against government, as indicated by the fact that he sought to accommodate the Nazi regime within it, it does provide the outline of a procedural requirement for law. The importance of procedure in Kelsen's schema as limiting what a regime can legally do is underlined by his statement, "the solution attempted here is merely the scientifically exact formulation of the old truism that right cannot exist without might and yet is not identical with might. Right (the law), according to the theory here developed, is a certain order (or organization) of might."[346]

The distinction between the gangster's order to give him money accompanied by the threatened use of a gun and a similar order of a tax collector lies in the fact that "the official's act is authorized by a tax law, whereas the gangster's act is not based on such an authorizing norm."[347] Also, the tax law, unlike the gangster's command, gets its authority from the basic (constitutional) norm which is presupposed. When the gangster issues his command, there is no presupposed basic norm because the gangster's order does not have the lasting effectiveness that the tax law does. Unlike the tax law issued in accordance with the appropriate procedure,[348] once the gun is removed there is

---

It is this presupposed basic norm which authorizes the procedure by which legal content is developed: "the constitution ordinarily does not predetermine the content of laws, but only the procedure of legislation." *Id.* at 88-89.

346. *Id.* at 214.

347. *Id.* at 8. Also, under the principle of legitimacy "[t]he norms of a legal order are valid until their validity is terminated according to the rules of the legal order." *Id.* at 209. "[T]he constitution prescribes for its abolition or amendment a procedure different from and more difficult than the procedure provided for ordinary legislation." *Id.* at 214. Two exceptions to the procedurally provided changes in either the constitution or ordinary legislation are: (1) revolution; and (2) the law's losing its validity by never being applied or obeyed. *See id.* at 208-214.

348. "A norm belongs to an order founded on...a basic norm, because it was created in a fashion determined by the basic norm." *Id.* at 197. "A legal norm is not valid because it has a certain content...but because it is created in a certain way — ultimately in a way determined by a presupposed basic norm." *Id.* at 198. "The basic norm is the presupposed starting point of a procedure: the procedure of positive law creation." *Id.* at 199.

no longer any reason to obey the gun person's command.[349] In short, if there is no appropriate procedure, there is no law.[350] "[T]he basic norm, in a certain sense, means the transformation of power into law."[351]

Kelsen also noted that "every community must have organs... because a community can only function through organs, that is, through individuals determined by the normative order."[352] One such organ constitutes law courts that are made up of individuals called to perform this particular function.[353] One commentator has summarized Kelsen's view as, "[l]aws are norms addressed to courts."[354] Kelsen also explicated the decision making process of these law courts.[355] Although he allowed for self-help as coming within the no-

---

349. *Id.* at 47-48.

350. As Kelsen put it: "The basic norm delegates the first constitution to prescribe the procedure by which the norms stipulating coercive acts are to be created. To be interpreted objectively as a legal norm, a norm must be the subjective meaning of an act performed in this procedure." *Id.* at 50.

Also, "'[i]t is the task of the science of law to represent the law of a community, i.e. the material produced by the legal authority in the law-making procedure, in the form of statements' of a certain structure." Raz, *The Concept of a Legal System, supra*, at 72 (quoting Kelsen, *General Theory of Law and State, supra*, at 45).

Raz summarizes Kelsen's procedural hierarchy as follows:

> The existence of every positive norm presupposes the existence of another norm authorizing its creation. Kelsen thinks that an infinite regress is avoided and can only be avoided by assuming the existence of a basic norm in each normative order which is not created at all, for it is a necessary norm.

Id. at 130.

351. *Id.* at 134. Raz explicates this point by asserting that for Kelsen "the only difference between laws created by certain acts of will and orders is the relatively prolonged existence and the systematic interconnections of laws." *Id.*

352. Kelsen, Hans, *Pure Theory of Law, supra*, at 153.

353. *See id.* at 155.

"The constitution of modern states institute special legislative organs authorized to create the general norms to be applied by the courts and administrative organs." *Id.* at 224.

354. Raz, Joseph, *The Authority of Law*, 1979, at 44.

355. There is also a need to have an organ authorized to determine whether the basic law (or constitution) was being observed in a concrete case:

> [T]he constitution has to authorize some specific legal organ to decide this question.... If the constitution contains no provision concerning the question who is authorized to examine the constitutionality of statutes, then the organs competent to apply statutes, that is, especially the courts, *(cont. on next page)*

tion of a legal order, he found that there was an evolution in the modern state toward an independent judiciary: "[c]ollective security...exists when at least the question of whether in a concrete situation the law was violated and of who is responsible for it, is not answered by the parties involved, but by a special organ,[356] an independent court...[where a sanction]...can be objectively decided."[357] "The thief has to be ascertained by a court authorized by the legal order in a procedure determined by the norms of the legal order; the court has to pronounce a punishment, determined by statute or custom."[358] Thus, for Kelsen because in a modern state an independent court in a particular case acts in accordance with the procedures creating it and determining what laws it is to apply, the court does not have total discretion to render its decision.[359]

> have the power to perform this examination.

Kelsen, *Pure Theory of Law, supra*, at 271-72.

356. *Id.* at 37.

> The...law-applying organs have to be designated by the legal order, that is, it must be determined under which conditions a certain individual functions as a judge or administrative organ. Besides, the procedure has to be determined in which his function — the application of general legal norms — is to be exercised. [T]he general norms to be applied by judicial or administrative organs have a double function: (1) determination of those organs and of the procedure to be observed by them; (2) determination of the content of the individual norms to be created in the judicial or administrative procedure.

Id. at 230.

357. *Id.* at 37.

358. *Id.* at 56.

359. The legal order may authorize the organ to determine the procedure at his own discretion; but the organ and the procedure must be determined — directly or indirectly — by the legal order so that the general norm can be applied to the concrete case.

Id. at 239.

> If an organ whose nomination is determined by a general legal norm, has ascertained, in a procedure determined by a general legal norm, that facts are present to which a general legal norm attaches a certain sanction, then this organ ought to order a sanction determined in the earlier mentioned norm, in a procedure determined by a general legal norm.

Id. at 231.

"The court has to answer the *quaestio juris* as well as the *quaestio facti.* After these two ascertainments have been made, the court has to order *in concreto* the sanctions prescribed by the general norm *in abstracto.*" *Id.* at 237.

"The question of the legality of a judicial decision or the constitutionality of a statute, generally formulated, is the question whether an act that claims to be creating a legal

In summary, Kelsen, who sought to rigidly separate law from morality, described the concept of law as containing various elements that also fit within procedural natural law: law cannot both proscribe a juristic person's behavior and that person's obverse behavior; in the usual context dealing with juristic persons law deals with (very loosely defined) behavior rather than pure status; except for the basic norm each law is authorized through a given procedure, that is, by a higher norm, rather than arbitrarily created ad hoc; and whether there has been a violation of the law is determined by an independent court where a sanction can be determined according to applicable norms.

H. L. A. Hart

Unlike Hans Kelsen, who sought to completely separate law from other disciplines including ethics, the positivist H. L. A. Hart recognized that there are some connections between law and ethics. Hart asserted that law contains both a substantive and a procedural element that could be used by someone making a natural law argument. The substantive natural law argument rested on the contingent fact that humans are vulnerable to attack and, therefore, need protection against murder and other forms of violence, theft, and deception. Even in primitive societies, "rules must contain in some form restrictions on the free use of violence, theft, and deception to which human beings are tempted but which they must, in general, repress, if they are to coexist in close proximity to each other."[360] But Hart denied that what he called this natural necessity leads to a very extensive overlap between legal rules and moral standards.

---

norm confirms to the higher norm which regulates its creation or content." *Id.* at 276. "If... a general norm is not already created by legislation or custom, the organ must proceed in the same way as a legislator who is guided in formulating the general norm by a certain ideal of justice." *Id.* at 253.

> [T]he question why a certain decision is just is provided by the need to justify the decision, to give a reason for the validity of the individual norm established by it. And such justification or foundation of the validity is only possible by showing that the individual norm conforms with a higher general norm presupposed to be just. The norm constituting the value of justice must, according to its nature, have a general character.

Id. at 253.

"To say that a judicial decision or an administrative decision is unlawful can only mean that the procedure in which the individual norm was created does not conform to the general norm determining this content." *Id.* at 268.

360. Hart, H. L. A., *The Concept of Law*, 1961, at 89.

The procedural natural law argument (or what he called natural procedural justice) consisted in principles of objectivity and impartiality in the administration of the law (such as, treating like cases alike), but did not require justice in the law itself.[361] Nonetheless, he denied that these principles were very helpful in developing a natural law position. Elsewhere, he suggested that within a jurisdiction's scheme of punishing criminal conduct, some crimes would be thought more serious than others and as a consequence would correspondingly be punished more severely than these others. But he regarded this as a matter of commonsense rather than a reflection of natural law theory.[362]

Instead of taking a natural law position, Hart devoted himself to developing a purely descriptive analysis of the concept 'law.' Still, even within Hart's purely descriptive analysis one can find aspects of law which would give a person interacting with a government applying the concept some protection against possible government arbitrariness and irrationality. In short, even apart from Hart's own explicit version of natural procedural justice, which he found inadequate for the development of a sufficient procedural natural law concept, there are elements in his theory that limit what a regime in compliance with it can do to those persons living within its control.

One of these features is that law regulates behavior. As Hart put it, "the law of any modern country regulates the conduct of populations inhabiting territories with fairly well-defined geographical limits."[363]

Hart also accepted the notion of procedural requirements, beginning with the concept that in the modern legal state "[t]he rules are *constitutive* of the sovereign."[364] He divided legal rules into two types, which he called primary and secondary.[365] It is the structure resulting from the combination of primary and secondary rules that constitute the heart of a legal system.[366] Primary rules "impose duties" and "con-

361. *Id.* at 75-6.

362. Hart, H. L. A., *Punishment and Responsibility*, 1968, at 25.

363. Hart, *The Concept of Law, supra*, at 24.

364. *Id.* at 75.

365. *Id.* at 78-79.

366. *Id.* at 95.

> The main theme of [Hart's] book is that so many of the distinctive operations of the law, and so many of the ideas which constitute the framework of legal thought, require for their elucidation reference to one or both [primary rules of obligation or secondary rules of recognition, change, and adjudication] that

cern actions involving physical movement or changes...,"[367] whereas secondary rules are about primary rules[368] and "confer powers, public or private."[369]

He articulated three kinds of secondary rules. One of these constitutes rules of recognition. A rule of recognition authoritatively disposes of doubts and uncertainties as to the applicable primary rule.[370] The second of these constitutes rules of change. A rule of change determines the procedure by which primary rules are to be changed and a person or body of persons who are empowered to introduce new primary rules.[371] The third of these constitutes rules of adjudication. A rule of adjudication both identifies who is to adjudicate a dispute as to whether a primary rule has been broken and the procedures to be followed in deciding the dispute.[372] Hart's notion of legal procedure also includes the equivalent of Kelsen's basic norm: "[law involves] currently accepted fundamental rules specifying a class or line of persons whose word is to constitute a standard of behaviour for the society, i.e. who have the *right* to legislate."[373]

Hart also asserted that the rules of a legal system must, for the most part, be general and that they must communicate general standards of conduct:

> In any large group general rules, standards, and principles must be the main instrument of social control, and not particular directions given to each individual separately. If it

---

> their union may be justly regarded as the 'essence' of law, though they may not always be found together wherever the word 'law' is correctly used.

Id. at 151.

367. *Id.* at 79.

368. *Id.* at 92.

369. *Id.* at 78.

370. *Id.* at 92.

The use of rules of recognition by courts and others in identifying particular rules of the system is characterized by the internal point of view, that is, "those who use [the rules] in this way thereby manifest their own acceptance of them as guiding rules.... *Id.* at 99. The internal point of view, characterized by the "*use* of the rules as standards for the appraisal of their own and others behaviour," is to be distinguished from the external point of view, characterized by the use of rules by those who record and predict the behavior of others but do not themselves accept the rules. *Id.* at 96, 99.

371. *Id.* at 93.

372. *Id.* at 94.

373. *Id.* at 61. What Hart calls the ultimate rule of recognition "can neither be valid nor invalid but is simply accepted as appropriate for use...." *Id.* at 105.

> were not possible to communicate general standards of conduct which multitudes of individuals could understand, without further direction, nothing that we now recognize as law could exist.[374]

Here, Hart seemed to be asserting that in a mature legal system (at least one of a certain size) the institution of law would contain certain elements. Among these are the following: law is an instrument of social control; it is designed to control conduct (rather than status; to be an effective instrument of social control, the legal institution will have to communicate (publish) its rules so that the population it seeks to control can follow them.[375]

On the issue of whether treating similars similarly is an aspect of the concept 'law,' Hart distinguished between law and the administration of law. He asserted that there is a moral element which he called "justice in the administration of law" which would consist in a legal system's treating similar cases similarly. But this element of morality brought into an analysis of the administration of law does not apply to the law itself. A legal system could treat persons dissimilarly whom rational outsiders would regard as similar. Thus, Hart accepted the assertion that a justly administered legal system could still be substantively unjust. For example, a legal system that singled out African-Americans for consistently applied discriminatory treatment would be treating similars similarly in the administration of the law. Nevertheless, it could still be regarded by a rational outsider as an unjust legal system because there was no rational basis for treating African-Americans differently than others.[376]

But even though Hart explicitly rejected one of the assertions I make in this book, namely, that the very concept of law embodies a moral element that similars be treated similarly in relevant respects (and not just in the administration of the law), he also undercut his own rejection of this thesis. One way in which he undercut his rejection of this

374. *Id.* at 121.

375. Hart indicated that the communication can occur through the legislation of general standards of conduct in advance of their application or through precedent. *Id.* at 121.

376. *Id.* at 156-159. At one point he stated: "[i]ndeed there is no absurdity in conceding that an unjust law forbidding the access of coloured persons to the parks has been justly administered, in that only persons genuinely guilty of breaking the law were punished under it and then only after a fair trial." *Id.* at 157.

thesis was his admission, though grudging, that the concept 'law' could be used in our language in the very way that he rejected. He stated:

> The connexion between this aspect of justice [namely, that only those marked out by the law as relevantly alike are to be treated similarly] and the very notion of proceeding by rule is obviously very close. Indeed, it might be said that to apply a law justly to different cases is simply to take seriously the assertion that what is to be applied in different cases is the same general rule, without prejudice, interest, or caprice. This close connexion between justice in the administration of the law and the very notion of a rule has tempted some famous thinkers to identify justice with conformity to law. Yet plainly this is an error *unless "law" is given some specially wide meaning*; for such an account of justice leaves unexplained the fact that the criticism in the name of justice is not confined to the administration of the law in particular, but the laws themselves are often criticized as just or unjust. (emphasis added)[377]

What is clear from this passage is that Hart did not equate justice with treating similars similarly in the administration of the law, for the law itself could be unjust. But he went on to admit that if the concept 'law' were given a specially wide meaning, then it could be equated with justice. Thus, if the government were to act in accordance with law in the wide sense, then it would also be just. Though not altogether clear, what I think this wide sense of law includes is the government's treating as similar those whom we (as outside neutral observers) would regard as genuinely similar. Underlying my understanding is the assumption that Hart's view of justice ordinarily would be satisfied by treating rationally relevantly similar persons similarly because a regime would be most unlikely, in fact, to enact a rule that either treated everybody badly, including its own leadership elite or else treated its own leadership elite less favorably than it treats others. Thus, under Hart's rejected use of language the regime could not simply declare who was similar to whom, but would presumably have to demonstrate that the legally less favored were justifiably dissimilar from the legally more favored (the elite).

Under this view of what he is saying, for Hart the difference between himself and the procedural natural law theorist as to whether

377. *Id.* at 156-7.

the very concept of law (as distinct from how it is being administered) includes the notion that relevant similars are to be treated similarly is how broadly the term 'law' is being used. Hart obviously preferred to use a narrow version of this language: he applied the requirement that similars be treated similarly within the administration of the laws of an existing legal system and did not apply the requirement of treating similars similarly to examining whether the laws of the system were themselves consistent with the the ideal of the rule of law. But he admitted that the broader version could be used and indeed implied that he understood this use. At this point his disagreement with the procedural natural law position can be reduced to the fact that there is a version of language dealing with the concept 'law' that he understood but did not himself use.

Hart also undercut his thesis by implying that it was possible to engage in cross-cultural judgments of a particular regime's notion of what constitutes treating similars similarly. He stated, for example, that (ordinarily) "if... the law discriminated by reference to such obvious irrelevancies as height, weight, or beauty [, this] would be... ludicrous."[378] On what basis could he assert that a regime's distinctions based on such criteria as height, weight and beauty would be ludicrous if cross-cultural judgments were not possible?[379]

Another statment that weakened his refusal to include within his criterion for law a requirement that the similar treatment of similars

378. *Id.* at 157-58.

379. One might attempt to defend Hart by noting that he was asserting that certain criteria would be ludicrous within the particular legal systems with which he was familiar, namely, the Anglo-American. But this is not the same as asserting that such criteria would be ludicrous as applied to other legal systems.

But this defense will not work since Hart was describing a concept 'law' that could be applied cross-culturally. What I am asserting is that it makes sense to provide cross-cultural judgments as to whether a positive legal system's laws are rational and non-arbitrary. By asserting that some positive law's distinctions can be judged as ludicrous without limiting the context of his remark to Anglo-American legal systems, Hart seemed to be accepting this sort of cross-cultural critique. Thus, what he regarded as ludicrous could be judged cross-culturally and if a "legal" system had made some such ludicrous distinction this would constitute a basis for regarding the system as less clearly a paradigm example of a legal system.

Another point worth noting (though a minor one) is that on further reflection probably neither Hart nor I would want to assert that a criterion such as height is always legally irrelevant. Thus, it does not seem irrelevant for a legal system to apply a height requirement for joining the police force.

be based on genuine similarity (as distinct from the regime's similar treatment of those it asserts to be similar) is his remark that both law and morality are "permeated by the conception that in [certain] fundamentals... human beings are entitled to be treated alike and that differences of treatment require more to justify them than just an appeal to the interests of others."[380]

Indeed, Hart seemed to concede the central point when he stated: "so deeply embedded in modern man is the principle that *prima facie* human beings are entitled to be treated alike that almost universally where the laws do discriminate by reference to such matters as colour and race, lip service is still widely paid to this principle."[381] What he appeared to be asserting here is that there is a general agreement

---

380. *Id.* at 195-96.

381. *Id.* at 158. He made a related point even more strongly when he stated:

> No doubt the contention that a legal system must treat all human beings within its scope as entitled to certain basic protections and freedoms, is now generally accepted as a statement of an ideal of obvious relevance in the criticism of law. Even where practice departs from it, lip service to this ideal is usually forthcoming. It may even be the case that a morality which does not take this view of the right of all men to equal consideration, can be shown by philosophy to be involved in some inner contradiction, dogmatism, or irrationality. If so, the enlightened morality which recognizes these rights has special credentials as the true morality, and not just one among many possible moralities.

Id. at 201.

Elsewhere, Hart made the point using the language of natural rights:

> In "Are There Any Natural Rights?"... Hart asserted that the existence of the equal *right of all men to be free.* For Hart, the equal right to freedom ranked as a *natural right*, in the sense that it was based directly in the bare capacity of the human agent for rational choice and action. In its character as a natural right, he insisted, the equal right to freedom stood as the final ground of justification for the enforcement of the conventional rules of law and social morality which defined the particular distribution of individual rights and liberties in any given society.

Covell, Charles, *The Defence of Natural Law*, 1992, at 25.

Hart went on to point out that legal systems have flouted these "principles of justice." Hart, H. L. A., *The Concept of Law, supra*, at 201.

What much of this language indicates is that Hart recognized that there might well be a basis for a cross-cultural (or even objectively valid) judgment that a regime is violating a cross-cultural legal ideal when it irrationally discriminates in its treatment of seemingly similar persons. If a regime asserts that some humans are not worthy of equal treatment, then outsiders can judge that the regime is not correctly applying the (legal?) ideal criterion of similar treatment.

among educated people ("modern man") about what are relevant characteristics for distinguishing among human beings on the ground that they are relevantly dissimilar, and this agreement includes the understanding that race and color are irrelevant characteristics. This is really the same assertion as I make, namely, that a dispassionate outside observer (that is, one not connected to the regime) can judge whether the regime is making relevant distinctions and justifying these distinctions between those it favors based on race or some other criterion and those it does not.[382] The well educated outsider's judgment that the regime is applying an irrelevant basis to distinguish persons reflects her idea of how a legal system operates when it is functioning according to the ideal of legality because in such a case such people cross-culturally could be expected to make similar judgments about the practical logic of determining what constitutes relevant similarity.[383] Given that people, regardless of their culture, who are

382. Despite my assertion in the text that Hart is making an assertion similar to mine, Hart would reject this argument. He emphasized that a regime that treats people differently on the basis of their race, etc. is still a legal regime: "[I]t is plain that...the law need [not] extend [its] minimal protection and benefits to all within [its] scope," such as, to slaves. *Id.* at 196.

But I am not being inconsistent in both pointing out language from Hart that can be synthesized with my argument and also that Hart would reject this argument as not reflecting what he is trying to assert. For I recognize that we use language in two different ways. We understand using the language of law both from a positivist perspective such as Hart's ("this is a legal system even though it does not treat relevant similars similarly") and from a procedural natural law prospective ("a regime that does not attempt to treat relevant similars similarly is not acting in accord with the concept 'the rule of law'"). I also recognize that while Hart does develop his positivist perspective, he also provides language that can be used contrary to his preferred use of language to support the position that a regime is not acting in accordance with the rule of law if it cannot justify its dissimilar treatment of seemingly similar persons to a disinterested outsider.

383. In the context of discussing morality rather than moral-legality, Hart responds that "it is certainly possible to conceive of a morality which" treated people differently based on characteristics such as race. *Id.* at 158. He then refers the reader to Aristotle and Plato.

But his assertion is undone for me by his seeming admission that, unlike Aristotle and Plato, "modern man" (which presumably means that humans educated with an awareness of the relevant factors involved) can be expected to reject this conceived morality. Thus, for Hart, a moral code "repellant though it may be to *us*, might forbid Barbarians to assault Greeks but allow Greeks to assault Barbarians...." *Id.* at 161 (emphasis added). Hart's assertion that this moral code might (would?) be repellant to us seems to reflect the view that we (moderns), regardless of who we are or what culture we are part of, would share the same method of analyzing the issue.

educated in science and logic, develop similar understandings of how to apply practical rationality to the question of what constitutes treating similars similarly, this would generate general cross-cultural agreement as to whether a regime has rationally applied this concept.[384] When educated people not beholden to a regime intelligently decide whether a regime is justified in treating some people less favorably than others, then they make both a moral judgment about this regime and a judgment about the regime's adherence to the ideal of the rule of law.

Other aspects of procedural natural law that Hart recognized include a judiciary that is limited in its discretion to decide cases. Hart asserted, for example, that courts which applied rules in deciding cases were not free to ignore what the rules state. He likened a system where courts were free to disregard applicable rules to a game of scorer's discretion.[385] By contrast, like the scorer in the usual game, the court's role is "to apply [the rule] as best he can."[386] This would not preclude a court's making a mistake even if it were the court of last resort. In the latter case the court's decision would be final, but not infallible.[387]

---

384. The language of practical rationality which I use here might appear to be similar to that used by John Finnis in his *Natural Law and Natural Rights*. See Finnis, John, *Natural Law and Natural Rights, supra*, at 88-89, 100-33. In one important respect, the appearance of similarity seems well founded. In both instances of the use of the term 'practical rationality' there is involved a person's ability to think logically and clearly about issues that come to the person's consciousness. But the appearance of similarity is also misleading. Finnis' analysis concerns intelligently choosing one's own life style based on self interest, whereas here the concern is with a person's ability to engage in the judge-like task (sub species aeternitatis) of dispassionately reasoning through what constitutes relevant similarities in humans.

385. *Id.* at 139.

386. *Id.*

387. *Id.* at 139-40.

Hart went on to assert that law, like a game, has a core of settled meaning that the judge "is not free to depart from." *Id.* at 140. *But see* Fuller, Lon, "Positivism and Fidelity to Law—A Reply to Hart," 71 *Harv. L. Rev.* 630, at 661-669, Feb., 1958.

As Hart put it, if a judge of last resort were to misapply the law, it "would be treated by a preponderant majority as a subject of serious criticism and as wrong, even though the result of the consequent decision in a particular case cannot, because of the rule as to the finality of decisions, be counteracted except by legislation." Hart, *The Concept of Law, supra*, at 142-43.

In addition, Hart stated: *(cont. on next page)*

Hart also referred to the "judicial virtues" of "impartiality and neutrality in surveying the alternatives; consideration for the interest of all who will be affected; and a concern to develop some acceptable general principle as a reasoned basis for decision."[388] Why is it a judicial virtue to be impartial, neutral, empathetic and able to use reasoned general principles? If, contrary to Hart's view, a legal system could be viewed as incorporating within its decision making whatever arbitrary and irrational use of power a regime decides to engage in, then the judicial virtues in such a state seemingly would reflect a spineless compliance with the regime's demands. In such a "legal system" impartiality, neutrality, empathy and reasoned general principles would have nothing to do with the judicial role. The fact that Hart, who was not limiting his analysis to the concept of law in benign democratic states, asserted that impartiality, neutrality, empathy and reasoned general principles were judicial virtues suggests that he believed that these were paradigmatic characteristics of a legal system. He was not just discussing a more moral judiciary,[389] but a more lawlike judiciary as well.[390]

This position appears to be similar to that of the procedural natural law theorist, Lon Fuller. With one important exception,[391] Hart

---

> [T]here...remains a distinction between a constitution which, after setting up a system of courts, provides that the law shall be whatever the supreme court thinks fit, and the...constitution of any modern State. 'The constitution (or law) is whatever the judge says it is', if interpreted as denying this distinction, is false. At any given moment judges, even those of a supreme court, are parts of a system the rules of which are determinate enough at the centre to supply standards of correct judicial decision. These are regarded by the courts as something which they are not free to disregard in the exercise of the authority to make those decisions which cannot be challenged within the system.

Id. at 140-1.

388. *Id.* at 200.

389. "[F]ew would deny the importance of these elements, which may well be called 'moral'" *Id.* at 200.

390. Hart asserted that "critics...have found that judicial law-making has often been blind to social values, 'automatic,' or inadequately reasoned." *Id.* at 201. But to assert that courts should, but often do not, apply these judicial virtues is to make a legal, as well as moral claim. The claim is that courts complying with these judicial virtues are acting more in accordance with the legal ideal than those that are not.

391. The exception mentioned in the text refers to Hart's belief that the procedural natural law position is "compatible with very great iniquity." *Id.* at 202. The reason for this view presumably was his belief that procedural natural law works toward treating similars similarly in the administration of the law but does not require that the law itself be just.

(cont. on next page)

conceded the point. He indicated his acceptance of Fuller's inner morality of the law or what Hart called "the principles of 'Natural Justice.'"[392] These include "[1][intelligible] [2]general rules [[3]that control human behavior [4]which are] publicly announced [[5]and within the capacity of most to obey][393] and [which are [6] impartially [7]] judicially applied,"[394] that is, are applied without reflecting "prejudice, interest, or caprice."[395] Further, the general rules must "in general [8] not be retrospective, though exceptionally they may be."[396] Hart added:

> Plainly these features of control by rule are closely related to the requirements of justice which lawyers term principles of legality.... Again, if this is what the necessary connexion of law and morality means, we may accept it....
>
> However incautiously they may have formulated their general outlook, few legal theorists classed as positivists would have concerned to deny the forms of connexion between law and morals discussed [here].[397]

Thus, Hart, acting in the name of positivists generally and without obtaining their permission, conceded the point that there is a neces-

---

But for the reasons I indicated earlier in the text, he himself partly undercut this position. And as I indicated, my own approach rejects this objection altogether by asserting that law as an ideal requires that a neutral, outside observer do the judging of the actual. This observer is not governed by the regime's notion of who is similar to whom. The observer can and does ask, for example, whether the regime is distinguishing between persons based on what she considers relevant grounds, and whether the regime rationally justifies to her satisfaction the disparity in its treatment of those it favors as against those it does not. And rationality here cannot be equated with a regime's self interested effort to keep itself in power. Rather, it must make its distinctions comprehensible to the outside observer based on criteria of logic and science that apply cross-culturally. If the neutral observer cannot be persuaded of the rationality of the regime's distinctions between its elite and its elite's friends on the one side and the others on the other, then the regime is not perceived as treating similars similarly and is violating a principle of legality or procedural natural law. And the burden of persuasion is on the regime. Under this analysis, the Nazi regime would have had the burden of persuading a neutral, outside observer that the disparity in its treatment of Nazis and Jews was rationally justified.

392. *Id.* at 202.
393. *Id.*
394. *Id.* at 126.
395. *Id.* at 202.
396. *Id.*
397. *Id.*

sary connection between law and morality. Still, as far as I know, he was the first and only positivist to do so. Further, his acceptance of the necessary connection between law and morality, has had very little impact on moving the discussion forward. This is because legal scholars continue to view the positivist and natural law positions, procedural as well as substantive, as largely inconsistent with each other.[398] It is also because Hart differentiated between applying procedural concepts within the administration of a single legal system, which he accepted, and judging whether a regime genuinely applied the requirement that similars be treated similarly, which he rejected. Thus, in his own view his version of procedural morality precluded it from having as substantial cross-cultural scope as it otherwise might have had. As one commentary put it: "[Hart] recognizes that no universal system of natural law or justice can be based upon the principle of impartiality, or that of treating like cases alike."[399]

In summary, here are some of the aspects of Hart's descriptive analysis of the concept of law that can be viewed as reflecting a procedural natural law perspective: law involves intelligible, publicly announced general rules; law regulates behavior within the capacity of most to obey; the judge's role is to apply the legal rule as best as she can using reason and impartiality in doing so rather than disregarding the rule to be applied; and similars are to be treated similarly in the administration of the law without discriminating on the basis of obvious irrelevancies.

Joseph Raz

The fourth positivist to be discussed here, Joseph Raz, states that what he is doing is providing "a general study of legal systems" that "claims to be true of all legal systems."[400] Like Hart he also acknowledges that he is testing what exists against a theoretical model (con-

---

398. "Certainly one of the firmest tenets of the positivist jurists from Bentham and Austin onwards has been that positive law is quite distinct from and its validity in no way dependent upon morals." Lloyd, Lord and Freeman, M. D. A., *Lloyd's Introduction to Jurisprudence*, *supra*, at 56.

399. *Id.* at 135. But as indicated above, Hart did indicate that he regarded impartiality as a universal judicial principle.

400. Raz, Joseph, *The Concept of a Legal System*, 1970, at 1.

cept in his mind) of what he would expect to find in a legal system, that is, what ought to exist in a legal system regardless of culture:

> I have been treating the rule of law as an ideal, as a standard to which the law ought to conform but which it can and sometimes does violate most radically and systematically.[401]

> Th[e] requirement [that an individuated law not deviate too much from the ordinary concept of a law] is based... on the desire to make the theoretical concept of a law the starting point for the explanation of the common-sense concept of a law; the common-sense concept will be elucidated by an explanation of its deviations from the theoretical concept, which is in its turn justified as being the best (or a good) tool in the analysis of the law.[402]

Raz's position raises the question as to how he can accept something called the rule of law against which he measures what a government actually does. Based on a purely descriptive analysis of what is done by various regimes, there could be no ideal to violate. If as one would expect him to do based on his being a positivist, he is engaging in an empirically based purely descriptive enterprise as to what various regimes do, then the fact that some of them do different things from what is done in Britain (or in the West) could not justify his assertion that they violate the ideal of legality. Thus, Raz turns what I would have expected from a positivist on its head. Rather than an examination of the empirical data to build a theoretical model summarizing that data (as I would have expected from him before reading his writings), Raz admits that he judges the empirical data against a

---

401. Raz, Joseph, *The Authority of Law*, 1979, at 223.

In the same passage Raz goes on to assert:

> Fuller, while allowing that deviations from the idea of the rule of law can occur, denies that they can be radical or total.... It is, of course, true that most of the principles enumerated [in Raz's enunciation of principles making up the ideal of the rule of law] cannot be violated altogether by any legal system.

Id.

This makes the distinction between Raz and Fuller on the applicability of a conceptual ideal of legality, what I call procedural natural law, a matter of degree, if any, rather than of one kind. By his own analysis Raz seemingly would allow more deviation from the enunciated principles of legality than Fuller would have.

402. Raz, *The Concept of a Legal System, supra*, at 142.

theoretical model. If the empirical data does not fit the theoretical model, then so much the worse for the empirical data, that is, the data does not come within the concept 'law.' This is exactly the technique I use in positing the concept 'law' as a natural law concept based on the presence of certain procedural elements. Contrary to what I would have expected, Raz is adopting a procedural natural law position that is difficult to square with his positivism.

One aspect of Raz's ideal legal procedure is his emphasis on law's dealing with behavior rather than status. For Raz one of the "most general and important features of the law [is] that it is normative in that it serves, and is meant to serve, as a guide for human behaviour [rather than dealing with status]."[403] He puts this feature in various ways. "[Law provides] publicly ascertainable ways of guiding behaviour"[404] "Law is universally regarded as a special social method of regulating human behaviour by guiding it in various ways and directions."[405] "Evaluating behaviour according to standards set by legal norms is an essential part of the function of judges and other officials who are professionally concerned with treating people according to their behaviour evaluated according to law."[406] "A legal system which does in general observe the rule of law treats people as persons at least in the sense that it attempts to guide their behaviour through affecting the circumstances of their action. It thus presupposes that they are rational autonomous creatures."[407]

Another related aspect of his procedural ideal is that "the law must be capable of being obeyed."[408] This suggests that law must be

---

403. *Id.* at 3. Elsewhere, Raz states that: "[law] is a system for guiding behaviour and for settling disputes..." Raz, *The Authority of Law, supra,* at 121. And yet Raz allows for retroactive laws that perforce would not guide behavior: "I can...admit that retroactive laws are not (or not completely) norms and yet maintain that they are laws." Raz, *The Concept of a Legal System, supra,* at 125 n. 1. Still, this is not necessarily Raz's rejection of laws as governing behavior rather than status, for even retroactive "laws" can be confined to sanctioning behavior though not guiding behavior.

404. Raz, *The Authority of Law, supra,* at 51. But, according to Raz, the publicly ascertainable aspect of law does not preclude secret laws providing they are not altogether secret, that is, they are publicly ascertainable by officials who are charged with their enforcement. *Id.* at 51 n. 9.

405. Raz, *The Concept of a Legal System, supra,* at 145.

406. *Id.* at 124.

407. Raz, *The Authority of Law, supra,* at 222.

408. *Id.* at 213.

promulgated in advance so that people can govern their lives in accordance with it:[409] "[i]t must be such that [the people] can find out what it is and act on it."[410] *"All laws should be prospective, open and clear."*[411] Assuming that by using the verb form should he means that in order to comply with the ideal of law all laws must be prospective, open and clear, this understanding would preclude retroactivity.[412] "*Laws should be relatively stable.*"[413] "*The making of particular laws (particular legal orders) should be guided by open, stable, clear and general rules.*"[414]

In addition, Raz provides for a distinction between a ruler's use of power and law. 'Law,' unlike the use of power, involves applying procedural formalities. This is borne out in his criticism of Austin who (according to Raz) asserted that every command by the sovereign is law.[415] In contrast Raz points out that the command of the sovereign might not have the procedural formality associated with law.[416]

As part of his procedural formality requirement, like Kelsen before him, Raz postulates that the validity of a particular law depends on its fitting into a hierarchical system: "[t]he legal validity of a rule is established...by showing that it conforms to tests of validity laid

---

409. As noted in an earlier footnote, Raz does allow for an occasional exception, namely, laws promulgated only to officials and kept secret from the general public.

410. *Id.* at 214.

411. *Id.*

412. But as I noted in several earlier footnotes, Raz hedges a bit on this view. There Raz indicated that a retroactive law may not be a norm but can still be a law.

413. *Id.*

414. *Id.* at 215.

415. Raz does not do justice to Austin's view. For as I pointed out earlier in the text, Austin did not regard every command of the sovereign as exemplifying law, that is, what he called an occasional command was not law.

416. [I]t is usually the case even in states where sovereignty is in the hands of a single person, that laws are created only when the sovereign follows a certain accepted procedure of legislation. But according to Austin every expression of the sovereign's desire which is a command is law, so he does not allow for the fact that the sovereign can command in ways which differ from the accepted procedure, in which case his command is not law. When the sovereign is a body of persons, following the accepted procedure might be a defining characteristic of the sovereign body. When this happens the members of the sovereign body constitute a sovereign body and act as sovereign only when following the accepted procedure.

Raz, *The Concept of a Legal System, supra*, at 38.

down by some other rules in the system which can be called rules of recognition.[417]" He also repeats Kelsen's statement that "[l]aw regulates its own creation." Or as Raz puts it, using his own terminology, "every law has a source...[and] the validity of a law depends on its source."[418]

"The necessary internal relations existing in every legal system"[419] consists of a minimum content and minimum complexity together with the principles of individuation. Every proposed individuation principle can be tested by two requirements, the guiding requirements (mainly principles of selection) and the limiting requirements (mainly principles of exclusion).[420]

A legal system contains a structured relationship: "legal systems should be regarded as intricate webs of interconnected laws"[421] One feature of this structure is genetic. The genetic relationship is the relationship between a law and another law authorizing its existence.[422] Thus, a legal system requires the application of laws in accordance with a procedure of authorization.[423]

Another aspect of Raz's ideal of legal procedure is what he calls the "law's [two] secondary social functions [which concern] the operation of the legal system itself."[424] The first of these regulates the law's own creation by instituting the organs and procedures for changing the law. The second of these regulates the operation of law-applying organs, such as, the courts, the police, the prison system and administrative agencies.

In Raz's schema law has partial autonomy from the vicissitudes of the political system of which it is a part. "[Law] can and should be

---

417. Raz, *The Authority of Law, supra*, at 151-2.

418. *Id.*

419. Raz, *The Concept of a Legal System, supra*, at 141.

420. *Id.* at 141-42.

421. *Id.* at 183.

422. *Id.* at 184.

423. Recent positivists, such as Kelsen, Hart and Raz, all provide for a basic law from which the other laws in the system obtain their ultimate authorization, but are themselves not authorized by any other laws. Kelsen called this the basic norm. Hart referred to it as the ultimate rule of recognition. In Raz's terminology, it is called an original law. *Id.* at 188. Each of these positivists provide a procedural element to law by insisting on a proper method of law authorization.

424. Raz, *The Authority of Law, supra*, at 175.

treated as an autonomous system for many purposes but ultimately its boundaries are dependent upon the nature and boundaries of the larger political system of which it is a part.... [But] it is too easy to underestimate the importance of those autonomous considerations."[425] So, for Raz law is not altogether a mechanism available to the state's political elite to be used for its own aggrandizement, but rather occupies a quasi-independent status (semi-autonomy) within the government structure.

Further, every legal system must have courts to adjudicate disputes. "It is widely agreed...that a system of norms is not a legal system unless it sets up adjudicative institutions charged with regulating disputes arising out of the application of the norms of the system."[426]

Judges are appointed "because of their supposed abilities, or because they deserve it, and not because of their relations to the injured party or to the violator of the law."[427] "*The independence of the judiciary must be guaranteed.*"[428] "Since the court's judgment establishes what is the law in the case before it, the litigants can be guided by law only if the judges apply the law correctly."[429] "Courts and tribunals have power [to make an authoritative] determin[ation of] the rights and duties of individuals."[430] The court's function also includes providing open and fair hearings and deciding without bias.

"[L]aw is a sytem of reasons recognized and enforced by authoritative law-applying institutions,"[431] that is, courts. These courts are bound to apply legal reasoning "in accordance with [their] own customs and practices."[432] All of this suggests that for Raz legal disputes must be settled by independent judicial-like officials who have some patina of expertise and who make rational decisions according to rules, legal reasons, customs and practices.

---

425. *Id.* at 212.

426. *Id.* at 43. Raz makes related points at several places in his writings. "[E]very legal system must regulate the existence and operations of some courts." Raz, *The Concept of a Legal System, supra*, at 141. "[E]very legal system institutes law-applying organs [that is, courts] which recognize every law of the system." *Id.* at 191.

427. *Id.* at 194.

428. Raz, Joseph, *The Authority of Law, supra*, at 216.

429. *Id.* at 217.

430. *Id.* at 108.

431. *Id.* at 212.

432. *Id.*

In summary, here are some of the procedural natural law points enunciated by Raz: he has an idea of what a legal system ought to contain against which he measures the actual legal system; he views a legal system as a guide to behavior; law is distinguishable from power by virtue of its following certain accepted procedures; law is partially insulated from the vicissitudes of the political system of which it is a part; and disputes are adjudicated by independent judges applying rules and legal reasons.

What lesson has been imparted by this analysis of some of the positivist thinkers (Austin, Kelsen, Hart and Raz)? I hope what has been imparted is that all these positivists (to a greater or lesser extent) have accepted the basic point of procedural natural law, namely, that the concept 'law' is not infinitely malleable, that is, they accept that the concept does not occupy all of the conceptual space occupied by governmental power. Therefore, they accept that the concept 'law' limits what government can legitimately do when it acts in accordance with the concept.

The result is that those people who come in contact with government are protected to some extent against governmental arbitrariness and irrationality. For these people on the receiving end of governmental action, the legal protection enunciated by these positivists, though limited more than the recipients of governmental action or I would desire, is a good thing, even a morally desirable value. In short, although they would reject the label 'natural law philosophers,' even as they attempt to provide an analysis of the concept 'law' that is descriptive and not morally normative, Austin, Kelsen, Hart and Raz accept some aspects of procedural natural law

15

Responding to Radical Criticism of Procedural Natural Law

This section provides a brief response to some of the questions that one would expect to be raised by deconstructionists[433] or other radical critics of a central thesis of this book to the effect that in one version of language use, there is a procedural element to the concept 'law.' For the purpose of simplifying the analysis, an article by one radical deconstructionist critic, namely, Gary Peller's *The Metaphysics of American Law*[434] provides the basis for discussion.[435]

---

433. A deconstructionist approach would focus on the transcendental subject. The contention would be that that no such pure source is available as a basis for representational activity. The source, instead, is always already differentiated by social practice and constructed by the representational practice itself.

Gary Peller, "The Metaphysics of American Law," 73 *Calif. L. Rev.* 1151, 1221 (1985).

434. *Id.*

No effort is made here to provide more than a bare outline of some of the central points made in Peller's radical critique. An interested reader is invited to look at the Peller's article.

435. While I don't deal with it in the main body of the text, some mention of a feminist critique of the position set forth in this book deserves mention. One aspect of this argument is that the notion of the rule of law ignores women's values because, in part, it disregards women's economic value through their role as care givers. As a result of this disregard, women are impoverished. *See* West, Robin, "Jurisprudence and Gender," 55 *U. Chi. L. Rev.* 1 (1988).

I regard this critique (as well as an economic based critique by critical race theorists) as a reflection of the limitation of a procedural natural law approach and not an effective critique of what it does do. From this aspect of the critique it does not follow that procedural natural law theory, with its emphasis on rationality and its opposition to arbitrariness, is a mistake but only that it does not resolve many substantive problems plaguing society, particularly including the economic disparity between white men on the one side and women and black men on the other. It seems to me that the fact that women in the U.S. who rear children are economically less well off than men who don't is a reflection of our reliance on the capitalist system rather than our reliance on the rule of law. If this economic disparity is to be changed, I cannot see how getting rid of the rule of law would be the appropriate means to change it. *(cont. on next page)*

Here are some of the points made in the Peller article. Language is indeterminate.[436] Language is always embedded in a socially deter-

---

Another aspect of the feminist critique, however, is more directly targeted against the rule of law, namely, the latter's alleged masculine emphasis on autonomy, rationality and logic as distinct from feminine caring and empathy. As applied to legal decision making, this critique seems related to that lodged by the Critical Legal Studies professor, Duncan Kennedy. He suggests that individualized justice would be better served if courts were to apply standards (taking into account all the particularized relevant factors) rather than rules in their decision making. *See* Kennedy, Duncan, "Form and Substance in Private Law Adjudication," 89 *Harv. L. Rev.* 1685-1778, 1776.

I am not writing in direct opposition to this thesis, however. What I am asserting is that a governmental bureaucracy, including its judiciary, that conforms to rules offers a definite plus that standards do not, namely, people can more easily plan their lives with the expectation that if they do what the rules demand, they will not be sanctioned by government. The satisfaction that comes from people (females as well as males) being able to plan their activities in accordance with what government rules tell them to do (or not do), thereby escaping from unwanted governmental intrusion into their lives, offers a kind of security that is well worth having. Thus, I am making a different point and not a denial of the criticism that a person who has already allegedly committed a rule violation might receive a more just substantive verdict if the fact finder were to apply individualized standards rather than rules. (Of course, rules can themselves be applied more contextually and justly as well as less so.)

436. "I will . . . argue that meaning is necessarily indeterminate." Peller, *The Metaphysics of American Law*, *supra*, at 1158.

Both Gordon and Balkin make remarks similar to Peller's:

The same body of law, in the same context, can always lead to contrary results because law is indeterminate at its core, in its inception, not just in its applications. This indeterminancy exists because legal rules derive from structure of thought, the collective constructs of many minds, that are fundamentally contradictory.

Gordon, Robert W., *Critical Legal Histories*, Hutchinson, Allan C., *Critical Legal Studies*, 1986, at 98.

A similar point is make by Balkin in explicating Derrida's deconstructionism. Balkin suggests the possibility that "all readings of legal materials are actually misreadings." If that is so, "then law cannot be a rational enterprise and the Rule of Law is impossible to achieve." Balkin, J. M., "Deconstructive Practice and Legal Theory," 96 *Yale L. J.* 743, 775 (March, 1987).

What Balkin means by misreading is that there is no single way to read a text, that is, (to use his language) every reading of the text is partial. I agree that in many instances there are several reasonable ways to read a legal text. In such cases, a police officer, clerk or judge will have a fair degree of discretion. But there are limits to how much discretion one has in interpreting a legal text before the interpretation can reasonably be criticized as outside the permissible scope of interpretation. *(cont. on next page)* mined context.[437] This socially determined context is itself determined by those elements within the political society which control the mechanisms of power.[438] The language that is used reinforces the dominance of the politically powerful.[439] There is no distinction be-

---

437. "'Language,' as the form of communication, can never escape its own textuality.... It is intertwined with the content of communication and contains its own substantive messages apart from that which it purports to represent." Peller, *The Metaphysics of American Law*, *supra*, at 1160. "'Reality' is not carved up into categories that representational systems happen to match. Rather, 'reality' is constructed in the very process of description or representation." *Id.* 1176.

> ... [T]he interpretive constructs of an ideology abstract from the thick texture of the world to provide a structure that determines which aspects are seen. When particular representational categories for dividing up the world are reified and achieve a hegemony in a particular community, description is taken as "fact" rather than "mere" opinion or ideology. In such a context, the social conventions for representing the world are viewed as flowing from the way the world really is. Their contingent and provisional status is suppressed. Fiction is presented as truth.

Id. 1181.

"[I]t is impossible to translate exactly some concepts from one language to another." *Id.* n. 34, 1173.

438. [T]he search for ... meaning leads back to contingent social practices rather than to objective "reality." These social practices embody contingent choices concerning how to organize the thick texture of the world in consciousness. "Knowledge" is not an adequation of consciousness to the world. What gets called "knowledge" is the produced effect of social power institutionalized in social representational conventions.

Id. 1169-1170.

"The social power that I am evoking in the explication of the metaphysics of discourse is external to the self and more diffuse than the formal power of the state." *Id.* 1177.

One can extrapolate from another writer, Mark Tushnet, a related version of this critique. He implies that embedded in the concept of procedural natural law is the idea that the ideal judge would be constrained because she can be expectecd to apply generally recognized neutral principles. But any appeal to an ideal notion of neutral principles is bound to be illusory. The reason why an appeal to neutral principles is illusory is because it rests on a "shared understanding and acceptance of [the] constraints." Tushnet, Mark V., "Following the Rule Laid Down: A Critique of Interpretavism and Neutral Principles," Hutchinson, Allan C., *Critical Legal Studies*, at 169. But this shared understanding rests on an acceptance of the dominant political system (in the U. S., liberal capitalism,) to the exclusion of other alternatives to which some members of the society might also adhere (such as, socialism). *Id.* at 168-177.

439. The American legal realist, "[Felix Cohen,] was confident that dominant economic forces play a part in legal decisions, that judges usually reflect the attitudes of their own income class on social issues." *(cont. on next page)*

tween law and politics.[440] Thus, such terms as legal procedure[441] or the rule of law[442] can be used as rhetorical devices to reinforce the

---

Peller, *The Metaphysics of American Law*, *supra*, at 1248.

"[T]his metaphysical infrastructure is not simply an aspect of intellectual discourse in liberal societies. It forms the infrastructure for reproductions of the status quo authority in everyday life as well." *Id.* at 1274.

"[T]he discourse of reason and liberal authority...reflect collective motivations to reproduce existing terms of power and collective choices to side with institutionalized authority over social resistance." *Id.* at 1275.

440. "My aim is to demonstrate that legal reasoning is political and ideological." *Id.* at 1153.

"Legal thought differentiates itself from politics by suppressing the socially contingent metaphors upon which the legal representation of the social world depends." *Id.* at 1156.

"[Felix Cohen], argued that all legal decisionmaking is political in that all decisionmaking requires moral and ethical judgments which are not dictated by any preexisting rule or case." *Id.* at 1230-1.

441. Still,

> [d]espite the purported acceptance of the realist claim that law is political, something called legal reasoning continues to be used at judicial proceedings and taught in law schools. Legal reasoning is still perceived as a distinct way of thinking about (and being within) the social world. Boundaries segregate legal discourse from political, rhetoric, poetry, or late night conversations with friends. These boundaries are marked by signs at the borders of the discipline which announce what kinds of appeals will be taken as persuasive.

Id. at 1152.

> [Henry Hart and Albert Sachs] contend that the processes for resolving disputes are separate from and "more fundamental" than disagreement about the content of social arrangements since they are at once the source of the substantive arrangements and the indispensable means of making them work effectively. [I]mplicit in every such system of procedures is the central ideal of law — an idea which can be described as the principle of institutional settlement....In the process, the Hart and Sachs rhetoric implicitly delegitimates insubordination as it exalts subordination....This trace of the Hart and Sachs argument implicitly institutes a benign perspective on the status quo.

Id. at 1183-1185.

442. "This deconstructive, debunking strand of realism seems inconsistent with any liberal notion of a rule of law distinct from politics, or indeed with any mode of rational thought distinct from ideology." *Id.* at 1223.

Seemingly subscribing to the view of Felix Cohen, Peller states: "Legal concepts...are supernatural entities which do not have a verifiable existence except to the eyes of faith....Jurisprudence...is a special branch of the science of transcendental nonsense." *Id.* at 1226-7.

> Although the traditional concept of the rule of law requires that like cases be treated alike, in fact no two social events or cases are ever exactly alike. Every

dominance of the politically powerful, but otherwise have no value.[443] The effect of our understanding that law is an instrument of political power is to weaken the authority of law and the power of the political elites.[444]

> assertion that one case is dictated by a prior rule suppresses the fact that the treatment from case to case is based on rhetoric...

Id. at 1232. Again, Peller here seems to be both describing the view of Felix Cohen and subscribing to it.

"There could be no rational, as opposed to ideological, content to legal reasoning.... [A]ll [legal] categories...were simply rhetorical; they were not determined by any objective reality." *Id.* at 1239.

> [The] claim to impersonal and impartial authority, whether made in the name of reason, knowledge, or law, is always false. It inevitably depends upon the repression of the socially created character of meaning in favor of a meaning imagined to be free from contingency and the mere conventionality of language.

Id. at 1269.

443. The characterization [of the two experiences of being evicted and selling bonds,] as rational[ly coming under the single concept of property] as opposed to rhetorical, real as opposed to metaphoric, or legal as opposed to political, depends on a suppression of socially created and contingent metaphors upon which the connection rests. It is an act of social power to the extent it excludes as "merely" subjective, personal, or primitive all the ways that we experience the two events as different.

Id. at 1155.

> The [Critical Legal Studies] literature is united in rejecting the rule conception of society....If rules cannot constrain and channel conduct, the rule of law must be a fiction. If rules are just instruments of manipulation, then liberal legal philosophy, by its stubborn insistence that legal rules protect us from the state and from one another, is responsible for helping to hide the manipulation of law by judges and other powerholders.

Altman, Andrew, *Critical Legal Studies* (1993), at 151.

Still, even Peller, however consistent he is, at several points seems unwilling to apply his radical conclusion in its most radical form. At one point, for example, he states, "I do not mean to deny the authenticity of the sensation that doing legal reasoning feels different from writing poetry or participating in a riot." Peller, *The Metaphysics of American Law*, *supra*, at 1155. If legal concepts have no independent meaning, then why does it feel like they do? Elsewhere he states, "Of course, such a rule will seem absurd if the difference between the two cases is unimportant (e.g., in the names or heights of the two defendants)." *Id.* at 1231. On what basis can a difference be unimportant if there is no independent meaning to treating similar cases similarly?

444. From this perspective, critical realism contained the rhetoric for a broadly insurrectional movement.... Had this form of the realist struggle been pursued, it would have posed realism...against the metaphysics of legal authority itself....The critical realist message...was that law could not be divorced from politics, nor reason from myth....

Id at 1260-61. *(cont. on next page)*

Several points can be made in response to this radical attack against traditional legal concepts including the notion of legality, the rule of law and procedural natural law. One of these is to deal with the question of indeterminacy in language. A strong version, i.e., very radical understanding of this concept is to assert that no two humans ever understand each other. If this were so, it is difficult to imagine how people would come to understand a language for there would be no successful way to communicate what one was expressing to another. As Altman points out, such a position would be "self-refuting." This is because "...the charge that the liberal rule of law is a theoretical impossibility makes no sense. For theoretical impossibilities can exist only when words have determinate meaning."[445] Thus, to attack the rule of law on the ground that words do not have determinate meaning is based on the presupposition that the attack has determinate meaning. Indeed, Peller himself agrees. "I am not arguing that we never communicate or understand each other when we speak or act. That would be absurd."[446]

In support of this insight of Peller, let us recall Humpty Dumpty's remark to Alice: "[w]hen I use a word... it means just what I choose it to mean-neither more nor less."[447] The reason why this remark

---

"The social power exercised through the ideological grammar of social relations constitutes a significant force. Moreover, it constitutes a threat to the liberal definition of freedom as the subject's independence [from] objective restraint." *Id.* at 1287.

> [T]he problem is not language.... Rather, the task is to face the inevitability of politics..., to recognize the extent to which we are inevitably thrown into social struggle, as either reproducers or resisters of the reigning order and to face the prospect that we have no guarantees that any specific course is the correct one. We inevitably align with one group or another....

Id. at 1290.

"[T]he aim of Unger and his CLS colleagues is...to destroy the forces that currently block the potential of mass political mobilization to effect radical social transformation." Altman, Andrew, *Critical Legal Studies, op. cit.*, at 172.

445. *Id.* at 93.

446. Peller, *The Metaphysics of American Law, supra*, at 1170. "Clearly, no one is challenging the idea that English speakers use words in similar ways." Ramberg, Bjorn, *Donald Davidson's Philosophy of Language*, (1989) at 106.

As Balkin, who shares some of Peller's views, put it, "the deconstructive reversal has not demonstrated that all readings of Brown v. Board of Education, 347 U.S. 483 (1954) are equally legitimate." Balkin, *Deconstructive Practice and Legal Theory, supra*, at 776.

447. Carrol, Lewis, *Alice's Adventure in Wonderland & Through the Looking Glass*, 1981, at 169.

"Humpty Dumpty was wrong when he said that you can make words mean whatevseems humorous to us is because we know that words have fairly determinate meanings and in interpersonal communication they cannot be limited in meaning to what one person subjectively wants them to mean. Humpty Dumpty's statement seems almost as ludicrous as King Canute's suggestion about rolling back the sea.

But Peller does adhere to a weaker version of indeterminacy, namely, that language is always embedded in a political/social context and has no meaning outside of this context. As Peller puts it in a representative passage:

> In the terms of this deconstructive realism, when issues in legal argument were posed in terms of freedom, productivity, or regulation, they were not simply ideologically based; they were incoherent. The terms did not refer to anything except their relational play within the representational discourse. Thus neither political nor legal arguments could proceed by determining the absence or existence of one of these factors, because they did not "exist" independent from the social construction of their boundaries in the legal discourse.[448]

Under this version of the incoherence theory, any legal concept including that of procedural natural law has meaning only within a political/social/legal context of a particular culture. If accepted, does not this version of the incoherence theory render the procedural natural law concept I have developed in this book useless as a cross-cultural verbal tool for attacking what governments do when they violate procedural requirements?

How one deals with this question depends, in part, on how seriously one views the point being made.[449] Linguistic terminology and

---

er you want them to mean." Hart, Jr., Henry M. and Sacks, Albert M., *Purposive Interpretation, The Legal Process*, (1958) at 1375.

448. Peller, *The Metaphysics of American Law*, *supra*, at 1238.

449. Here is one commentator who does not take the deconstructionist or post-modernist critique very seriously:

> Postmodernism is a movement which, in addition to contingent flaws—obscurity, pretentiousness, faddiness, showmanship, cultural name-dropping—commits major errors in the methods it recommends: its penchant for relativism and preferential attention to semantic idiosyncrasy blind it to the non-semantic aspect of society, and to the immensely important, absolutely pervasive asymmetry in cognitive and economic power in the world situation.
>
> Postmoderinism ... is objectionable because it leads to *cognitive* nihilism,

concepts are often conventionally determined. As such, they would be subject to the patterns of analysis useful to the political/social power structure of a given community. But is this always the case? To believe this is to completely reject my view presented and discussed above[450] namely, that just as humans have similar sense organs and physiological mechanisms for processing pain, etc. regardless of their particular culture, so regardless of culture they also have similar brain/mind structures that enable them to process experiences and information in similar ways.

To make my point I refer you to Peller's remark that "[t]here is nothing in the object tree that marks it off as an object separate from the woods and bushes surrounding it."[451] And "[f]rom this perspective, the language of social roles is projected to have positive content, just as the word 'tree' is projected to have positive content as its socially produced status is suppressed."[452]

Contrary to what I gather Peller is asserting, I think it is more reasonable to assume that people, regardless of culture or the degree of their development, would be likely both to perceive trees as different from bushes and to have terminology that reflects this difference. To support this understanding I refer both to the reasonable assumption that human brains/minds are programmed to perceive things in similar ways, and to the reasonable assumption that if linguistic distinctions are useful in one culture they are likely to be useful in another culture.[453] Indeed, if humans did not adopt common ways of perceiving things, how could

---

> which is simply false, and also because it possibly misrepresents the way in which we actually understand societies and cultures. It denies or obscures tremendous differences in cognition and technical power, differences which are crucial for the understanding of current developments of human society. A vision which obscures that which matters most *cannot* be sound.

Gellner, Ernest, *Postmodernism, Reason and Religion*, 1992, at 70, 71-2.

450. See the discussion of Kant and Chomsky. (But a word of caution is in order. It is worth recognizing that a Kantian understanding of the commonality of how humans process experiences and information indicates an intersubjective similarity in human processing. However, it does not require a belief that what is being perceived is epistemologically an accurate rendition of what is out there independent of our sense apparatus.)

451. Peller, "The Metaphysics of American Law," *supra*, at 1165.

452. *Id.* at 1283.

453. I am reminded of the purported counter-example that the Eskimos have many different words for various kinds of snow while we English speakers are linguistically relatively snow deprived. But this counter-example, to the extent that it has force, ignores that Eskimos had (have) a special need to concentrate on snow that others living

one explain the cross-cultural application of mathematical and scientific concepts? Thus, I believe that viewing language as totally dependent on its political/social context is barking up the wrong tree.

If indeed, as seems obvious, humans have similar brain/mind structures regardless of culture, then this similarity might well predispose humans regardless of culture to adopt fairly similar concepts to articulate some of their basic ideas, at least after they have been exposed to these concepts. One example is the widely shared concept of religion. Although the content of one culture's religion often differs dramatically from that of the next culture, the cross-cultural commonality of the existence of the concept suggests that humans tend to think along similar lines.

Although not as obviously having cross-cultural application as, say, religion, a similar argument can be made with respect to the rule of law. While this concept might well have developed in the West, once introduced to the governed of other cultures it might well seem to have self-evident value to them.[454] It is like asking the governed, would you rather that your government treat you better or worse? That is what a government's following the rule of law amounts to, namely, treating the governed better, more fairly, less arbitrarily. The reason why this seems like a rhetorical question is because being treated better rather than worse is a self evident value. If humans generally preferred to be flagellated and abused, then their brain/mind structures would be different from what they are. But even granting the occasional exception, they generally don't.

Assuming that the point about the similarity of human brain/mind structures does not persuade you, let me focus instead on the value of the concept 'the rule of law.' Peller's assertion would deny that, regardless of culture, humans find certain concepts pragmatically useful, or would find them useful if they were made aware of them. By

---

in more temperate climates do not have. By contrast I would not expect similar disparities among the various language users in temperate climates would demonstrate a disregard for the differences between trees and bushes among the users of these languages.

454. It is not a tautology to assert that one would rather be treated better rather than worse. And assuming there are such, it is not a self evident truth. ("...we know that there are no self-evident truths." MacIntyre, Alasdair, *After Virtue*, 1981, at 69.) I think, however, that almost all of humans would regard it as a positive value to be treated better rather than worse.

contrast I assume that regardless of language, culture or government, people who do not belong to the power elites of their particular societies would find the terminology of procedural natural law a useful verbal tool by which to measure and gauge the regime's responsiveness to their need to plan their lives without being subject to sanctions based on governmental irrationality and arbitrariness. Even if the concept 'the rule of law' is not indigenous to a particular culture, once people within that culture learn of it they would find it a worthwhile concept to use.

Only if one rejects both of my responses to Peller's linguistic indeterminacy argument, namely, that humans possess similar mechanisms for processing experiences and information (what I call the rationality basis for procedural natural law) and that a concept developed within one culture can have cross-cultural usefulness (what I call the pragmatic basis), that Peller's assertion seemingly has force. But even if one rejects these two responses, Peller's position can be attacked, for to "suppose... [as Peller does] that legal rules have no meaning at all when regarded in isolation from the body of legal rules and doctrines" leaves inexplicable "how a language... is learned or how communication occurs."[455] One is not dependent on having learned the whole of legal rules (or any other language) before one can begin to communicate using that part of legal rules one has already learned.

Regardless of the weaknesses in Peller's view of indeterminacy, one can still take seriously his view that the concept of procedural natural law has no value other than to reinforce the status quo of the dominant political/social power structure.[456] Peller goes on to assert that legal concepts cannot be separated from the broader political power struggle in which they are used to reinforce the dominance of the status quo:

> [T]he "problem" is not language.... Rather, the task is to face the inevitability of politics in the fullest sense, to recognize the extent to which we are inevitably thrown into social struggle as either reproducers or resisters of the reigning order and to face the prospect that we have no guarantees that any specific course is the correct one. We

455. Altman, *Critical Legal Studies, supra*, at 97.

456. If Peller were right that the use of 'the rule of law' concept simply reinforces the dominance of the ruling elite, then from my perspective it has no value worth writing a book about whether or not it could be given cross-cultural application.

> inevitably side with one group or another; there is no place free from the play of social practice, where we could flee from the existential condition that we create our world on the basis of a prior context that we can never fully grasp.[457]

For Peller everything is political. This seemingly would entail that there is no basis for distinguishing between legal rationality and governmental arbitrariness. Rather, the only analysis depends either on our self-interest or some psychological preference: regardless of the context in which the "legal" issue arises, we either side with the status quo or with those seeking to undermine and destroy it. Some, probably including Peller, identify with the powerless, whereas others, presumably including anyone like myself who is so benighted as to write a book defending procedural natural law, would be expected to identify with the ruling elite.

Since I take Peller's argument seriously on its own terms, I have to respond to the idea that legal process cannot be separated from politics broadly understood. One response to Peller's position is that legal process is something learned in law school whereas political theory is learned in political science departments or departments of philosophy. There is a separate discipline called legal procedure that is learned in law school, not in political science department. This discipline can be applied to states that adopt socialism or a strong social welfare system as well as to laissez faire capitalism.[458] While political values certainly play a role in every aspect of law including the procedural aspects discussed here, we can and do examine the legal processes separate from their broader social and political context.[459]

---

457. Peller, *The Metaphysics of American Law*, *supra*, at 1290.

458. [I]f interpreted in strictly *formal* terms,

> Fuller's principles of legal morality sufficed neither to confer a special normative status upon the individual rights to private property and economic choice which Hayek associated with the free market, nor to preclude the implementation by a government of legislative policies in matters of economic management and welfare provisions which gave concrete effect to the egalitarian rights central to the Rawlsian theory of distributive justice.

Covell, Charles, *The Defence of Natural Law*, 1992, at 67.

459. A less radical understanding of the political nature of legal process would be easier to accept. The use of one scholar's effort to explain deconstructionist terminology, if applied to Peller's insistence that law and legal process always involve politics, might render it more explicable. *(cont. on next page)*

Let us assume *ab initio* for the sake of analysis that Peller is right to assert that law, including legal procedure, is politics by other means. Let us assume further that our use of legal terminology tends to reinforces the dominance of the power elite. Still, one factor mitigates the thrust of these assertions, namely, that the value of using the terminology of the rule of law is in its providing the user with a verbal tool for attacking and undermining the status quo. It can be and is used to attack what a government does as violating legality, not simply as a means to reenforce government power. It is a verbal tool available to the underclass for promoting the mitigation of economic and social inequalities and even revolutionaries.[460]

Use of the rule of law, however, does not attempt to change human nature. If, as I believe, there is a human tendency for the strong to exploit and dominate the weak, economically and otherwise, applying the rule of law would not change this tendency. Unless forced to do so, lions do not peaceably lie down with lambs. And assuming the existence of a capitalist state, there would be the economically and politically strong who would not be required by the rule of law to provide distributive justice to the weak. Even so, if the rule of law existed within a state, and sometimes it does exist within a state, it would limit the ability of the strong to exploit and oppress and would enable the weak more easily to get through the governmental bureaucratic maze. This is all that is provided. But I suspect that al-

---

> To say that A [say, law] and B [say, politicss] form a nested opposition is not to say that A is identical with B, or that it is impossible to tell A and B apart in a particular context. Indeed, the concept of a nested opposition only makes sense if we assume that there are points of difference between A and B; otherwise we could not see these concepts as opposed. Therefore it is a misuse of deconstructive arguments to claim that one can abolish all distinctions and demonstrate that all forms of intellectual endeavor lack coherence. For deconstructive argument itself rests upon the very possibility of those distinctions and those coherences.

J. M. Balkin, "Book Review: Nested Oppositions," 99 *Yale L. J.* 1669, 1677 (1990).

460. Admittedly, if and when the revolution becomes successful and the new government then complies with the rule of law, the suggested legal terminology would then reenforce the status quo of the victorious revolutionaries.

But if the new revolutionary government made up of members of the old underclass proved to be just as violative of the rule of law as the old government, then the new underclass (perhaps including members of the old ruling elite) could assert that the rule of law had been violated.

most everyone outside of the ruling class would regard this at preferable to its absence.

One asks the radical critic of the rule of law, "if you were raised in the Anglo-American legal culture but found yourself in the clutches of a regime that you regard as consistently acting arbitrarily and irrationally, would you refuse to use 'the rule of law' concept as a verbal weapon to attempt, if you could, to protect yourself against the regime's attack?" I suspect that you would agree with Mark Kelman who states:

> The contrast we typically learned to draw back in civics class is between a regime of impersonal rules and a regime of personal domination; a world of known duties and a world of surprise demands made by unreadable bureaucrats; formal equality against feudal status; formal equality and autonomy against Stalinist terror. At that level, the choice of the Rule of Law seems unexceptionable.[461]

The concept 'the rule of law,' as explicated here, does not carry us to perfect justice in general or in individual cases, but it is a useful verbal tool by which to judge and, if necessary, to attack what regimes do. Like the atheist who allegedly professes belief while being shot at in the foxhole, when needed the radical can benefit from using this tool even if, epistemologically, she does not believe it refers to something having cross-cultural value. If nothing else, it has rhetorical value. Referring to it as having rhetorical value (what I have referred to as the conventionality basis for procedural natural law) is not to denigrate it for it is not the use of language of sophistry designed to obfuscate the issue. For the person in extremis who uses the language of procedural natural law is using a concept both that at the moment she is likely to believe in and one she hopes will resonate with her hearers even if they belong to the bureaucracy of the oppressive regime.[462]

---

461. Kelman, Mark, *A Guide to Critical Legal Studies*, 1987, at 294.

462. Here are several observations which suggest that the rule of law does not always serve those in power. One observer points out the rhetorical value of the use of legal terminology in British history.

> The law may be rhetoric, but it need not be empty rhetoric. [T]he rulers were, in serious senses, whether willingly or unwillingly, the prisoners of their own rhetoric; they played the games of power according to rules which suited them, but they could not break those rules or the whole game would be thrown away. And finally, so far from the ruled shrugging off this rhetoric as a hypocrisy, some part of it at least was taken over as part of the rhetoric of the plebeian crowd, of the "free-born Englishman" with his inviolable privacy, his *habeas*

Allow me now to briefly sum up some of the ideas expressed in this section. I began by articulating certain deconstructionist assertions which can be made against the thrust of this book. These assertions include: 1. that language is indeterminate, 2. that to the extent the concept 'the rule of law' can be given any meaning at all its meaning is culturally dependent and 3. that the concept has no value except to shore up the power of the political and social elite.

My response to the first assertion (the language indeterminacy assertion) is in large measure to wonder how the deconstructionist can make such an assertion if language is so indeterminate. My response to the second assertion (the culturally determined assertion) is twofold. On the one hand I suggest that concepts have cross-cultural application because human brains/minds are structured in similar ways regardless of culture. Assuming this to be so, this structuring might well include a preference on the part of the governed for their government to follow the rule of law rather than to act out of pure arbitrariness, irrationality and whim. I call this the rationality basis for procedural natural law. On the other hand I also suggest a pragmatic basis for procedural natural law, namely, that regardless of culture it

---

> *corpus*, his equality before the law. If the rhetoric was a mask, it was a mask which John Wilkes was to borrow, at the head of ten thousand masked supporters.... [T]here is a very large difference... between arbitrary extra-legal power and the rule of law. And not only were the rulers (indeed, the ruling class as a whole) inhibited by their own rules of law against the exercise of direct immediate force (arbitrary imprisonment, the employment of troops against the crowd, torture, and those other conveniences of power with which we are all conversant), but they also believed enough in these rules, and in their accompanying ideological rhetoric, to allow, in certain limited areas, the law itself to be a genuine forum within which certain kinds of class conflict were fought out.

Thompson, E. P., *Whigs and Hunters*, 1975, at 263-5 (describing 18th Century British law).

Michael Foucault provides a cross-cultural observation along the same lines as Thompson:

> It will be said no doubt that law (*droit*) in Western societies has always served as a mask for power. This explanation does not seem wholly adequate. Law was an effective instrument for the constitution of monarchial forms of power in Europe, and political thought was ordered for centuries around the problem of Sovereignty and its rights. Moreover, law, particularly in the eighteenth century, was a weapon of the struggle against the same monarchical power, which had initially made use of it to impose itself.

Foucault, Michael, *Power/Knowledge*, edited and translated by Colin Gordon, 1972, at 140-1 .

is a useful verbal tool by which the governed can attempt to limit their government's arbitrariness and irrationality. The reason for the governed to prefer the rule of law regardless of culture is that it enables them to attempt to conform their behavior to the government's demands. This response to the deconstructionist's second articulated criticism also constitutes the response to the third articulated criticism to the effect that the procedural natural law concept is a weapon of those in power against the powerless. The response takes the form of demonstrating the rhetorical advantage to the politically weak in using 'the rule of law' concept to castigate their government for oppressing them in violation of the concept.

16

Conclusion

This book attempts to fortify those who express their outrage at the atrocities committed by the leadership and trusted hench people of totalitarian, authoritarian and, on occasion, even democratic regimes. Based on our ordinary use of language, it notes that we have an idea of the concept 'law' that contains a number of procedural elements that, if applied by internal and external critics, can be a basis for attacking these oppressive regimes. The critic can point out that a regime's abusing those whom it governs also constitutes its failure to adhere to law and its procedural elements. Obversely, a regime's adhering to law means that those governed by it can more easily plan their lives without government interference. Legal procedure reduces the room available to a regime to act arbitrarily and irrationally.

The idea of law as procedurally based includes such content as providing general rules, treating similars similarly, setting forth these rules publically in advance of their being used to sanction violaters, confining the rules to dealing with behavior rather than status, avoiding any resort to torture as a means of determining whether to apply a sanction and conditioning any sanction imposed to a prior determination by an impartial fact finder that there had been a breach of the rules.

This procedural element of law constitutes a moral concept as well as a legal one. Why? Because those who come in contact with a regime would regard it as preferable for that regime to comply with these and other legal procedures. They would regard it as something they could rely on. Just as a person's keeping her promise has a moral dimension so a regime's complying with its legal procedures constitutes a moral good and its absence as a moral evil. And because the procedural element of law is part of the description of the concept rather than a prescriptive addition to the concept, the idea of law does not violate the principle that an ought cannot be derived from an is.

While those legal philosophers (Austin, Kelsen, Hart and Raz) who have engaged in describing law without attributing to it any necessary moral element have rejected natural law theories, if they focused on this procedural version of natural law, it would be more difficult for them to dismiss it than the substantive versions they rejected. This is because their own descriptions of law contain some of the very elements that constitute the procedural idea of it articulated originally by Fuller and developed in this book.

Finally, an analysis of a radical deconstructionist critique demonstrated that it was no barrier to the use of procedural natural law terminology as the basis for a cross-cultural verbal attack on those regimes that engage in atrocities in violation of this concept. So, contrary to what I assume you believed before starting this book, I have set forth a limited version of natural law that is intellectually defensible and attractive. Will wonders never cease.

Index to Proper Names